Therapeutic Recreation:

its theory, philosophy, and practice

Therapeutic Recreation:

its theory, philosophy, and practice

Virginia Frye and
Martha Peters

STACKPOLE BOOKS

Library of Congress Cataloging in Publication Data

Frye, Mary Virginia, 1918–
    Therapeutic recreation: its theory, philosophy,
and practice.

    Includes bibliographical references.
    1. Recreational therapy. I. Peters, Martha,
1919–   joint author. II. Title.
RM736.7.F78   615'.8515   70-179610
ISBN 0-8117-1735-6

TO

CHARLES K. BRIGHTBILL

whose concepts of the nature and value of
recreative living permeate this book

Contents

Part I   History and Philosophy

Part II Therapeutic Values and Applications

Part III Professional Matters

Part IV Looking Ahead

A Word About The Writing of This Book

CHARLES K. BRIGHTBILL, who contributed so much to the literature of leisure and recreation, had long wanted and planned to develop a major publication concerning the field of therapeutic recreation and the relationships between recreation and health. This was to be his next project following completion of his *Educating for Leisure-Centered Living.* His invitation to co-author the proposed book was accepted as a signal honor by one of the current authors. The basic approach and outline had been developed and Professor Brightbill had begun the drafting of materials for several chapters shortly before his death.

The book as it now appears has been developed essentially on the original plan and outline. Professor Brightbill's influence and, indeed, his words appear throughout the contents. Yet no one can speak—or write—for another. Responsibility for this book—with all of its many shortcomings or limited merit—resides with the authors. We offer what follows humbly as a tribute, imperfect and inadequate, but with deepest sincerity to all that Charles K. Brightbill brought so eloquently to the goal of raising the quality of life through recreative living.

For the use of materials and notes from Professor Brightbill's files, we are deeply grateful to his family. Their continuing interest and encouragement have meant much in the preparation of the manuscript.

Martha Peters and
Virginia Frye

Foreword

IN THE MEDICAL and paramedical professions as well as within the recreation profession, there is a growing recognition and acceptance of the significant role recreation can play in the lives of the ill and the disabled. The purpose of this book is to provide a comprehensive view and a better understanding of recreation in relation to medicine and rehabilitation, and to suggest principles and guidelines for those persons who are interested in maximizing the therapeutic benefits of recreation.

Part I sets the background, historically, of therapeutic recreation, and establishes the philosophical foundations upon which the principles and practices are based.

In Part II, the therapeutic possibilities of recreation are related to the effects of various illnesses and disabilities upon the individual's capacity to realize his fullest potential socially, physically, intellectually, and creatively. This is the heart of the book, where major benefits that can accrue from recreation experiences are *identified* and *applied* to helping overcome incapacities. The presentation is organized around the benefits of recreation experiences as they apply to the *effects* of handicapping conditions rather than around medical or diagnostic categories as such.

Part III deals with the practical matters involved in the organization, administration, and provision of therapeutic recreation services in a variety of settings, including those in the community outside the hospital. Suggested criteria for personnel, for administrative patterns, for program planning, and for facilities are given.

Part IV concludes with a discussion of various research studies and their application to the practice of therapeutic recreation, together with some indications of the issues and trends of the future.

This book is unique because of its comprehensiveness and its point of view. Unlike previous publications, the material is not limited to a specific age group nor to specific diagnostic entities. Its approach is from the viewpoint of the recreator rather than an addendum to the medical point of view.

The book is intended for use by professional practitioners, including not only recreators but also occupational therapists, physical therapists, special educators, rehabilitation counselors, social workers, nurses, and others. It is particularly geared for use as a text for basic courses in therapeutic recreation. It should also be a useful reference for undergraduate and graduate majors in general recreation, adapted physical education, special education, occupational therapy, hospital administration, and the like.

Part I | HISTORY AND PHILOSOPHY

1 | Historical Sketch

Antecedents

EARLY IN THE development of human civilization, recreation—play—became integral to man's expressions of his health beliefs, aspirations, and practices. With rituals and festivals he supplicated the gods for health and healing and gave thanks when his petitions were answered. With games and contests he sought the agility and fitness essential for his survival. The identity of play and ritual was asserted in Plato's eighth book of *Laws* in the fourth century B.C., and reaffirmed in Johan Huizinga's *Homo Ludens* in the twentieth century A.D.[1] Concern for the human body, the temporal dwelling of the soul, has always been a vital tie between health and religion. Linked to both of these, recreation has played essential roles, not only in relation to health on the one hand and religion on the other, but also in providing an avenue of communication, a connecting pathway between them. Moreover, recreation, in the sense of re-creative living—of living creatively over and over again—is inseparably bound to basic concepts of both health and religion.

Thus it is not surprising that we look to religious history for early evidences of the relation of recreation to medicine and rehabilitation. Two thousand years before Christ, the ancient Egyptians found pleasurable occupation a mental health restorative. Temples dedicated to the relief of "melancholias" offered games and other forms of recreation activities to high-born and influential people who came in large numbers to seek health-restoring relief from their problems. Some of the Egyptian priests of that ancient culture would not be strangers to the contemporary concept of milieu therapy; for it is said that the therapeutic potentials of environment and atmosphere, of elements such as lovely lotus gardens and ritualistic songs and dances performed by the temple maidens, were fully recognized by certain of the religious leaders of the times and offered as effective dispellers of morbid moods.

No other form of the arts, or indeed of human expression, has more pervasive effects upon mood and feelings than has music. Listener or performer may find in music pleasant persuasion to restorative relaxation and rest, pulsing motivation to activity, rhythmic aid to coordination, or a therapeutic medium of emotional release. In Greek and Roman mythology, Apollo was the god of music and poetry as well as of medicine. Judeo-Christian annals offer early testimonial to concepts of music as a pleasurable healing agent in the familiar biblical account of Saul, the king who was relieved of the evil spirit, refreshed and made well as he listened to the music of David's harp. The histories of primitive peoples and of ancient and classical cultures abound with evidences of man's belief in the curative powers of music and of its use in treating the ill and injured.

In ancient Greece, Apollo's son, Asclepius, or Aesculapius as he was known to the Romans, was the god of healing. Temples and shrines built to him and to his daughters, Hygieia, goddess of health, and Panacea, goddess of remedies, were the principal medical centers of Greece. By the fifth century B.C. some of these temples had assumed many of the characteristics of modern health spas. The most famous was at Epidauros, not far from Athens. Here, for seekers of the Greek health ideal of a balanced state of well-being in mind, body, and soul, were provided not only places of worship, lodging, and a hospital, but also gymnasiums, libraries, a stadium for twelve thousand spectators, and a theater, with a seating capacity of sixteen thousand, reported to be one of the most beautiful of all the Grecian outdoor theaters. The scenic natural site in the midst of sacred groves of trees was enhanced by the gleaming white marble of the buildings. At Epidauros and the other Asclepian health temples a ritual developed. As defined by the dream oracle it included rest followed by purifying baths, massages and oil annointments, catharsis or blood-letting, dietary programs, and other hygienic measures. To be sure, an aura of magic permeated the ministrations of the Asclepiades (temple priests) and their ceremonies, which were designed to gain entrance for the supplicant via dreams to the presence of the healing god. Nevertheless, there was also a hygienic emphasis in the routine and full advantage was taken of the fresh air and sunlight available in the surroundings. It seems not unlikely that many who enjoyed the temples' ample provisions for instructions, bathing, exercise, and entertainment, along with the restful, relaxing regimen and atmosphere, may have felt an improvement in their general health and spirits even before being "admitted to the mysteries."[2]

Little has been revealed by historians of the part that recreation may have played in medical developments of ancient civilizations in Asian countries or among the early inhabitants of the American continents. The association of religious beliefs with early health practices in these regions, as elsewhere, has been well documented, however. Huizinga's contention that all culture arises in the form of play suggests a primary relationship of play to medical-religious aspects of cultural history and a logical hypothesis or starting point for further inquiry and research into the relation of recreation to the medical practices of Oriental peoples and American Indians.

The Age of Pericles marked the rise of rational medicine in Greek scientific history. The transition away from the magical to the scientific was led by Hippocrates, himself the son of a priest-physician and one of the Asclepiades.[3]

Although Aesculapian temples were built in Rome on the Greek model, the conquerors of Greece also imported other facets of her medical science. For their own part, the Romans made particular progress in promoting personal and public hygiene. In this connection, the famed public and private baths afford an example of an important tie between recreation and health. The bath houses were apt to include libraries, gymnasiums, and dining rooms and served actually as social centers or clubs for Roman citizens, both men and women.[4]

Through the period of Roman ascendancy and the long centuries of the Middle Ages that followed Rome's decline, evidences are scarce of conscious efforts to provide recreation or other occupations for the sick. It is true that there appeared from time to time proponents and programs for treating illness by occupation of some kind, including the "work cure" as well as diversional and recreational activity. Galen, for instance, a second century A.D. Greek teacher of anatomy and physician to the gladiators of Rome, is credited with having recommended employment as nature's best physician and essential to human happiness.[5] By A.D. 100 military medicine was well developed and twenty-four surgeons were assigned to every Roman legion. Hospitals were established near military camps and first aid and field ambulance services were organized. Roman physicians also opened private hospitals, which were the forerunners of public hospitals in the Middle Ages.[6] The rise of Christianity brought humanitarian ideals to the care of the poor and the sick, and the Church and its leaders took up the building of hospitals. However, through the centuries the medieval Christian Church became more and more occupied with things spiritual, to the point that lack of emphasis upon the physical being became a virtue. Under these circumstances little value was placed upon medical care and medicine in general declined.

The early modern period, from about 1500 to 1700, was, in many respects, a time of transition. New scientific knowledge was largely unapplied in medical practice. Hospital conditions were deplorable. Particularly tragic was the treatment of the mentally ill who were tortured and burned in the witch-hunting frenzy stirred by religious zealots.

Not until the latter part of the eighteenth century is there evidence of a renewal of interest in the potentialities of work and recreational activities as aids in helping those suffering from nervous disorders. By the late 1700's and early 1800's records indicate the use of occupations as a form of treatment in

Italy, Spain, England, and the United States. At Aversa, Italy, for instance, moderate work combined with amusement was described as "the best cure." Employments in which the patients engaged included printing, translating, music, husbandry, and manufacturing of woolen cloth.[7] The great French humanitarian and leader of reforms in the care of the insane, Dr. Phillippe Pinel, wrote in 1791 of his observation of a patient who, in his judgment, had been restored to full command of his faculties through a program of moderate employment and regular exercise that cooperated with the energies of nature in achieving therapeutic results. Although exercises that were looked upon as useful—work— were considered to have greater therapeutic benefits than diversions or amusements, Dr. Benjamin Rush, first superintendent of the Pennsylvania Hospital of Philadelphia, expressed some understanding of the therapeutic values that might come from activities of a recreational nature. "Man was made to be active," Rush is quoted as stating in his book published in 1812. "Even in paradise he was employed in the healthy and pleasant exercises of cultivating a garden." Rush held, furthermore, that activity that was wholesomely stimulating to " . . . the passions by alternate hope, fear, and enjoyment, and by rendering bodily exercise or labor necessary, is calculated to produce the greatest benefit. Absence of occupation is not rest, a mind quite vacant is a mind distressed."

A paper read in 1815 before the board of the New York Hospital by Thomas Eddy is credited with having inspired the institution of many progressive treatment measures as well as the building of a hospital for the mentally ill. Along with his recommendations for various prescribed activities and employment, Eddy believed that melancholic patients should be able to participate freely in such exercises as walking, riding, innocent sports, conversations, and other amusements. He stressed those employments that involved considerable bodily action, were agreeable to the patient, and that contrasted with the illusions of the disease. Interestingly, Eddy also suggested that patients ". . . should be gratified with birds, deer, rabbits, etc." Following the opening of the New York Hospital in 1821 the deputy-keeper and the female keeper were assigned definite responsibility for seeing that patients, selected by the doctor or the Committee of the Asylum, participated in approved exercises, employment, or amusement.[8]

The records of McLean Hospital in Waverly, Massachusetts, for 1822 include a report by a Dr. Wyman of amusements provided for the "lunatics" that include draughts, chess, backgammon, ninepins, swinging, sawing wood, gardening, reading, writing, and music. Wyman held such activities to be therapeutic on several counts: for the diversion afforded from unpleasant subjects of thought; for the mental and physical exercise involved; and for the tranquilizing effect upon the mind which could result not only in breaking up wrong associations of ideas, but also in inducing correct habits of thinking and acting.[9]

In England, the *Illustrated London News* of May, 1843, carried a description of facilities of a recreational nature provided at the Hanwell Asylum. There were airing courts with summer houses where patients could sit, read newspapers, smoke, and converse and where the listless and depressed could be encouraged to walk out of doors. Bowling greens were located in the airing courts, as well as a novel type of equipment—rocking horses large enough to accommodate as many as five people! The rocking horses were credited with providing not only a means of amusement and exercise, but also an alleviation of maladies. This exercise, it was reported, seemed to cause the patients to forget their troubles and irritations and might even lull some of them to sleep. In 1848 the same newspaper commented upon the value of music in treating mental patients and reported that the hospital was supplying pianos, flutes, clarinets, and violins for the patients' use. Wards for disturbed male patients were brightened by fiddle music and patients were often stimulated to spontaneous dancing. A small band formed by some of the attendants played for winter evening parties for the patients and there were also sometimes entertainments on a large scale.[10]

At the mid-point of the nineteenth century, Florence Nightingale, the "Lady with a Lamp," not only led the way to modern nursing, but lighted new paths in serving the recreational needs of those who were hospitalized. As she worked to better the care and treatment of soldier patients in the hospitals in Scutari and the Crimea, she introduced innovations that have since become an established, and in some instances, essential part of military life. To Nightingale, the greatest horror of the war was the drunkenness and demoralizing behavior she saw. Her way of combatting such excesses was to furnish for the men classrooms and instruction, reading rooms and recreation huts. Later Florence Nightingale's friend, Sir Sydney Herbert, who was Secretary of War in the British Cabinet, appointed a committee to investigate how best to provide day rooms for the soldiers. The committee reported in 1861 that every barracks should be provided with a separate room where the men could meet with their comrades, read the paper, drink coffee, play innocent games, or write letters. In large camps it was recommended that the men might well have a club of their own outside the barracks.[11]

Notes on Nursing by Florence Nightingale was published in 1873. This small volume should be reviewed by all recreators who serve the ill or the disabled and particularly by those who work in a hospital or clinical setting. Nightingale devoted a section of her book to a plea for providing variety for the patient. Stressing the reciprocal relation of mind and body, she regretted that, "The effect in sickness of beautiful objects, of variety of objects, and especially of brilliant colour is hardly at all appreciated." She rejected the notion that the effect of the esthetic is only a fancy of the mind. "It is no such thing," she declared. "The effect is on the body, too. Little as we know about the way in which we are affected by form, by colour, and light, we do know this, that they have an actual physical effect." Nightingale had specific advice for visitors to patients, including appropriate and inappropriate topics of conversation. Her recommendation that babies be brought to visit patients and even laid upon the sick-bed may be an echo from a less antiseptic, germ-conscious past; however, other suggestions she made have continued as worthy of consideration as they were in 1873. For example, Nightingale thought a small pet animal an excellent companion for the sick, particularly for long chronic cases. "A pet bird in a cage is sometimes the only pleasure of an invalid confined for years to the same room. If he can feed and clean the animal himself, he ought to do so." In other sections of her book, Nightingale commented on the effect of music upon the sick and recommended stringed and wind instruments, including the human voice, because they are "capable of a continuous sound." The pianoforte and other instruments having "no continuity of sound" she believed might actually aggravate the illness of the listener.[12] Although this little book is in many ways a quaint reflection of an unsophisticated past, ideas championed by the humanitarian rebel who wrote it seem to echo—or at least, are being rediscovered—a century later in the surge of interest and effort that have developed rapidly in relating recreation to the keeping or regaining of health.

Early Developments in the United States

In the United States toward the end of the nineteenth century a recreation movement began to take shape. Its main focus in the beginning and its major thrust for some time was directed toward the provision of leisure facilities, programs, and services in large cities and particularly in those urban areas having high indices of economic and social problems. Parallel with the growth of community recreation were the development and expansion of recreation facilities and programs for patients in mental institutions, particularly in state hospitals such as those established in Illinois in the last half of the nineteenth and early years of the twentieth centuries.[13] However, recreation programs and services provided for patients in hospitals and institutions remained for many years outside the mainstream of the community-based recreation movement.

World War I brought a considerable expansion of recreation services to patients in general medical and surgical—as well as in psychiatric—hospitals. Soon after the entry of the United States into the war, the American Red Cross provided some recreation services incidental to its other responsibilities to patients in military hospitals. Before the war's end, recreation activities and programs were being offered in wards and in convalescent houses. Recreation leaders were employed and assigned to military and veterans hospitals during the 1920's. By 1930 there were 117 Red Cross hospital recreation workers. In 1931 responsibility for the recreation program in veterans hospitals was transferred from the Red Cross to the United States Veterans Bureau.[14]

Other fields closely related to recreation for the ill and disabled were also developing. The first school of Occupational Therapy opened in Chicago in 1915.[15] By 1919 the librarian of Barnes Hospital in St. Louis observed that, while the use of hospital libraries as a therapeutic resource was not new, there was, at that time, added attention being given to more definite and positively planned use of books by patients.[16] A number of persons have entered the recreation profession, particularly in relation to medicine and rehabilitation, from a background of preparation in social group work. The first course for this branch of the social work family was offered in 1923 at Western Reserve University, and course work was also offered during the 1920's at Carnegie Institute of Technology, Northwestern University, and George Williams and Springfield Colleges.[17] Music and medicine have had close contacts through the ages. World War I gave great impetus to the use of music as a diversion in hospitals. However, music therapy is a more recent development, with college preparation in this specialization dating only from the late 1940's.[18]

One of the earliest significant studies in recreation for the handicapped was carried on at the Lincoln State School and Colony in Illinois. In June, 1929, a Department of Recreation was created ". . . to conduct a program of activities consistent with the interests and abilities of mentally handicapped children, this program to serve as a substitute for former repressive measures of control. The objective was the development of the individual child through active participation in play activities, in small homogeneous groups, which averaged twenty each in size." As a result of an evaluation of the project by the Director of the Illinois Department of Public Welfare after the first year of experimentation, the Superintendent of Lincoln State School officially recognized the recreation department in his institution. The experimental project continued for two years. At the end of that period a report was prepared by Bertha Schlotter and Margaret Svendsen and published in 1932.

Reissued in 1951 and again in 1956 and 1959 with some additions and revisions by Schlotter, the report includes observations and analyses of the responses of mentally retarded children to various play activities; suggestions concerning play equipment; classifications of play activities according to mental age, degree of motor activity, social organization, and the like. One chapter is devoted to a socio-psychological analysis of play activities that were used in the experiment. The authors suggested that this analysis indicated ". . . the possibility of more discriminating use of game material for psychotherapeutic purposes with the mentally ill, as well as with the socially maladjusted in the community." In a foreword to the third printing in 1956, Dr. Otto L. Bettag, then Director of the Illinois Department of Public Welfare, recognized the historical significance of the study:

> This marks the third printing of a publication that is in many ways a historic document in the field of recreational work. It is one of the earliest presentations showing the value of recreation as a tool in teaching social skills to mentally retarded children. For those who regard the enjoyment derived from play as a valuable end in itself, this material is a source of invaluable help and guidance.[19]

Decade of Expansion, 1940-1950

World War II brought tremendous acceleration to the hospital recreation movement. Recreation gained recognition for its contribution to the morale and total treatment of hospitalized servicemen. The American National Red Cross, in its unique position as a quasi-governmental agency chartered by Congress,[20] was charged with the responsibility for providing recreation services to patients in military hospitals, both in the United States and overseas. To meet the unprecedented demand for hospital recreation personnel, the Red Cross recruited large numbers of young women from allied professional fields—teachers of the arts, social sciences, physical education, as well as social group workers, and others. A training program was established and headquartered at the American University in Washington, D.C. There, newly employed staff were enrolled in an intensive four week "Basic Recreation" course that included preparation for those who were to be assigned to the wartime Red Cross leave area clubs for able-bodied servicemen, as well as to the military hospitals. The faculty employed by the Red Cross included some of the illustrious names of the recreation movement to that time—Ott Romney, John Scherlacher, Mary Breen Lawson, and Thomas Rickman, to name a few. From a low point of seven recreation staff during the depression years just prior to 1940, the number of Red Cross hospital recreation workers had soared to a peak total of 1809 by the end of the war.[21] Medical approval was required for all recreation offerings for the servicemen patients and their hospitalized dependents. Red Cross recreators worked closely with and under the guidance of medical officers. Emphasis was placed on offering and encouraging patients to participate in as wide a range of recreation activities as possible within the boundaries of the medical treatment program, limitations caused by the illness or disability, and the capacities and interests, known or developed, of the patient, himself. Individualized as well as group activities were conducted indoors on wards, in recreation halls, auditoriums, craft shops, game rooms, and the like; outdoors on lawns surrounding the hospital as well as in other areas such as picnic grounds or small parks often provided on military installations. Off-post trips to nearby communities and to various special events were popular with convalescent patients. Large numbers of volunteers were recruited, trained, and used to help supplement and extend the efforts of the paid recreation staff.

Following the war, hospital recreation became a permanently established part of the peacetime as well as emergency Red Cross services to the armed forces, taking its place alongside the longer established social case work service of the agency. Although the number of personnel employed decreased after World War II, the Red Cross recreation program in military hospitals continues as an important part of the whole movement in recreation for the ill and the disabled.

Another major impact in the development of therapeutic recreation after World War II was made by the Veterans Administration. Before 1945, recreation in VA hospitals was characterized as ". . . an honest but fragmentary offer of diversional amusement for hospitalized veterans." Offerings were unequal from hospital to hospital and inadequate from the standpoints of program, personnel, and financial support. With the cessation of hostilities, the increase in number of veteran patients required rapid expansion in the hospital and treatment programs. In November, 1945, the Veterans Administration established the Recreation Service as a function of its Hospital Special Services Division along with the Canteen, Library, Chaplaincy, and Voluntary Services.[22] The Recreation Service operated a program at each VA hospital and domiciliary institution. In 1960 recreation programs and services were organized administratively as a Recreation Section in the Physical Medicine and Rehabilitation Service.[23] The purposes and objectives of the recreation service in the VA hospitals were summarized as follows:

> The purpose of the recreation program in Veterans Administration hospitals is to provide, as an integral phase of the total medical program, a comprehensive, well-balanced, and professionally executed range of recreation activities to meet the needs, interests, and capabilities of all patients. All activities offered by the recreation program require medical approval.
>
> The recreation program is planned to assist the doctor in getting his patients well and to make life as satisfying and meaningful as possible for those patients who must remain in the hospital for long periods of time. The diversified activities which constitute the program are designed to accomplish the following objectives:
>
> a. Assist in facilitating patients' adjustment to hospital life and medical treatment.
> b. Provide doctors with opportunities to observe patient behavior and response to activity.
> c. Assist in orienting patients in their physical limitations and potentialities.
> d. Contribute to the development and maintenance of normal physical condition during the patients' stay in the hospital.
> e. Develop interests and skills in so-called "carry-over" activities; that is, activities in which patients may participate safely and beneficially during their stay in the hospital as well as after their discharge from the hospital.
> f. Contribute to the total social and psychological readjustment of patients.
>
> Primary consideration is given to the needs of patients as determined by appropriate medical authority. Following this determination, patient interests and capabilities as well as program resources are ascertained so that appropriate activities may be selected to meet these patient needs.[24]

Mid-century Highlights

The story of recreation as a professional field of service to the ill and the disabled after the mid-point of the twentieth century can be told better in terms of important areas of development than from a purely chronological standpoint. Much of this development resulted from the efforts of those employed as recreators in hospitals to identify and improve the caliber of the personnel, to examine their mission, and to refine and extend their services.

Professional and Service Organizations

As Roy Sorenson pointed out, one of the hallmarks of a profession is that it seeks to improve itself by organizing into guilds or societies.[25] The first push toward professional association of hospital recreation personnel came in 1948 during the annual meeting of the American Recreation Society. Approximately thirty-seven recreators from veterans, military, and private hospitals who were attending the meeting felt the need for a means whereby recreation personnel from hospitals across the country might come together as a professional group. An interim committee was appointed to do the necessary exploratory and preliminary work. In 1949, the Hospital Recreation Section of the American Recreation Society was established during the Thirty-first National Recreation Congress in New Orleans. This was the first special interest section formed within the Society since its founding eleven years earlier in 1938.[26]

Community and hospital recreation, as previously pointed out, had developed quite independently of each other in their early stages. The rapid growth of recreation in hospitals during and after World War II created new demands for experienced and knowledgeable leadership. However, there were few recreators who had had experience in working in medical settings. Thus community recreators were called upon, in many instances, to apply their knowledge and experience in the organization of programs as well as the recruiting and training of staff for hospital service, particularly in military and veterans hospitals. This nucleus of experienced recreators were aware of, and felt an identity with, the larger recreation movement, and it was they who were largely responsible for the formation of the Hospital Recreation Section within the American Recreation Society. A framework was thus established for bringing two facets of the movement—community recreation and recreation for the ill and the disabled—into close professional association.

One of the valuable contributions made by members of the Hospital Recreation Section of ARS was the study, examination, and preparation of a publication dealing with *Basic Concepts of Hospital Recreation*. The first edition was published as a result of the work of a committee chaired by Clifford C. Bream, Jr., in 1953-1954. Subsequent revisions were prepared by other committees through the years with copies of their reports being distributed to the Section membership and made available to others. The last revision, made before the merger of the American Recreation Society with the new National Recreation and Park Association, was completed in 1962.

Although the membership of the American Recreation Society's Hospital Recreation Section had increased to 593 by 1964,[27] this figure by no means represented the total number of persons employed throughout the nation as therapeutic recreators. The National Association of Recreation Therapists was formed in 1952. Through the remainder of the decade and the first half of the 1960's, this organization continued to be a growing and active group. Many recreators employed in different kinds of institutions, particularly the increasing numbers of professional recreators in state psychiatric hospitals and mental health departments, found stimulating opportunities for professional association and discussion in the organization's national and regional meetings. The official publication of NART, *Recreation for the Ill and Handicapped*, was widely distributed and well received for the quality of its content.

Also in 1952, a Recreation Therapy Section was established in the Recreation Division of the American Association for Health, Physical Education, and Recreation. Among members of this group were some who came into the therapeutic recreation field via the physical education route. Opportunities for association with the teaching profession, particularly with physical educators, were assets offered by this organization. For several years a column or more was devoted to "recreation therapy" in each issue of the Association's *Journal of*

Health, Physical Education, and Recreation. Section meetings on "recreational therapy" were held during the Association's national conference, as well as its district meetings.

Soon after the formation of the latter two groups, it became apparent that there was a need for establishing a channel of communication and cooperation among the three major national organizations which represented the interests of the therapeutic recreation profession. The Council for the Advancement of Hospital Recreation was formed for this purpose in November, 1953.[28] Membership on the Council consisted of representatives of each of the three participating organizations—the National Association of Recreation Therapists, the Recreation Therapy Section of the American Association for Health, Physical Education, and Recreation, and the Hospital Recreation Section of the American Recreation Society. The major achievements of the Council were the development of basic standards of qualification for hospital recreators and the establishment, in 1956, and subsequent operation, of a program of National Voluntary Registration for Hospital Recreation Personnel. This was the first national plan to be effected within the entire recreation movement for setting minimum standards of qualification and identifying professional recreators. It marked a significant forward step in the development of therapeutic recreation professionally and had an effect upon the employment policies of a number of agencies and institutions.[29] Several state recreation societies adopted statewide voluntary registration plans for therapeutic recreators, and some of these plans (as in Illinois) were modeled upon, and provided reciprocal arrangements tying into, the national plan.

While the Council for the Advancement of Hospital Recreation provided some means for joint action and communication among professionals represented in the rolls of the three member groups, it was evident that progress in the therapeutic recreation movement was seriously impeded by the lack of a single, unified, strong organization to represent and speak for this whole professional area. As early as 1958 the question of a possible merger of the three national organizations was raised. Representatives from each of the three groups met as a Committee on Merger. After four years, however, the goal had not been achieved and the Committee was disbanded.

As with the setting of standards and registration of recreators, the question of unity was a concern that stretched across the entire recreation and park movement. In 1965 five national organizations dissolved and united as the National Recreation and Park Association.[30] The new organization was structured to provide for active participation and membership of lay or volunteer as well as professional leadership in the movement. Branches were formed to accommodate special areas of interest. Accordingly, members and the Executive Committee of the former Hospital Recreation Section of the American Recreation Society, meeting at the National Recreation Congress in Minneapolis in October, 1965, expressed interest in seeking separate branch status for their specialty. Interest was also revived at this time in the possibility of bringing the memberships of the National Association of Recreation Therapists and the former ARS Hospital Recreation Section together in the new organizational structure. By June, 1966, both organizations reported a favorable response from their members to referendums on the question of joint action to develop a Branch within the NRPA. Machinery was accordingly set in motion for the official action taken during the National Park and Recreation Congress in Washington, D.C., in October, 1966. The National Therapeutic Recreation Society thus formed was heralded as a milestone in the unity and progress of therapeutic recreation as a professional specialty.

The discussion to this point has been concerned with membership organizations whose main purposes are to provide for association of professionals and spokesmanship for the field. Another type of organization rather loosely defined as a service organization also developed with the recreation movement. The National Recreation Association, founded in 1906, fell into this category. Before merging with other organizations in forming the NRPA, the National Recreation Association had, since 1953, offered a consulting service in "Recreation for the Ill and Handicapped." A national staff consisting of a consultant and one or more assistants was employed. Among the services provided was a regular column or page of current information concerning recreation for the ill and handicapped in the NRA magazine, *Recreation.* Special funds from government grants and other sources were used in demonstration projects and studies of various kinds concerning recreation for ill or handicapped people, including a nation-wide survey in the late 1950's of the status of hospital recreation.

Comeback, Inc. was established in 1960. Its functions were similar to those performed by the NRA consulting service in "Recreation for the Ill and Handicapped." The attention of Comeback was directed toward promoting, through recreation, the social rehabilitation of the aged, ill, and handicapped. It employed a professional staff; published literature; participated in and sponsored workshops, demonstrations, and research projects; and offered a scholarship program. After the establishment of the National Therapeutic Recreation Society, Comeback was gradually phased out of existence.

Organizations such as the National Association for Music Therapy, Inc., the American Association of Rehabilitation Therapy, Inc., the Association of Hospital and Institutional Libraries, the American Occupational Therapy Association, the American Physical Therapy Association, the Group Work Section of the National Association of Social Workers, and others, include among their membership many who work in close relationship to therapeutic recreation and some whose major function lies in that area. Many voluntary and governmental health agencies also provide services, often, but not exclusively, in the form of grants of money for studies, research, projects, or demonstration programs in therapeutic recreation. Examples are the Children's Bureau, Office of Aging, Rehabilitation Services Administration, Bureau of Education for the Handicapped, National Institutes of Health, and other divisions of the Department of HEW in the national government; various state departments of mental health or welfare; the National Association for Retarded Children, Inc.; the National Easter Seal Society for Crippled Children and Adults; the American Foundation for the Blind; the Kennedy Foundation; the International Society for

Rehabilitation of the Disabled; the International Recreation Association; and the National Multiple Sclerosis Society.

Professional Preparation

Academic preparation in the therapeutic recreation specialty became available only after World War II. Before that time, such specific orientation or training for recreation personnel serving the ill or disabled as was provided was offered by employing agencies and institutions through staff development or in-service programs, conferences, and meetings of various kinds. Non-academic programs of this nature continue to provide an essential part of the training and education of therapeutic recreators, and will always be needed to extend and supplement academic education. University recreation departments and faculties have participated, in recent years, in various types of workshops, short courses, and training programs sponsored either by agencies such as state departments of mental health or by one or more of the recreation service or related private or governmental groups. Nevertheless, major responsibility for non-academic training continues to be assumed by employers in programs for their employees.

During the 1950's, biennial institutes in hospital recreation or recreation for the ill and disabled were held on the campuses of the universities of Minnesota and North Carolina. These continued throughout the 1960's under the title of Southern Regional Institutes at the University of North Carolina during the spring of odd-numbered years. Publication by the North Carolina Recreation Commission of papers, addresses, and proceedings from these institutes has made a valuable contribution to the literature in therapeutic recreation.

As recreation curriculums developed in colleges and universities in all parts of the nation following World War II, some of the institutions of higher learning began to offer opportunities for special preparation in therapeutic recreation. Among the first were master's degree programs established by 1951 at the universities of West Virginia and Minnesota.[31]

A national survey of recreation in hospitals was undertaken by the National Recreation Association in the mid-1950's and published in 1959 under the title, *Recreation in Hospitals: Report of a Study of Organized Recreation Programs in Hospitals and of Personnel Conducting Them.* From a partial survey of colleges and universities offering preparation in this field, the study indicated inconsistency in the approaches and degree requirements. As a follow-up, a Therapeutic Recreation Development Conference was held in February, 1961, in New York City. The conference was sponsored by the National Recreation Association's Consulting Service on Recreation for the Ill and Disabled, financed by the Avalon Foundation, and the report was published and distributed by Comeback, Inc. The conferees devoted attention to the traditional and changing concepts of the role of the specialist in therapeutic recreation, and to needs, trends, and problems related to preparing such specialists. Prerequisites to graduate education and competencies at the graduate level were indicated and general suggestions and guidelines proposed for institutions offering a curriculum in therapeutic recreation.[32]

Again, as in other facets of the rapidly developing recreation profession, the establishing of standards for the education of recreators became a matter of growing concern to the entire profession as well as to the specializations within it. The Federation of Professional Organizations for Recreation[33] agreed in 1963 to sponsor a Recreation Education Accreditation Project. The purpose was to develop the basic rationale, standards, and evaluative criteria for recreation education at undergraduate and graduate levels, including such specialized areas as therapeutic recreation.[34]

Thus in the latter 1950's and through the decade that followed, therapeutic recreation as a specialization within the total recreation profession was moving toward the establishment of professional standards and criteria for its practitioners and its educational foundation. Approximately fifty-five of the colleges and universities granting degrees in recreation were known to offer undergraduate preparation (options, minors, special courses, etc.) and/or graduate specialization in therapeutic recreation. New dimensions in the educational preparation of recreators and of specialists in therapeutic recreation were introduced with the rapid expansion of community or junior colleges throughout the country in the latter half of the 1960's. The impact of these two year programs was only beginning to be felt by the close of the decade.

Financial Support and Research

Availability of scholarships is an important factor in attracting able students and in making it possible for them to attend college, pursue advanced study, or engage in research. Scholarships for a given field of study also indicate recognition of that field as a profession. It is worthy of note, therefore, that scholarship funds have been earmarked for students in therapeutic recreation. Examples of these include: scholarships granted by agencies to their employees, such as those offered by the American National Red Cross to its hospital recreators for graduate study; funds made available by agencies seeking to employ qualified people, such as the Illinois Department of Mental Health Employment-Education grants for juniors, seniors, and graduate students in a variety of professional and paramedical fields, including therapeutic recreation; and special scholarships such as those of the Joseph P. Kennedy, Jr. Foundation for students preparing to work with the mentally retarded. The Rehabilitation Services Administration (formerly the Vocational Rehabilitation Administration) in the Department of Health, Education, and Welfare in 1963 instituted a program to award supportive funds for graduate study and teaching to selected colleges and universities offering specialization in therapeutic or rehabilitative recreation. In 1969 additional funds for developing new approaches in graduate programs in therapeutic recreation were made available through grants to selected universities from the Bureau of Education for the Handicapped in the U.S. Office of Education. In addition, grants to individuals, universities, and service agencies for study, research, demonstrations, and projects of various kinds have been made by governmental and private agencies including the Rockefeller Foundation, Avalon Foundation, Kennedy Foundation, National Association for Retarded Children, National Foundation for the Blind, National Institutes of Health, and others.

As short as the history of therapeutic recreation is, the record of research in the therapeutic-rehabilitative aspects of play and recreation is even briefer. Studies and developments in research are discussed in Chapter 11.

In Summary

The history of therapeutic recreation is as old as antiquity and as recent as yesterday. The story of recreation in relation to man's health, to his health beliefs and practices reaches back to the earliest known civilizations—a rich and needed area for research. On the other hand, recreation as a professional area of service to the ill or disabled is a matter of contemporary history spanning no more than fifty years, including the decade ending with 1969.

Recognition of the needs for recreation in the lives of the ill or disabled developed rapidly in the United States after World War I. Yet it was not until World War II and the ensuing fifteen to twenty years that concerted effort was directed toward developing and expanding professional leadership and services. Accomplishments during these post-World War II decades were largely matters of organization and activities of professional groups; initiation of curricular offerings, both undergraduate and graduate; development of minimum standards of qualification and establishment of a voluntary registration plan for therapeutic recreators; and of multiplication, extension, and, to some degree, refinement of recreation services of a therapeutic nature.

Of importance historically, also, are the basic philosophical questions raised and debated during this period concerning the relationship of recreation to medical treatment or therapy. These issues, however, are fundamental to, and thus more properly incorporated in, the subject matter of the following chapter.

Likewise, discussion of major current trends and problems of therapeutic recreation in the late 1960's is reserved for the final chapters as an appropriate indicator of the direction in which therapeutic recreation may be moving.

Notes, Chapter 1

1. Johan Huizinga, *Homo Ludens* (Boston: The Beacon Press, 1950), pp. 18-19.

2. Elizabeth M. Jamieson and Mary F. Sewall, *Trends in Nursing History: Their Relationship to World Events* (Philadelphia: W.B. Saunders Company, 1949), pp. 58-65; Richard Shryock, *The History of Nursing: An Interpretation of the Social and Medical Factors Involved* (Philadelphia: W.B. Saunders Company, 1959), pp. 41-42.

3. Jamieson and Sewall, *op. cit.*, p. 66.

4. *Ibid.*, p. 78.

5. Louis J. Haas, *Practical Occupational Therapy for the Mentally and Nervously Ill* (Milwaukee: The Bruce Publishing Company, 1944), p. 3.

6. Will Durant, *The Story of Civilization: Part III, Caesar and Christ* (New York: Simon and Schuster, 1944), p. 312.

7. Norah A. Haworth and E. Mary MacDonald, *Theory of Occupational Therapy*, 3rd ed. (Baltimore: The Williams and Wilkins Company, 1946), p. 3.

8. Materials in the preceding three paragraphs from Haas, *op. cit.*, pp. 6-9.

9. William Dunton Rush, Jr., *Occupational Therapy: A Manual for Nurses* (Philadelphia: W. B. Saunders Company, 1915), p. 12.

10. Haworth and MacDonald, *op. cit.*, pp. 4, 32.

11. Shryock, *op. cit.*, p. 276; Sir Edward Cook, *The Life of Florence Nightingale*, Vol I (London: Macmillan and Company Ltd., 1913), pp. 276-282; 396-397.

12. Florence Nightingale, *Notes on Nursing: What It Is, and What It Is Not* (New York: D. Appleton and Company, 1873), pp. 57-59, 95-104.

13. William F. Robins, "A Study of the History of Recreation Activities in Selected Mental Hospitals in Illinois, 1850 to 1930" (unpublished thesis in the University of Illinois Library), *passim.*

14. Lillian Summers, "The American Red Cross Program of Recreation in Military Hospitals" (unpublished thesis in the University of North Carolina Library), *passim.*

15. Haworth and MacDonald, *op. cit.*, p. 5.

16. Elizabeth Green and Sidney L. Schwab, "The Therapeutic Use of a Hospital Library," *The Hospital Social Service Quarterly*, Vol. I, No. 3 (August, 1919), pp. 147-157.

17. Ernest V. Hollis and Alice Taylor, *Social Work Education in the United States* (New York: Columbia University Press, 1951), p. 16.

18. Myrtle Fish Thompson, "Music Therapy," in Gerald D. O'Morrow, comp. and ed., *Administration of Activity Therapy Service* (Springfield, Ill.: Charles C. Thomas Publisher, 1966), p. 78.

19 Bertha E. Schlotter and Margaret Svendsen, *An Experiment in Recreation with the Mentally Retarded*, rev. ed. (National Mental Health Funds, 1951, reprinted by authority of the State of Illinois, 1956), *passim.*

20. The American Red Cross, nationally and locally, is, however, a voluntary agency in terms of its financial support.

21. Summers, *op, cit., passim.*

22. "The Recreation Service, Special Services, Veterans Administration" (duplicated paper, November, 1947).

23. The organization and administration of recreation services in VA hospitals are discussed in Chapter 9.

24. Special Services Pamphlet 6-3, Veterans Administration, *Recreation Services* (Washington, D. C.: United States Government Printing Office, n.d.).

25. Roy Sorenson, "Professional Maturity," American Recreation Society, *Quarterly Bulletin*, Vol. V, No. 1 (May, 1953), p. 19.

26. History Committee, Hospital Recreation Section, *History, Hospital Recreation Section, American Recreation Society, Inc., 1948-1964*, pp. 1-2. Publication of the American Recreation Society.

27. *Ibid.*, p. 5.

28. *Ibid.*, p. 3.

29. For further discussion of the National Voluntary Registration of hospital (therapeutic) recreators, see Chapter 8.

30. The merger became reality on January 1, 1966, when the National Recreation and Park Association actually began to function. The five merging organizations were the National Recreation Association, the American Recreation Scoiety, the American Institute of Park Executives, the National Conference on State Parks, and the American Association of Zoological Parks and Aquariums.

31. History Committee, Hospital Recreation Section, *op. cit.*, p. 3.

32. *Therapeutic Recreation Curriculum Development Conference*. February 16-18, 1961 (New York: Comback, Inc., n.d.), *passim.*

33. Member organizations of the Federation of National Professional Organizations for Recreation included: the American Association for Health, Physical Education, and Recreation; the American Camping Association; the American Institute of Park Executives; the American Recreation Society; the Association of College Unions-International; the National Association of Social Workers; the National Association of Recreation Therapists; the National Industrial Recreation Association Conference on State Parks; and the Society of State Directors of Health, Physical Education, and Recreation. The Athletic Institute and the National Recreation Association were consultants to the Federation.

34. Progress and current status of the Recreation Education Accreditation Project are discussed in Chapter 8.

2 | Philosophical Considerations

IN ANY PROFESSIONAL field, philosophy is the rudder that gives guidance and direction. Guidelines for planning, decision, and action in education, research, and practice are based upon a profession's philosophical foundations. Coherent and effective action of professionals depends in large measure upon their knowledge, understanding, acceptance, and consistent application of the basic philosophical tenets of the profession they represent. Professional identity—the why, what, and who of the field and its practitioners—stems from philosophical roots.

Problems

The philosophy of a human service profession is appropriately evolving, rather than static in nature. As one writer put it, "The aim of a true philosophy must lie, not in futile efforts towards the complete accommodation of man to the circumstances in which he chances to find himself, but in the maintenance of a kind of candid discontent, in the face of the very highest achievement."[1]

In a professional field as young as recreation, nevertheless, the major problem has been one of developing sound guidelines for new and rapidly expanding endeavors and areas of service. Recreation is itself a human experience, and as such has been seen as a philosophy—a way—of life. Thus any philosophy of the recreation profession and its practice must be accommodated to this fundamental concept. This may indicate a difference between a philosophy of recreation as a profession in comparison with some of the older service professions such as medicine, law, and social work. On the other hand, some parallels might be drawn between recreation—as both a way of life and a professional area—and education.

With a philosophy of the recreation profession as a whole in only a rudimentary stage of development, specializations began to emerge and soon demanded some definition of the rationale for their existence. By the mid-point of the twentieth century, as pointed out in the previous chapter, recreators serving the ill or disabled in hospitals and institutions of various kinds had formed the first special interest section of the American Recreation Society. The Hospital Recreation Section of the ARS was soon followed by the National Association of Recreation Therapists and a Recreation Therapy Section in the Recreation Division of the American Association of Health, Physical Education, and Recreation. Terms used in the titles of these three organizations were indicative of differing philosophical orientations among their memberships.

The relationship of recreation to medical treatment or therapy posed concepts that were embraced by some, rejected by others, and debated in professional journals and meetings. An "either-or" dilemma characterized many of the arguments. To some it was recreation *versus* therapy; diversional *or* purposeful activity; voluntary *or* prescribed and structured participation; medical approval *or* medical prescription; fun *or* therapeutic goals; recreator *or* therapist; and so on. Although some of the discussion might be dismissed as merely subjective and emotional expression, or as rather superficial exercises in semantics, nevertheless basic issues were involved.

Progress

By the early 1950's controversy was developing concerning the relationship—or lack of it—between recreation and therapy. As indicated in the preceding chapter, a committee was appointed in the early 1950's in the Hospital Recreation Section, American Recreation Society, to conduct a study on the Basic Concepts of Hospital Recreation. The committee, composed of leading recreators employed in hospitals, sent letters to selected physicians and to other recreators soliciting their ideas and comments on the following points:

1. Definition of recreation.
2. The application of the definition to the recreation program in a hospital.
3. The place of the recreation program in a hospital.
4. Opinion of the use of medical prescription in relation to the participation of patients in the recreation program.
5. The function of the physician in relation to determining the activities to be included in the recreation program. For diagnostic groups. For individual patients.[2]

The report of the study was published in 1953 with the following proposed as a statement of tenet:

STATEMENT OF TENET, HOSPITAL RECREATION SECTION, AMERICAN RECREATION SOCIETY

WE BELIEVE,

That wholesome recreation is an essential ingredient of mental, emotional, and physical well-being.

That in keeping with the modern medical concept of treating the whole man, recreation, under medical guidance, has a vital and an important role in the treatment, care, and rehabilitation of ill and disabled people.

That recreation assists the physician in his work of helping the patient get well by:
1. Facilitating favorable adjustment of the patient to treatment and hospital environment.
2. Contributing to the development, restoration, or maintenance of sound mental, emotional, and physical health.
3. Providing the physician with opportunities to observe patient response to medically approved recreation activities.

That as hospital recreation leaders we have the responsibility of:
1. Adapting and conducting medically approved recreation programs that satisfy the needs, capabilities, and interests of all patients in varying degrees of illness or disability.
2. Developing topmost professional standards and leadership qualities.
3. Continually improving and refining program content.
4. Developing factual evidence of program effectiveness through objective evaluation and scientific research.
5. Continually apprising the physician of recreation resources available to assist in the treatment, care, and rehabilitation of patients.[3]

Although this proposed statement of tenet, which constituted the major recommendations of the committee, was quite general and non-specific in nature, the study report was a landmark, setting the stage for continuing attempts to probe the problems more deeply and examine the issues more critically.

Some of the quoted responses from various individuals included in the study are significant because of their lasting influence upon the development of philosophical guidelines in therapeutic recreation. Others were indicative of cleavages in basic beliefs among various professionals.

The inspirational teacher and pioneer among recreation educators, Ott Romney, was quoted as stating that "recreation in a hospital is cut in a different pattern [as compared with other settings] and is subject to factors which shape and limit—but . . . it is cut out of the same cloth." Romney continued, "I could better understand the role of the recreationist in relation to therapy or the therapeutic dividends of recreation than the role of the 'recreation therapist,' but I believe we will do well to make sure we are not engaging in semantics but are analyzing content and method professionally."[4]

Ralph Rossen, M.D., Commissioner of Mental Health, Minneapolis, Minnesota, saw recreation in the hospital as ". . . somewhat different from the ordinary connotation of community recreation in that its only justifiable means of existence is the treatment of the patient." A speech therapist from Little Rock, Arkansas, Clara Mae Frederick, also emphasized that in the hospital "Recreation is a therapy which is a socialized, diversional combination of other therapies."[5]

In the same study, Dr. Howard A. Rusk was quoted as believing firmly "that both individual and group recreation activities for hospital patients have a direct relationship upon their recovery—these [hospital recreation activities], in my opinion, are definitely adjunctive therapy, as are all the environmental forces within a hospital, and would be under definite medical supervision. I do not believe, however, that they should be termed 'recreational therapy.'" However, the medical Director of the National Association for Mental Health, George S. Stevenson, expressed his view that "Recreation really re-creates. It affects the individual deeply, is somewhat akin to therapy, but is more positive than therapy. Recreation is pointed less toward the correction of a disorder than toward the elevation of the quality of living. Recreation may be therapeutic but that is a by-product. Its goal is not therapy and its therapeutic value is apt to be greater when the person is least conscious of its therapeutic influence."[6]

Several leading professionals in the recreation field have pointed out that some of the differences in opinions, such as those cited above, might be partially ascribed to the presence of dual motivations at work in recreation with the ill or disabled—that of the leader or recreator, and that of the participant, in this case usually a patient. In other words, for the participant, be he sick or well, able-bodied or disabled, in or out of a treatment center, the major aim and outcome of recreation is the pleasurable or satisfying nature of the experience. To the recreator in the medical setting, however, there is the added, or perhaps more consciously sought goal of therapeutic benefits that may accompany or be achieved through the recreation experience itself.

Major contributions to the philosophical dialogue concerning hospital—or therapeutic—recreation have been made by various medical men. Several whose statements were included in the 1953 Basic Concepts report have been referred to previously. Notable among others are psychiatrists Paul Haun and Alexander Reid Martin, cardiologist Joseph B. Wolffe, and physiatrist A. B. C. Knudson. A few excerpts from the writings of these men will indicate their views. Each has helped to elucidate points of view important to the development of concepts and guidelines for recreation in relation to medicine and rehabilitation.

Alexander Reid Martin:

> When asked to talk about a philosophy for hospital recreation, I faltered somewhat . . . A more appropriate title would be "A psychiatrist makes some suggestions for a basic philosophy of all recreation."
> I asked myself the question—whether a philosophy for recreation can be one thing within a hospital for sick and disabled individuals, and another thing outside the hospital for everyday individuals.

. . . .

Two elements prevail in the hospital situation, which are not characteristic of the extra-mural situation. One—the existence of disease or disability, and two—because of these, the high degree of dependency on the recreation worker implicit in the relationship. Regarding the first—for effective rapport, the hospital recreation worker must be more intent upon maintaining a holistic approach than he would be extramurally; that is, he must be more careful to relate himself to the whole person and not to the disease.

. . . .

Regarding the . . . element of dependency, this enters much more strongly than in the everyday situation of the hobby shop, game room, camp, or playing field.

. . . .

. . . I am convinced that any and every philosophy for recreation that is worthwhile, must have as a prerequisite, as a common central core, an appreciation and clear conception of the true nature of recreation, its real meaning and value to mankind, its indispensability for all healthy growth and creativity and its dynamic and inseparable relationship to relaxation and leisure. I would like to call this common, basic component of all worthwhile recreation philosophy the *humanistic component.*

. . . .

. . . the psychiatrist is now focusing considerable attention upon this whole subject [recreation] and, more and more psychiatric problems are approached, formulated and treated in terms of leisure, relaxation and recreation. This frame of reference has provided us with new insights into the neurotic process and has necessitated our closer integration with the specialist in recreation.

. . . .

. . . broadly speaking, our therapeutic goal is to help the patient live leisurely and not compulsively.

. . . .

It seems to me our aim should be to strive always for recreation in its ideal, its wholesome and healthful sense, in its humanistic sense, and that we examine carefully what we are calling recreation.

. . . .

Until we in Medicine stop relating ourselves primarily to disease and start to relate ourselves primarily to health promotion, health conservation, health protection, we cannot really join hands with recreation because these have always been the ideals of recreation.[7]

Joseph B. Wolffe (one of the earliest to report an observational study in quantitative terms):

In the area of education and health, where recreation is coming to be recognized more and more as a vital modality in both preventive medicine and therapeutics, the non-MD—you, the recreator—have an historic role to play.

. . . .

A survey of 1000 patients has shown that carefully selected recreation to suit the patient's problem and personality resulted in reduction both in drug requirements as well as length of hospital stay, when compared to the control group in the institution without the program.

In over 200 cases of organic cardiovascular disease, with anxieties attributable either to fear of their conditions or definite iatrogenic factors, . . . there was better than a 50% reduction in the need for drugs among those who received recreation therapy. In neuro-circulatory asthenia (effort syndrome) there was a 35% reduction in the need for sedatives and tranquilizers.

To a lesser, but very definite extent, there was a reduction in the need for drug therapy in angina pectoris, coronary heart disease, fistular heart disease, and essential hypertension. This is particularly noteworthy in disease where the need for rest has been universally emphasized in the past.

In the management of cardiovascular diseases associated with diabetes mellitus the daily maintenance dose of Insulin was materially reduced. In milder cases Insulin was dispensed with and a normal blood sugar level maintained on diet alone. . . . There is also ample scientific evidence that recreational physical activities stimulate the cortex of the adrenal gland, which is intimately associated with the protective mechanism against undue stress reactions, whether due to organic disease or emotional disturbance.

On the other hand, in cases where tranquilizing drugs were indicated and patients indulged in mentally stimulating recreation activities, particularly close to bedtime, there was a tendency to a greater degree of restlessness.

These observations suggest that there are definite indications and contra-indications for recreation activities, and only suitable forms of activity will do good, while others may in some instances aggravate the condition.

We also found that the average hospital confinement was reduced by approximately 15% in the institution where recreation therapy was an important part of the management. Most of the patients have learned through such activities, both directly and indirectly, that they are not hopeless invalids and can return to normal life. Activity, therefore, must be chosen as carefully as are potent medicinals.[8]

A. B. C. Knudson:

. . . "Is recreation *therapy?*" Since the word "therapy" has different meanings for different people the answer requires a distinction. If therapy is defined as prescribed or medically guided participation on the team mobilized for a potential therapeutic attack on illness, then most assuredly recreation is frequently therapy. But recreation cannot be labeled as therapy in the sense of a precise cure for a specific ailment.[9]

Probably no other medical person, and few within the recreation profession, have contributed more than did the late Paul Haun to the literature of therapeutic recreation, particularly with respect to its philosophical connotations. The following statements are indicative of his point of view:

In defining the place, and the very important place, that recreation plays in total patient care I would single out the fact that it is extra-clinical.

In such a setting the unique value of providing recreation services to patients lies in their *not* being clinical.

Contemporary medicine is coming to think less about the disease and more about people with disease. The strength of the recreation movement is that it thinks about people, and in so doing goes beyond the limitations of medicine. Perhaps I should say it thinks about individuals rather than people, for it is one of the peculiar virtues of recreation to individualize.

. . . .

I like to think of recreation . . . as an important means of increasing the effectiveness of therapy. While not curative in itself, it helps create the milieu for successful treatment.

. . . .

It is my belief that "recreational therapy" cannot successfully answer the rigorous questions that must be put to it if it is to be taken seriously as another form of treatment. If the recreation worker claims access to the sick primarily as a therapist and fails to demonstrate the equivalence, if not the superiority, of his contribution fairly measured against that of other supportive medical disciplines, it would seem unwise for hospital administrators to devote their always limited financial resources to such programs or even to the salaries of recreation personnel. It seems both hazardous and unnecessary to me for those interested in recreation to place their figurative eggs in so gossamer a basket as "therapy;" hazardous because I know of no evidence that recreation is an effective treatment instrument and unnecessary since I am persuaded that highly relevant arguments can be advanced for providing recreation services in terms other than therapy. I am so fully persuaded of the value of recreation *as recreation* for the ill or disabled person that I am alarmed at the possibility of its being unjustly discredited through laying claim to an effectiveness it cannot possess.[10]

Although there was a tendency among recreators working with the ill or disabled to look to and depend upon medical men for the definition and justification of their service and role, articles written by recreators did appear from time to time in the journals of the various organizations. Of the small company of recreators who have authored major publications on the philosophy of leisure and recreation, Charles K. Brightbill was one of the most influential and respected. In each of his widely read and acclaimed books, *Man and Leisure: a Philosophy of Recreation,* and the paperback edition, *The Challenge of Leisure,* Brightbill devoted a chapter to an exposition of concepts and philosophy of the relation of recreative uses of leisure to health—ideas and beliefs he had gained through long experience, observations, and study both in the United States and abroad.

Brightbill was a strong advocate of the therapeutic values and potential of recreation. "Therapeutic recreation," he said, "refers to the use of varied forms of recreation in the therapeutic process. It is carefully structured and medically applied recreation directed toward goals—treatment and rehabilitation aims— which, of course, transcend those of patient enjoyment and satisfaction."[11] The flavor of Brightbill's ideas and arguments are indicated in the following excerpts from a series of questions which he posed as being the kind those who are ready to use the term "therapeutic recreation" would ask:

If recreation can help upgrade the self-concept of the patient, is not the process therapeutic?

Is recreation therapeutic if it contributes to the patient's adjustment in any way?

If recreation by definition is re-creation, refreshment of mind, spirit, and body, how can it be anything but therapeutic?

If illness disrupts the harmonious performance of the human organism which includes recreation and relaxation as well as work and rest, what are recreation's therapeutic implications?

In certain types of mental disorders, can recreation serve as [a socially acceptable] outlet for aggressive drives . . . ? If so, is it therapeutic?

Is recreation an outlet to compensate for feelings of worthlessness, inferiority, insecurity, and non-recognition? If it is applied in such a way as to reduce such feelings of inadequacy, is it contributing to the treatment aims?

How important is communication in the treatment of mental disorders? Can recreation expedite communication? If it can, is it therapeutic?

Do attitudes and values have anything to do with patient recovery? If so, can recreation be blocked out of the therapeutic family?

Do certain types of recreation nurture the sense of belonging? If so, is recreation a valuable instrument in the therapeutic process for certain types of mental disorders?

If it is true that loneliness, anxiety, and boredom are among modern man's most bothersome problems, multiplied and sharpened when one is ill, is recreation a partial answer in helping to make them less devastating?[12]

A concerted effort by professionals to develop a philosophical position statement for therapeutic recreation was begun by a study group which met concurrently with the Ninth Southern Regional Institute on Therapeutic Recreation at the University of North Carolina in 1969. Later in the same year, participation in the discussions was extended to include all interested members of the National Therapeutic Recreation Society in attendance at the National Congress for Recreation and Parks. Further development and refinement of the statement was the purpose of a follow-up invitational work-study conference held in the spring of 1970 at Indiana State University.

By the end of the 1960's, the term "therapeutic recreation" was in wide use, generally replacing such terms as "hospital recreation" and "recreation therapy." "Continuum" and "process" appeared in papers and discussions attempting to elucidate concepts basic to an understanding of therapeutic recreation.

Toward a Philosophical Statement

In setting forth the philosophical guidelines for the content of this book, the authors recognize that a definite statement of a philosophy of therapeutic recreation is in an evolving stage and remains in need of continuing efforts toward more rigorous analysis, deeper comprehensions, and broader consensus. The influence of concepts from sources described in preceding pages will be apparent to the reader. Likewise, important contributions made by various recreators in relation to the development of a position statement for therapeutic recreation, referred to above, figure in the discussion that follows.

A look at the term, itself, at the words used, the concepts involved, and the way in which they are combined provides a logical starting point for stating a philosophy of therapeutic recreation. The phrase consists of two words—a noun and an adjective. This connotes that the basic concepts involved are those conveyed by the noun, "recreation," with the adjective, "therapeutic," indicating an adaptation or modification of the generic element in the expression.

Recreation is defined as experience derived from participation in voluntarily chosen pursuits engaged in during unobligated time (leisure) primarily for purposes of personal satisfaction or enjoyment. The foundation for a philosophy of recreation may be found in principles such as the following:

1. Recreation is a pleasurable, satisfying human experience.
2. Recreation involves the exercise of voluntary choice and participation by the individual.
3. The primary motivation and goal of the individual (participant) lies in the pleasurable, satisfying nature of the experience itself.
4. Recreation is a highly internalized, individual experience.
5. Recreation may be gained through or from any form or type of activity.
6. Certain conditions are necessary to an experience that is uniquely recreational in nature, including:
   a. the leisure (unobligated or free time) to make possible individual choice and freedom of activity
   b. resources (including personal knowledge, skills, and attitudes) and opportunities for making choices.
7. Recreation is an experience involving the whole person.
8. Recreation has meaning, purpose, and value to the individual.
9. Recreation usually, if not always, involves concomitant effects that, although secondary to the pleasurable nature of the experience, are integral to it.

Principles such as these embody concepts that remain constant even when the generic term "recreation" is modified, as in the phrase "therapeutic recreation." Addition of the adjective "therapeutic" therefore, rather than altering the basic philosophical tenets of recreation, denotes addition to the recreative experience of effects of a specific nature. Principle nine as stated above can thus be seen to indicate the basic rationale for the relationship implied in the term "therapeutic recreation."

The word "therapeutic" refers, of course, to a healing or curative process or agent. The term may be used in a general, broad sense to describe anything of a positive or beneficial nature. Understood in this light, all desirable recreation may be looked upon as therapeutic, and all recreators assumed to be dedicated to therapeutic recreation as their basic professional commitment. Somewhere between such a generalized view and a specific medical interpretation and use of the term lies the concept that the difference between recreation and therapeutic recreation is mainly a matter of degree, particularly with respect to the increased responsibility of the therapeutic recreator to direct conscious effort toward emphasizing potential beneficial effects of recreation.

In the medical sense, therapy is defined as the treatment of disease, and therapeutic pertains to the art and science of healing. Predictable results are fundamental to the concept of treatment. A strict medical construction would hold, then, that recreation could be considered therapeutic only to the extent that specific beneficial effects of a recreative experience could be identified, predicted, and achieved.

The foregoing discussion is indicative of dual concepts and usages of both recreation and therapeutic recreation. As pointed out by the study group that continued the work begun on a position statement at the 1969 University of North Carolina Institute, the term "recreation" is used to describe both an experience and an area of professional service. Based upon the rationale that the quality and nature of recreation as a human experience and its meaning to the individual remain unchanged regardless of life's vicissitudes, and with an understanding of the relationship of possible therapeutic benefits to the recreative experience as indicated in the ninth principle above, the authors agree that therapeutic recreation may most readily and properly be understood as a special area of recreation services.

Viewed from this perspective, therapeutic recreation becomes ". . . a process which utilizes recreation services for purposive intervention in some physical, emotional, and/or social behavior to bring about a desired change in that behavior and to promote the growth and development of the individual."[13] "Process" may be defined, according to Webster, as "a continuing development involving many changes." This definition has been used effectively by Doris Berryman, Research Scientist, New York University, in developing a conceptual model of therapeutic recreation ". . . suggested by the double helix structure of the DNA molecule." Berryman sees in this approach a dynamic interpretation that takes into account the concept of a continuum in therapeutic recreation service implied in the above definition of process. The continuum here suggested, however, is not represented by a straight line, but rather is viewed ". . . as an infinite, fluid movement . . ." that provides ". . . for the constantly changing relationship between self and environment and the relationship of recreation thereto." In describing her imaginative and provocative conceptual model, Berryman continues:

> If, for example, we view the self as one helix and the environment as the other helix, then recreation can become experiential bonds linking the self together with his environment.
>
> In the therapeutic process, as recreation activities are introduced into the environment, the patient reacts. If his reaction is one of withdrawal no bonding can take place. We must then introduce new activities and/or other leadership techniques until there is some positive reaction on the patient's part which will establish a firm experiential bond between him and his environment.
>
> As these bonds are established, the self and environment take on a new relationship. This new relationship opens the way for new activity experiences to be introduced and, hopefully, the creation of new bonds between the self and environment.
>
> At some point, the self with its strong bonds to the environment, actually expands and so, automatically, does the environment. This mutual expansion opens up new avenues of approach for the practitioner, and for the patient, new ways of reacting and internalizing the recreative experience to create new bonds with his environment.

At some further point in this constantly changing and expanding relationship between the expanding self and his expanding environment, the patient no longer needs the in-put into his environment provided by the practitioner. On his own volition, he enters into recreational pursuits which become recreative experiences providing him with positive emotional rewards and new experiential bonds between himself and his environment.

However, the moving and intertwining continuum does not stop. The self actualization process continues ad infinitum with recreative experiences creating ever new bonds between the self and his environment and Self and Environment continue to establish new relationships and additional expansions.[14]

Another interpretation of the continuum concept as applied to therapeutic recreation has been contributed by Edith L. Ball, recreation educator and Professor of Education at New York University. She sees this as a progressive scale along which the individual may move through various levels until he reaches a true recreative experience. Ball charts her scale as follows:

Experience	Type of time	Major Motivation
1. Activity for sake of activity	Obligated time	Drive is outer directed
2. Recreation Education	Obligated time	Drive is outer directed
3. Therapeutic Recreation	Unobligated time	Motivation is inner directed but choice of experience is limited
4. Recreation	Unobligated time	Motivation is inner directed

As indicated by the chart, an individual might move from the first level, activity for the sake of "reality participation," through the recreation education stage in which, according to Ball, the individual ". . . develops attitudes toward the use of free time, and learns knowledge and skills about activities that he may use in his free time. In recreation education . . . the individual is specifically counseled into activities based on a careful assessment of his needs and interests." Moving into the therapeutic recreation phase, the individual, "Having learned the basic elements of the selected experiences in the recreation education phase . . . then begins to make choices of therapeutically oriented recreation experiences in which he wishes to participate." Thus he is moving toward a true recreation experience which he will choose on his own volition in his unobligated time. Ball points out further that any individual may be participating at different levels of the scale with respect to various aspects of his life experiences at any given time. Also, it is probable that ". . . all people need, at one time or another, to have exposure to each phase of the recreation scale."[15]

Still another dimension of the continuum along which therapeutic recreation may be seen to function was developed by graduate students in a class taught by one of the authors and submitted by the students for consideration in the development of the therapeutic recreation position statement referred to previously. The diagram below was adapted from a basic idea of Robert Tannenbaum and Warren H. Schmidt concerning the change of authority and freedom in a managerial type relationship.[16]

Therapeutic Recreation—A Continuum

Clinical	Clinical	←___ Special ___	Community
Setting	Setting	Populations	Setting
Therapeutic	Recreation	Recreation	Recreation
Recreation ———→			

Use of authority
by the recreator

Area of freedom
for "patients"

↑	↑	↑	↑	↑
Recreator administers highly structured program under medical orders	Recreator "sells" program to patient, motivates patient to participate	Recreator and patient construct program together	Recreator advises patient and community	Patient free to participate in any activity available to him

A question frequently raised concerning therapeutic recreation has to do with the principle of voluntary choice as a requisite for a truly recreative experience. It is apparent that the capacity for making choices or for volitional action may not be possible for some who are extremely ill or disabled such as those who are profoundly mentally retarded, severely brain damaged, or acutely ill—mentally or emotionally. Concepts of therapeutic recreation as a service and of the various dimensions of the continuum along which the service or process may function imply a differentiation between short- and long-term goals. While the immediately attainable goals with individuals such as those indicated above may preclude the achievement of a true recreative experience, the overall objective of the therapeutic recreator will be to assist these people along a continuum leading toward the fullest recreative experience their capacities will allow.

Not only are concepts broadening concerning the nature and range of therapeutic recreation services to include areas such as leisure counseling and leisure habilitation or rehabilitation, but also concerning the population to be served. Therapeutic recreation services are no longer conceived as being offered only within the treatment or institutional setting. Concepts of recreation as a continuum in the individual's total life experience make the offering of effective service to the hospitalized patient improbable without regard for both his pre- and post-hospital leisure life pattern. The population with whom therapeutic recreation is concerned are referred to as "the ill or disabled." "Illness" as defined by Webster refers specifically to an unhealthy condition of the body or mind, sickness, or disease. "Disability" has a broader connotation, however. A person may be disabled from any of a number of standpoints—social, cultural, economic, educational—as well as from physical or mental impairments. Therapeutic recreators thus are concerned, along with their community recreation colleagues, with serving individuals within broad segments of the total population who may benefit from certain of the concomitant effects or values to be gained through recreative experience.

On the basis of the foregoing concepts and principles of recreation as a human experience and of therapeutic recreation as a special area of service within the total field of recreation services, a statement that succinctly defines the term "therapeutic recreation" may appropriately be proposed. Although the concepts involved may be variously expressed, the authors believe that, simply stated, therapeutic recreation is a process through which purposeful efforts are directed toward achieving or maximizing desired concomitant effects of a recreative experience.

Some of the major benefits that may accrue to the individual through recreation experiences are identified in Part II. Discussion in each chapter focuses upon the therapeutic potential that may be achieved when such values are purposefully sought and emphasized according to the individual's specific needs as related both to his capacities and to the effects of various illnesses and disabling conditions. There are, of course, numerous additional benefits that come along with various recreation experiences. Many of these that have particular therapeutic significance are included in the discussions of the major topics of various chapters. For example, the values of recreation as a channel of communication, involving non-verbal as well as verbal expression, enter into the discussion of social implications, educative values, and opportunities for self-realization. The preventive potential of recreation as a health-maintaining as well as a health-restoring way of life can be considered as both foundation and point of departure for all of the concepts expressed in Part II. Finally, while the emphasis in this book is upon the kind of benefits that may be considered human values, the importance of other contributions that recreation may offer in relation to illness and disabling conditions is recognized. Opportunities recreation affords to other treatment areas, for example in the observation of patient behavior and the like, are related more appropriately to later sections of the book.

Notes, Chapter 2

1. Walter Pater, *Marius the Epicurean* [1885], Chapter 25 (as quoted in John Bartlett, *Familiar Quotations*, 13th rev. ed., Boston: Little, Brown and Company, 1955), p. 702.

2. Hospital Recreation Section, American Recreation Society, *Basic Concepts of Hospital Recreation*, (n.p., 1953), p. 2.

3. *Ibid.*, p. 21.

4. *Ibid.*, pp. 5, 7.

5. Ibid., p. 6.

6. *Ibid.*, pp. 6, 7.

7. Alexander Reid Martin, M.D., "A Philosophy of Recreation," in *The Doctors and Recreation in the Hospital Setting*, Bulletin No. 30 (Raleigh, N.C.: The North Carolina Recreation Commission, 1962), pp. 5, 6, 7, 8, 10, 14.

8. Joseph B. Wolffe, M.D., "Recreation, Medicine and the Humanities," *Ibid.*, pp. 17, 19-20.

9. A. B. C. Knudson, M.D., "Concepts of Recreation in Rehabilitation," *Ibid.*, p. 40.

10. Paul Haun, *Recreation: A Medical Viewpoint*, Elliott M. Avedon and Frances B. Arje, comps. and eds. (New York: Teachers College Press, 1965), pp. 53, 54, 55, 60-61.

11. Charles K. Brightbill, from unpublished manuscript on "Philosophy, Concepts, and Principles" [of Therapeutic Recreation], p. 3. In his full definition of the term, Brightbill describes therapeutic recreation as "the medical application of an activity, voluntarily engaged in during a period of treatment or convalescence, that is enjoyable and satisfying, even though the activity and the participation are structured to achieve a predicted result beyond the participant's enjoyment and satisfaction." Harold D. Meyer and Charles K. Brightbill, *Community Recreation: A Guide to Its Organization*, 3rd ed., (Englewood Cliffs, N. J.: Prentice-Hall, Inc., 1964), p. 36.

12. Charles K. Brightbill, unpublished manuscript, *op. cit.*, pp. 20-21.

13. Unpublished paper prepared by committee of participants in Ninth Southern Regional Institute of Therapeutic Recreation, University of North Carolina, 1969.

14. Doris L. Berryman, "Therapeutic Recreation . . . A Conceptual Model," unpublished paper presented at Ninth Southern Regional Institute on Therapeutic Recreation, University of North Carolina, 1969.

15. Edith L. Ball, "The Meaning of Therapeutic Recreation," *Therapeutic Recreation Journal*, Vol. IV., No. 1 (First Quarter, 1970), pp. 17-18.

16. Cynthia Bertholf, James Brademas, Laura Jarvis, Cheryl Reeves, "Therapeutic Recreation—A Continuum," unpublished paper, 1969. Adaptation of concept and diagram of change of authority and freedom based upon Robert Tannenbaum and Warren H. Schmidt, "How to Choose a Leadership Pattern," *Harvard Business Review*, Vol. 36, No. 2 (March-April, 1958), pp. 95-101.

Part II

THERAPEUTIC VALUES AND APPLICATIONS

In this section of the book the authors have departed rather sharply from the presentations of other writers. Thus, an additional word concerning the rationale and organization of the following chapter topics and discussions may be helpful to the reader.

First, no matter what the approach, there is agreement that recreation is a whole experience of the whole person. Individuals are complex beings; recreation experiences are multi-faceted. Although various aspects of each must be studied to determine the relationship and effect of one upon the other, such analysis must always be done within the context of the totality of the being and of the experience. As it is difficult, albeit necessary in some instances, to treat separately aspects of the individual's social, physical, or emotional being, so the task of examining components of the recreative experience is complicated but, we believe, essential to a consideration of recreation service in relation to the therapeutic process.

Discussions of development and delivery of therapeutic recreation services are usually organized around diagnostic classifications or disability designations. This approach tends to draw attention first to the disability or illness and only then to recreation as it may relate to ameliorating the effects of such conditions.

The authors propose that, as therapeutic recreators, we have the responsibility of first examining elements of the total recreative experience that may have therapeutic potential and then of exploring how such elements may relate to helping people who are ill or disabled develop, regain, or maintain their capacities for full living.

Some of these elements that are representative of the types of values or benefits that come along with or are concomitants of recreative experiences have been selected as the topics of the following chapters and their therapeutic potential discussed in relation to the effects of various illnesses and disabling conditions. As we acknowledge that social, physiological, psychological aspects of life are an interrelated whole, and recognize the impossibility of compartmentalizing physical, mental, or emotional disorders as discrete entities, so the various benefits that come with recreation are intertwined. Thus there is bound to be some overlap in the discussions that follow as, for example, between the educational and social values of recreation in the therapeutic process. No claim is made that all of the potential therapeutic values of recreation are discussed in Part II nor that all aspects and possible applications of those that are identified have been presented. The intent has been to point out some basic concepts along with suggestions for their application to specific situations as a stimulus to further thinking, study, and action along these lines toward the goal of increasing the effectiveness of therapeutic recreation services.

3 | Social Implications

IN THIS DISCUSSION the term "social" is used to refer to the relation of one individual to another, or to a group of individuals. Patterns of such relationships, having become established and passed on from one generation to another, may be referred to as a "culture."

To the person who has an illness or a disability, it may seem that such an experience is a highly individualized phenomenon. His pain, his disease, his physical or mental condition are very personal and may seem to have little to do with his interpersonal relationships. Certainly the invading germs recognize no social or class distinctions in their choice of hosts. From this viewpoint, the possibility of any significant relationship between illness and social condition seems remote.

Yet illness, disease, and disability extend beyond the domain of medical science. There are social implications in the patient's attitude toward illness and disability, in the course he chooses to follow in doing something about his illness, in the effects of his illness or disability on other people's attitudes toward him, even in the very definition of illness. The recreator deals with the patient as a person and as a social being. He can leave to the medical profession the deep concern for the natural laws of medicine, and take up his concern with the patient as a person, recognizing that the personality of the patient and his social condition may constitute elements of his illness.

Definitions of Illness and Disability in the Social Context

What constitutes illness? In most societies health is the norm and illness is a departure from the norm. But as MacLachlan points out, there is a great variation of concepts of normal health among the world's many culture groups. "Normal" is what is usual, expected, understood in its frame of reference, and generally regarded as desirable.[1] Thus a physiological condition which is common to the majority in one culture will be regarded as usual, expected, and a state of normal health, while in another culture such a condition will be found only in isolated cases and considered a deviance from the norm, highly undesirable, and, consequently, will be considered an illness. An example is the universal infestation of hookworm in areas of southern North Africa at one time. Anemia in children caused by the hookworm was considered normal, and outside efforts to eradicate hookworm were met with considerable resistance.[2] Also cited are such conditions as schizophrenia or epilepsy which are considered to be serious conditions of ill health in some cultures, but in others are regarded as enviable states. In fact, disease or disfigurement, as defined by modern scientific medicine, is in some cultures considered desirable and is deliberately cultivated. Some examples are "the deliberate inducement of hysterias such as the 'dancing madness' of the Middle Ages, the painful attainment of hallucinations among some American Indian tribes, the adulation of addicts in some of the societies in which addiction is related to ritual,"[3] the conception that obesity is esthetically desirable in Africa and the Near East, the custom of footbinding in China, the attenuation of the neck among the Congolese, and lip stretching among the Ubangi.

What constitutes illness or disability, then, depends to some extent on what is considered normal and desirable in the given culture, and what is expected of each individual within the social role structure. Parsons defines health as the state of optimum capacity of an individual for the effective performance of the roles and tasks for which he has been socialized.[4] He equates mental health primarily with role performance, and physical health with task performance. Illness is the disturbance of this capacity. Clearly, then, as roles and tasks differ from group to group, the concept of illness differs.

Concepts of illness vary not only in widely differing cultures, but variations are found in the social classes within one culture. Koos' study of Regionville revealed that social class tended to dictate the attitude of its members toward symptomatic indications of illness. The respondents were questioned about the following symptoms: loss of appetite, persistent backaches, continued coughing, persistent joint and muscle pains, blood in stools, blood in urine, excessive vaginal bleeding, swelling of ankles, loss of weight, bleeding gums, chronic fatigue, shortness of breath, persistent headaches, fainting spells, pain in chest, lump in breast, and lump in abdomen—all symptoms considered by medical science to warrant the attention of the doctor. Class I, upper class members, consistently recognized the importance of the symptoms and indicated they would usually seek medical advice or assistance upon the appearance of almost all the listed symptoms. Class II, middle class people, were less concerned, while Class III, lower class people, showed marked indifference to the symptoms as indications of illness and were least inclined to seek medical assistance.[5]

The effect of the symptoms on the efficient occupational functioning of the individuals determines to some extent whether or not the symptoms will be considered illness. Persistent headaches, for instance, will be viewed with greater alarm by a college professor whose occupation is chiefly concerned with "brain work," than by the blue collar worker whose job depends more on brawn than brain. Along with occupation goes the status in the family—the age, sex, and role of the afflicted person and the importance of his health as compared with other needs and desires of the family.

The economic aspects of illness influence the definitions of illness in each of the classes. As the ability to pay for medical attention decreases, the reluctance to accept symptoms as indications of illness increases. The introduction of health insurance plans has often modified the concept of illness in this respect, particularly in the lower middle class.

Beliefs, not only about what constitutes illness but also about what causes illness, have varied from one historical period to another and from one culture or sub-culture to another. Blum gives an interesting account of historically developed beliefs which persist to varying degrees in almost all societies. These beliefs he calls animistic, religious, and scientific.

Animistic belief ascribes life to objects and events. "That the spirit of the disease must come from the outside seemed logical; since the man with the disease had not willed his illness, another force must have willed it for him. The other force would be the spirit of the illness itself, or perhaps the more powerful will of another person or demon."[6]

The animistic concept of disease began in primitive times, but has continued to some extent through history. In medieval times, the ills of the mind and flesh were attributed to devils and witches. Voodoo hexing is another example. Even modern man is subject to animistic views at times. Magical qualities are sometimes ascribed to medicine, and the doctor himself is often thought of as a kind of magician who can control disease.

Religious beliefs attribute bodily disorders to the willful intervention of the Deity. The disease can be considered a sign of God's esteem and blessing, a test of the patient's spiritual endurance, or a punishment for sin. Illness as a blessing from God or a test of faith is less prevalent today than the idea that illness is a punishment. "Taught that sin brings retribution, it is hard for patients to avoid interpreting the presence of pain as retribution. . . . He assumes that the appeal to God through prayer, promise, and penance is the treatment of the cause, whereas the ministration of the physician is treatment of the symptom only."[7]

Modern medical scientific beliefs are characterized by biological determinism. It is much less personal than animistic or religious viewpoints. Disease is defined biologically and is capable of remedy through physical means. Health is an ideal state and the elimination of pain or defect is in itself a worthy goal. Biological determinism is being challenged to some extent, however, by the ideas of psychosomatic medicine, which again gives individuality to the causes of disease and importance to the "spirit" as well as the body function in both cause and cure.

Although these three belief systems about illness are progressive historically, any one or all may exist at the same time in a class, culture, sub-culture, or individual.

Attitudes toward Illness and Disability

Each person's own cultural and environmental background has considerable bearing on his attitude toward illness, hospitalization, and/or disability, and on his consequent behavior. This background includes his family, his social class, his ethnic group, his educational level, his occupation, his religion, and his leisure pursuits. The beliefs, customs, superstitions, prejudices, attitudes, demands, and perceptions of these background components are influential in conditioning the person's attitude. "Having the force of habit or the backing of social censure, they carry an emotional impact that makes them resistant to change. Being almost automatic in operation they are also unobtrusive."[8]

The American culture is made up of many sub-cultures. Members of a patient population in any hospital may come from a number of these sub-cultures. Hospital staff members do not necessarily have similar cultural backgrounds, either, and theirs may differ greatly from that of the patients. For the recreator, such a variety of cultural backgrounds may be a positive factor in giving scope and color to the recreation program. But he should also be aware of the many influences culture has on behavior, not only the patient's behavior but his own as well. He should recognize each person's right to his own beliefs and attitudes, and realize that they will be held with tenacity and the assurance that they are quite right and adequate.

The patient's family, his position in and relationship with the family, and their attitudes may have effect on his attitudes and behavior. For instance, the patient who was a "spoiled brat" may find in the sickbed a happy substitute for the pampering he enjoyed as a child.[9] Or another patient may find it difficult to accept illness because the family has never done so, and he fears losing parental acceptance.[10] Some families have an almost traditional suspicion of doctors, hospitals, injections, innoculations, or some other hospital procedure. This suspicion, passed on to the patient, cannot help but influence his behavior in the hospital. The family's attitude about hard-earned money spent for such luxuries as hospitalization, or about "giving in" to sickness, or the opposite attitude— that of panic at the slightest ache or pain—all affect the patient's perception of illness.

Family culture is derived to a large extent from the culture of the ethnic group to which it belongs. Group cultural traditions may show up in beliefs about the value of food in sickness, in attitudes toward modesty and exposure of the body, and in attitudes toward and responses to pain.

Cultural patterns do play an important part in determining attitudes and consequent behavior, and may be among the most difficult factors for the hospital staff to recognize and deal with, because they themselves have their own cultural background exerting influence on their own behavior and attitudes.

The patient's, and his family's, attitudes toward illness, disability, and hospitalization must be taken into consideration by the recreator. The patient's willingness to give attention to and participate in recreation, or any activity not obviously bearing on his physical condition, is often determined by his attitude toward illness and hospitalization.

Response to Illness and Disability

Faced with the threat or reality of illness, almost everyone will do *something*. But what each individual does is determined to large extent by cultural and social influences.

King suggests that the types of treatment people seek may be divided into three general classifications: primitive, folk, and scientific medicine.[11] Magic is the basis of primitive medicine. Although it bears little relation to modern scientific medicine, it is complex and detailed. Folk medicine is that vast body of beliefs held by the non-professionals in any society concerning the causes of illness and the ways of treating it.[12] Traditional remedies and empirical evidence from specific cases and from nature, passed on from mother to daughter, are the basis of folk medicine. Characteristics of folk medicine vary greatly with the "folk," but almost all societies make wide application of this type of treatment for illness. Folk medicine is not based on magic, as primitive medicine is, nor is it based to any extent on scientific fact. Probably more than anything else it is based on experience, and modern folk medicine probably on advertising.

The central feature of scientific medicine is the rational explanation of natural events in terms of cause and effect. It is determined by the scientific method, and predictions can be made and verified or dismissed through experimentation.[13]

Generally, primitive medicine is resorted to by primitive cultures, folk medicine by peasant and agricultural cultures, and scientific medicine by modern industrial and sophisticated cultures. However, two or all three of these systems may exist at the same time in any social group, or even in an individual. Usually the dominant belief system will be tried first, and if that fails, one or both of the others will be tried. One of the authors recalls an experience during an assignment in an Air Force hospital in the Philippine Islands. Among the patients were a few members of a native tribe, the Negritos, a pygmy sized, primitive folk who were employed to guard the perimeter of the Base and were thus authorized hospitalization. Occasionally when their "primitive medicine" failed to bring the desired results, they availed themselves of the opportunity to try "scientific medicine" and checked into the Air Force hospital.

It works the other way too, as evidenced by those sufferers of chronic ailments for whom scientific medicine has been able to effect no cure, who then seek the ministrations of a faith healer, for instance, or a mechanical appliance or some other folk remedy.

Along another line, social structure has had some effect on what people do about illness. Certain features of the modern American urban family, as contrasted with the large, far-reaching family structure of other societies and previous times, tend to push the sick person out of the home and into the hospital. This extrafamilial care, according to Roth,[14] is good in that it provides protection of the family against the disruptive effects of the illness; it directs the passive deviance of illness into closely supervised medical channels; and it facilitates the therapeutic process. Although large family structures could provide protection and absorb the difficulties of illness, the small urban family unit cannot.

An attempt to provide for the patient the benefits of hospital care and at the same time preserve the benefits of his remaining at home is evident in the establishment of community health centers, particularly mental health centers. With professional medical help close at hand, the patient oftentimes may remain at home without unduly disrupting the lives of the other family members.

Another attempt to help keep intact the family relationships during periods of illness is demonstrated in the care-by-parent concept which was developed at the University of Kentucky Medical Center, and is being adopted by a number of other hospitals. In the pediatrics section of the hospital, children who have no contagious disease or no acute illness requiring a registered nurse's care may be admitted to the Care-by-Parent Unit. An adult, usually the mother, is admitted with the child. Following instructions from the resident child-care assistants, the parent takes care of the child, recording medications given, temperature, special activities, and other notes for the physician. Thus the trauma of mother-child separation is eliminated and the mother has the opportunity to acquire skill in caring for the sick child and to practice these skills under medical supervision. The continuous presence of the mother in the hospital with her child gives the recreator an opportunity to establish patterns of recreation activity appropriate to the child's condition which can be instigated and supervised by the mother after discharge from the hospital, as well as during hospitalization.

Social Structure of the Hospital

Although large numbers of ill or disabled persons are residing outside hospitals, and some groups of disabled, such as the mentally retarded, may never have been hospitalized, still a majority of the special population about which this book is concerned are or have been hospitalized sometime during the course of their illness or injury. Again, although therapeutic recreation is more and more extending beyond the walls of the hospital, the concentration of therapeutic recreation services is in the hospital or treatment center. Thus the social condition of the patient in the hospital, and the social structure of the hospital itself are important considerations.

A hospital has a social structure all its own. This structure is well understood and accepted by the people working in the hospital, but for the new patient it may seem bewildering, artificial, and undemocratic. The patient may seem to be the focal point of hospital activity, the most important person there, yet he has the least to say about what goes on. It is an authoritative system with the physician making pronouncements and issuing orders which others scurry to obey. Yet the overall manager of the hospital may not be a physician at all. The hospital has been termed a dependency culture, with a distinct "we-they" relationship between patients and staff. The patient is not permitted to cross this dividing line, even though in ordinary life he may be on equal or superior social terms with certain members of the staff. He will find too that the hospital hierarchy has definite ranks with attending privileges. He may note that the atmosphere of the hospital is one which places great value on human life, in fact is dedicated to prolonging life, yet maintains strict emotional neutrality. Until the patient can find his own proper place in the hospital social structure, sort out the varied kinds of people and their functions, and determine how to act toward different personnel, the hospital will be a strange, bewildering, and possibly frightening place. The more elaborate the equipment, organization, and specialization in the hospital, the more this is true.

The recreator may be of considerable help to the patient in easing him into the social structure of the hospital. Although the recreator is a member of the hospital staff, his social relationship with the patient may be a bit more relaxed than that of some other staff. As a staff member he understands and can explain to the patient the hospital structure, and why it is the way it is.

The patient often finds that he is not able to order his social relationships in his own way as he would at home. He is no longer the source of control himself. His social contact with hospital staff is limited, and he has little control of visitors. He can neither initiate desired social contacts nor escape undesirable ones, except with his fellow patients.

Such a reversal of roles can be disconcerting, particularly since it is related to lack of privacy, loss of power and prestige, and restrictions of movement. His privacy is invaded in many ways. "Upon admission, the patient is divested of his clothes and is frequently given a kind of gown to wear that offers but little cover for most of his body. His anatomy is exposed repeatedly for examinations by the doctor. . . ."[15] If he is on a ward, he is living intimately with strangers, who may view his every action. Even in a private room he is subject to invasion by anyone who feels he has business there, from the surgeon to the window washer. During visiting hours he is at the mercy of any well-wishers who care to visit, unless visitors are limited by "doctor's orders." Such lack of privacy is taken for granted by hospital personnel, but it can be a demoralizing factor for the patient. The recreator, however, need not contribute to such demoralization. The recreator, whose concern is not with enemas or chest thumpings but with morale, can respect the patient's right to whatever privacy he wants and is afforded. He should not take advantage of his position on the hospital staff to impose himself and his activities. The recreator's relationship with the patient is such that the normal social amenities can be observed.

Never does a person suffer such restriction of movement and contact with people as he does in a hospital. The bed patient's life space is highly restricted. His world becomes very small and consequently his attention is focused on smaller and smaller details. Even the ambulatory patient "is limited to the places he can go on foot or in his wheelchair. He feels rebuffed by the mysteries of closed doors and areas that are 'off limits'. Hospital personnel always appear to be suspicious of the movements of patients."[16] Thus the recreation area can be a haven for the patients. Its atmosphere is one of welcome. Here the patients may meet on equal social terms and feel at home.

Another loss which some patients feel keenly is that of external power and prestige. The patient is expected to give up the right to make his own decisions about ordinary details of everyday living as well as about what medical treatment he is to have. The attitude of the hospital is that all patients are equal and all will receive the best that the institution has to offer. All are sick people, and external power and prestige have little to do with the business of recovery. But for the patients who have enjoyed a full measure of power and prestige outside the hospital, there may be difficulty in relinquishing these things. This is especially noticeable in military hospitals when a patient, an officer of high rank, must obey the orders of his doctor who is possibly of lower military rank. However, in recreation activities in the hospital, the patient's self-respect in freedom of choice can be left intact. Even when recreation activity is prescribed by the patient's physician, the skillful recreator preserves some elements of control and choice for the patient.

There is a certain social role attendant on illness in all societies, involving certain rights and duties. The degree to which the patient assumes the sick role as decreed by his own society has some bearing on the way he is treated. In the American culture, the sick role carries two specific rights. The first is exemption from all normal social and business responsibilities. "Lying behind the right is the prestige of the doctor neatly phrased in the term, 'doctor's orders.' Society . . . frees the sick person from his ordinary duties and obligations in order that he may concentrate on the process of getting well."[17]

The second right of the sick role is the right to be taken care of. The obligation for this falls primarily on the family. When care is beyond the capability of the family it then becomes a responsibility of society in general through such agents as public and private hospitals, voluntary health and civic societies, social work agencies and the like.

The sick role also carries certain duties on the part of the patient. Illness is considered to be an undesirable state, and the patient is expected to want to get well. He is expected to seek competent assistance and to cooperate in the process of recovery so that he may resume his normal function in society as soon as possible. The patient who does not carry out these duties is considered a drag on society and may be denied the rights of the sick role.

Adherence to the rights and duties of the sick role allows for a certain amount of prestige to be built up within the patient group in a hospital. A study was made of the factors which contribute to patient prestige. "In this society, the sickest had the highest status. . . . The rights of those who constituted the aristocracy were simple; to be left alone, to initiate conversation and social interaction only when they wished to do so. In return, their duty seemed to be to provide the horrible example of greater suffering to those less seriously injured."[18] Other contributions to prestige were the length of hospitalization, the rarity of the disease, the time the doctor spent with a patient during ward rounds, and speed of recovery. "Congeniality and forcefulness of personality without unnecessary aggressiveness were also highly regarded, as were special talent which contributed in some measure to life on the ward."[19]

The recreator may find that the patient's concept of illness, his feeling about his rights and particularly his responsibilities in the sick role, may have particular significance in his willingness to participate in recreation activities. A patient who considers recreation frivolous or something that has to be earned might well hesitate to "indulge" in recreation activities for fear that he is not carrying out his duties in the sick role. He may feel his rights as a sick person will be threatened if he does not pay strict attention to his sick role duties. He may feel guilty about enjoying himself while others are working so hard to make him well. The recreator then has the responsibility to help the patient understand that recreation has rightful value in itself and that it may well aid in the patient's eventual recovery. He will often be working against odds represented in the patient's pre-hospital background. But when the sick role threatens to become a permanent role for the patient, the recreator has a large responsibility in offering incentive to the will to get well.

Effects of Illness and Disability on Social Condition

Important as social and cultural factors are in the recreator's understanding of patients' attitudes and responses, even more important are the effects of illness and disability on a person's social condition. The effects may be minimal for the short-term patient who enjoys complete recovery, and may be limited to a temporary change of status while in the hospital, as described above. But long-term or chronic illness, injury or surgery resulting in permanent, visable, physical disability, mental illness, and mental retardation all have serious and far-reaching social effects. One function of the therapeutic recreator is to minimize or alleviate harmful or negative effects on the patient's social condition. Although other professionals working with the ill or disabled carry some responsibility for this task too, the recreator is in a particularly advantageous position to be effective.

The different categories of illness and disability tend to produce somewhat different effects on interpersonal relationships and social interactions. Thus they will be considered separately.

Mental Illness

The manifestations of mental illness are frequently seen in the areas of behavior and of interpersonal or social relationships. Mental illness may often be recognized by an individual's marked deviation from the norm in his relation to others, by the severe disturbance of his role performance.

This disturbance is seen as early as the first two years of life in the autistic child, whose difficulty is in part a serious lack of contact with people. A corresponding symptom of adolescent and adult schizophrenia is the patient's poor ability to communicate with others, and his lack of affective contact and lack of desire to conform with those around him. This disturbance is seen in a different way in the behavior of the sociopathic personality who actively violates the codes and conventions of society. The effect of mental illness or emotional disturbance on an individual's social condition can indeed be profound.

Much of the aim of psychotherapy is directed toward re-establishing social contacts, developing social relationships, and eliciting "whatever social inclinations may still be stirring in the patient."[20]

The role of the recreator in a mental hospital or in any situation dealing with the treatment of mental or emotional disturbances is not necessarily to help in getting at the causes of such disturbances. But the provision of recreation experiences can be effective in a number of ways in reversing the trend toward social isolation or maladjustment.

Recreation activity may serve as a vehicle by which social contact is made almost as a by-product. This is illustrated by a situation in which a person, withdrawn from voluntary and meaningful contact with others, finds inanimate objects harmless and is willing to try a handcraft project. Although his conscious attention is on the craft item, the momentary interactions with others necessary for the completion of his project—obtaining materials, sharing tools and instruments, receiving instruction, perhaps even exhibiting the finished product—serve to ease his way into more conscious and sustained social contact.

Because of the very nature of much recreation activity, it can provide a natural climate or atmosphere for resocialization. Social recreation in the form of a party, for instance, presents a pattern or framework already established by custom in which the acceptance of the individual as a social being is taken for granted, and the expected behavior is that of friendly, pleasant social interchange. The essence of many games, folk dances, and musical groups is that of cooperative, non-threatening interaction and mutual enjoyment.

Recreation offers the patient the opportunity to test reality. Recreation or play—for adults as well as children—can be regarded as an experience in make-believe. Games, with a prescribed beginning and end, with rules and roles established by generations of players, may be considered to represent capsulated life experiences, played in virtual rather than real time and space. The patient who is not yet ready to commit himself to the social give and take of the work-a-day world finds, in the circumscribed experience of a game, the opportunity to test his ability to relate to others on a limited basis.

Again, the patterns of action established by the rules of the game, the form of the music or dance, the rules of etiquette, provide a background against which the patient may practice his social role. The repetitive, or re-creative, quality of much recreation activity gives him a chance to strengthen and stabilize his shaky role.

Perhaps of most importance is the incentive that recreation offers the patient to re-enter the real world. The patient who learns that the enjoyment to be found in recreation often involves mutual enjoyment of those around him may be less inclined to withdraw from social contact. Of course the enjoyment of the activity itself is enticing. But a greater incentive may be the patient's realization that mentally healthy people step aside occasionally from life's stresses and strains and consciously enter, for a little while, into a world of make-believe socially acceptable as recreation or play. The beginning of a preference for the socially accepted fantasy of play with other people rather than the isolated fantasy world of mental illness is a step toward recovery.

The mentally ill person who has recovered sufficiently to be discharged from the hospital often continues to have difficulty in returning to his former social role. His own fragile hold on reality is strengthened not at all by the stereotyped attitude of many people toward mental illness. The therapeutic recreator can function effectively here in two respects. While the patient is still hospitalized, the recreator introduces him to recreation activities in which people from outside the hospital are involved. This limited, controlled, and buffered contact with the attitudes of "normal" people other than therapists can be extended then toward more exposure in the form of recreational excursions away from the hospital, and contact with more people and with people who have not necessarily been briefed for such contact. The patient often finds that interest and attention, his own as well as the "outsider's," is focused on the recreation activity—the base hit, the action on the stage, the picnic food—overriding attention on him as a mental patient.

In a second respect the recreator's responsibility includes purposefully shaping the attitudes of the general public toward former mental patients in a more positive way. Capitalizing on the shared enjoyment inherent in recreation, on the circumscribed aspect of most recreation activity—that is, a known beginning and end, known rules and roles—the recreator gives the normal person a chance also to test and practice his relationship with the patient, to see him as a person, and to accord him a normal social role. The recreator in the hospital does not carry this responsibility alone. His colleagues in community recreation agencies have the opportunity and responsibility to influence general attitudes toward the social condition of those who have suffered from mental illness and to help alleviate the ill effects of negative attitudes.

Physical and Medical Disability

Previous sections of this chapter have described some of the social problems encountered by persons hospitalized because of physical illness or injury. The effects of such illness or injury do not always terminate upon the patient's discharge from the hospital. When the cause for hospitalization results in a permanent physical disability or a chronic medical condition, the patient often finds his attempts and ability to establish or re-establish a desirable social role outside the hospital are seriously affected.

One of the factors which may have bearing on his social condition is that of restricted mobility. The ability to move about from place to place freely and normally is restricted for persons who are crippled, paralyzed, blind, or who have neurological or muscular disorders affecting motor performance. Similarly, the ability to carry on normal physical activity may be seriously restricted by crippling orthopedic conditions, paralysis, neurological conditions, blindness, damaged heart or lungs, and so on. Another factor affecting social interchange is the restriction on communication imposed by impairments in hearing, sight, and speech.

Chronic medical conditions such as tuberculosis, heart conditions, diabetes, hemophilia, ulcers, and so on, carry some less obvious but seriously restricting factors. Decreased strength and the required adherence to dietary restrictions and to other schedules of activity or medication are some such factors.

All the factors listed above may affect the social behavior of both the disabled person and those around him. Too often a characteristic behavior of the disabled person is social withdrawal. For some, withdrawal may be caused by physical appearance. Others withdraw because their physical or medical conditions make it difficult to perform even the simple actions expected in social situations. Or withdrawal may be caused by fear that meeting the demands of social interchange with others will have a harmful effect on an already precarious physical or medical condition.

The necessity for adhering to a dietary schedule, to a schedule of treatment or medication, to a specified schedule of alternating activity and rest causes some to feel that attempts at normal social relations with others are just not worth the effort.

The therapeutic recreator who notices that a patient has such a tendency to withdraw should begin working with the patient while he is still in the hospital. Having secured from the patient's physician the limits of physical activity and exertion that are safe for the patient, the recreator can then try to draw the patient into recreation activities which will promote socialization, by whatever method is most effective.

At least three qualities of recreation can be capitalized on here. One is the quality of enjoyment and pleasure—fun—that is inherent in all recreation activity. Oftentimes, in spite of their fears and difficulties, reluctant patients can be enticed into recreation activity by the fun it promises and delivers. This is illustrated by the young girl in a crippled children's hospital who was confined to a wheelchair. Unwilling to exert the effort necessary to learn to transfer herself from her wheelchair to a bed, car, etc., she had required attendants to lift her whenever it was necessary for her to be moved. Her attitude changed, however, when plans were announced for the children in the hospital to take a trip to the circus. The recreator in charge of the trip told the patient that she was getting too big for the recreator to lift her in and out of her chair, and that if she wanted to go with the other children, she would have to learn to transfer. The prospects of a pleasure trip proved to be the incentive she needed. She mastered this skill, went to the circus, and subsequently on numerous other recreation outings.

Another quality of recreation of advantage here is the wide range of activities and experiences it encompasses. For patients who withdraw because of their appearance, recreation activities can be found in which appearance is irrelevant. Even though some activities—even activities of daily living—are difficult because of physical and medical disabilities, among the wide variety of things to do in recreation everyone can find some activity which does not involve the impaired or disabled part of the person, and in which the patient may participate on a par with the able-bodied. For those who hesitate to become involved for fear of worsening their condition, again among the vast array of activities that are recreative are some which offer no threat.

A third quality of recreation is one previously discussed in connection with the mentally ill. This is the play or make-believe aspect of much recreation activity. Social activity which has this characteristic, which may be entered into and left at will, is often the fearful patient's first step toward socialization. Too, the patient whose life is regulated by a medical schedule finds that the play quality of recreation activity makes it possible for him to have some social involvement with others without the necessity for commitment in time and energy which other types of interpersonal activities may require.

While withdrawal is often a behavioral effect of illness and disability on the disabled person, a concurrent response to disability manifested by those around him may be rejection. Some of the causes of social rejection of the disabled by the able-bodied are the same as those which cause the disabled person's withdrawal. For instance, physical appearance which is not normal—an amputated leg, a palsied hand, paralyzed facial muscles, unseeing eyes—often triggers rejection. Although such behavior is cruel, it can often be accounted for by people's natural tendency to reject that which is strange or unfamiliar. The recreator has good opportunity to reverse the tendency toward rejection due to unfamiliarity. Purposefully arranging trips for the disabled can promote, even force, the intermingling of able-bodied with disabled persons at recreation events which are open to the public—sports events, stage performances, the county fair, museum visits, and the like.

Another reason for rejection is the various psychological feelings the able-bodied may have—fear of hurting the patient, fear of "catching" whatever the patient has, feelings of guilt or shame, ignorance of the nature of the disability. Neither the therapeutic recreator nor the community recreator need feel he must deeply analyze such feelings, but both should be aware they exist and both should know what they can do to alleviate their harmful effects. Providing for recreation activities and experiences which can be participated in by both disabled and able-bodied, the recreator can emphasize their mutuality of interests and can promote specifically those activities which permit participation on equal terms. As the able-bodied allow themselves to regard the disabled as people and not oddities, their feelings of rejection may be relaxed.

Rejection is sometimes caused by impatience. Physical disabilities often mean that the disabled can't move or talk with normal speed. Not wanting to be slowed down, the able-bodied again reject the disabled. Recreators, along with all others who are interested in the physically disabled, should work toward the elimination of any architectural barriers which make it difficult or impossible for the disabled to move about freely with other people. The recreator should perhaps concentrate on this problem in recreation areas, but join hands with city planners and others to eliminate barriers in the total environment.

Further the recreator can work individually with his disabled clients to devise means by which the disabled person may be able to keep up with his able-bodied friends in social and recreation activities. Such means may be as simple as a card holder for the one-handed bridge player, or it may involve hours of practice and training for the paraplegic to learn to handle a bow and arrow, a pool cue, or a ping pong paddle from a sitting position in a wheel chair.

In the area of social recreation activities, the recreator should determine when it is reasonable for the disabled to expect help from the able-bodied in the pursuance of their mutual activity. He should promote realistic attitudes among both the disabled and able-bodied toward the kinds and extent of assistance needed.

Because verbal communication is one of the chief means of social intercourse, any physical impairment which interferes with verbal communication has considerable effect on one's social condition. Physical and medical conditions resulting in speech impairment, as well as hearing impairments, greatly affect oral communication. Similarly, blindness prevents ordinary communication by the written word. The opportunities for non-verbal communication and self-expression in recreation are discussed in Chapter 6. As many as possible of such opportunities should be provided for persons with sensory impairments which present barriers to normal communication and affect social relations.

Perhaps one of the most unfortunate effects of illness and disability is the tendency to group disabled persons by their diagnosis, disability, or degree of mobility. Such grouping is often made for purposes of efficiency in treatment. But social grouping drawn along these lines is often inappropriate, ineffective, and artificial. Other than a common physical ailment, the people so grouped may have no other mutual interest on which to base a social relationship.

In order to help his disabled clients to break away from such confinement to a diagnostic group, the recreator needs to use his skills in a number of ways. This responsibility has been mentioned several times previously, and applies to the recreator in the community as well as in the hospital.

The recreator uses his counseling skills to find what the interests and enthusiasms of the patient or disabled client are. As a person acquainted with a wide variety of recreation activities, he can determine what is required physically for participation. In collaboration with his colleagues on the medical or treatment team and with the patient himself, he assesses the physical capacity of the patient. Combining the factors thus ascertained, he uses his skill as a motivator, teacher, and recreation leader to direct the disabled person toward those recreation experiences which may be most appropriate and rewarding.

The recreator uses his organizational skill to bring together into social groups those people who have mutual recreation interests and capacities. He must give consideration to the feasibility of integrating the disabled with the able-bodied —what concessions may need to be made and whether or not such concessions can be overridden by the pleasure of the shared experience. One such successful experiment along this line is described by Williams in the *Therapeutic Recreation Journal*. The recreation department of the Westchester Lighthouse for the Blind had a drama group made up of blind and partially sighted persons. Although the group had successfully presented dramatic productions to churches, clubs, and little theater groups, the performances were largely viewed as a kind of novelty and attempts on the part of the blind actors and actresses to participate in local, sighted drama clubs were met with no success. An experiment in integration was then made by the Westchester Lighthouse recreation personnel, who formed a new group, the "Spotlight Players." Sighted persons from a number of community organizations throughout the county were invited to audition for parts. The object was to have half the parts played by sighted persons and half by visually handicapped persons. An ample number of both sighted and blind persons tried out for the parts so that this objective was met. Their primary reason for wishing to participate was the chance to act, not necessarily to participate in a project in integration. The socializing effect of their mutual interest in drama is described, however, by Williams:

> As rehearsals progressed, there was a gradual merging of the two groups which resulted in a joint concern for the production. During rehearsals, participants were busy on stage most of the time which left little chance to socialize or informally bridge the gap between the sighted and blind participants. To help overcome this, the blind and visually handicapped people were encouraged to act as hosts and hostesses at sandwich and coffee time following the morning's work. This was a big help in getting the group to become acquainted.[21]
>
> Following the last production . . . the sighted actors and actresses . . . stated their initial reactions to the blind actors was that they were probably not only blind but retarded as well and "needed to be led around like children." As the drama sessions continued, these attitudes were rapidly changed and replaced by ones of complete acceptance and knowledge that the blind and visually handicapped participants were indeed individuals with some of the same problems, shortcomings, fears, needs, and desires of us all. They further stated the "act and react situation" involved in drama became a greater challenge to the sighted actor since the visual rapport was not possible and a true acting response had to be obtained. They all concurred that the blind or visually handicapped thespian could participate in sighted local theatre groups. This conviction, they stated, had only resulted from their active role in this program.[22]

Mental Retardation

Although mental retardation is not primarily a medical condition, it is a disability that warrants the same kind of attention that other physical, medical, and mental disabilities do. What constitutes the condition of mental retardation depends to some extent on the discipline in which it is being considered, and the focus of that discipline's attempts to help the disabled person. All definitions, however, indicate that some degree of below-normal intellectual functioning is present. The sub-normality, or retardation, may range from mild to profound in different individuals. Generally, the greater the degree of retardation the greater the effects of retardation on the individual's behavior in all areas of living, including interpersonal or social relationships.

There are many more mildly and moderately retarded children and adults than severely and profoundly retarded. Children who are retarded to a lesser degree are often not identified until they enter school, where their difficulties with the abstract concepts of academic subjects become evident. When they graduate or leave school, they tend to lose their identity as mentally retarded, and to blend into the general population. For such persons, their social problems may be most acute during their school years when learning is a major activity and their difference in ability to learn sets them apart. When they advance beyond school age and the spotlight is off academic learning, their social condition may well become stabilized and approximately normal.

Persons with greater degrees of retardation have more serious problems of interpersonal and social relationships. These problems tend to increase as the child grows older and the difference between his rate of mental development and consequent social behavior and that of the normal child becomes greater. For the person whose retardation is serious enough to require institutionalization, there are obvious social effects.

The effects of mental retardation on the individual's social condition may be described in terms of the retarded person's behavior as well as the behavior of those around him. These effects depend not only on the degree of retardation but also on the preventive and supportive measures that have been taken on the retardate's behalf.[23]

Even in this supposedly enlightened age, a reaction to mental retardation that is often seen, especially among children, is ridicule and teasing. Such actions, as well as other more subtle forms of social rejection, are sometimes reactions to the physical appearance of the retardate caused by an abnormal condition of which mental retardation is only one part. Some examples are the enlarged head of the hydrocephalic, small head of the microcephalic, certain physical stigmata of the mongoloid and cretin, and the uncoordinated or spastic movements of some retarded people.

As is true with the physically disabled and mentally ill, social rejection on the part of others may be caused by a fear of the strange or unusual and a vague fear of "contamination." Or the retardate may be ridiculed or rejected because of his pattern of failure in so many things he tries to do. Verbal communication is difficult for the mentally retarded, becoming increasingly more difficult for the more severely retarded. Thus the child, and adult too, who cannot readily understand others or make himself understood, and who has difficulty doing things or keeping up with his normal contemporaries, is likely to bring on an exasperated impatience in those contemporaries.

The retardate's behavioral reaction to his retardation, in a social sense, may be withdrawal from social interaction, or it may be aggressiveness. This is especially true of the person whose mental capacity is not so low that he cannot recognize ridicule or the frustration of his own limited abilities. The difficulty in understanding and doing what seems to be expected, in making himself understood, the frustration of repeated failures, and the rejection by others often make the retardate feel that attempts toward normal socialization are just not worth the effort. Or, in anger and frustration, he may react by exhibiting unacceptable behavior patterns of aggressiveness.

Although in most cases mental retardation is irreversible, it is important that supportive intervention be instituted early. Retardation is more than an education problem—it is a social problem as well—and should not be borne entirely by educators. The therapeutic recreator, for instance, is in an excellent position to help in the socialization process for the retardate.

Fortunately, social acceptance is not based necessarily on academic achievement. Achievement in play activities carries high status for children, and can be important for the adult retardate as well. Dunn points this out in relation to the educable mentally retarded children:

> Both because it will help them develop a feeling of worth and because of the increased time free from work which they are likely to have in the future, it is important that the retarded be taught the leisure arts. . . . The retarded need to develop hobbies and the habit of participating in community esthetic functions. Too, they need to learn the joy of serving on community projects for the welfare of others. These leisure arts are not likely to develop unless they are specifically and systematically taught.[24]

The recreator who is involved in teaching the leisure arts and in providing social and recreation experiences for the retarded must realize that, even in play activities, retarded children may have to be taught many of the basic perceptions and skills that normal children acquire without guidance. For example, one of the authors recalls an instance in which one of her students was introducing a group of elementary school boys to some of the intricacies of basketball. The group included a mentally retarded boy. The rest of the group seemed to have no difficulty in matching action to casual verbal instruction or description. But the retarded child, when told it was his turn to dribble the ball down the court, had no idea what to do until he was told and shown, "This is how you dribble."

Much of what is recreative involves motor activity and the senses more than it involves intellectual concepts. The therapeutic recreator must know the essential nature of the recreation activity he is providing for the retardate. He should know whether the enjoyment is tied in with the physical activity involved, as in most sports; or with esthetic involvement, as in music and dance; with fantasy, as in drama and story telling; or with problem solving, as in chess. Those activities which involve abstract concepts and problem solving provide little enjoyment for the retardate, are potentially frustrating and should not be included in programs for the retarded.

Retarded persons are often successful in learning by means of imitation and repetition. Once an activity is learned they are often quite happy to repeat it again and again. Recreation and play activities essentially are participated in for the pleasure of the doing and not for the results they bring. Thus, once a play skill is learned by a retardate, his participation in such play can be for the same purpose and on a par with his normal friends.

It has been noted that retarded persons are sometimes avoided because of their lack of social graces and their unpleasant behavior. As in the other areas of life, socially acceptable behavior patterns need to be consciously taught to the retarded. With children, the make-believe of play can often be a good vehicle for such instruction. A more direct approach can be taken with young people and adults, as is illustrated by a project undertaken by the Duval County Recreation Department. A charm school for trainable mentally retarded girls was conducted at Pine Castle School in Jacksonville. By demonstration and practice, "the girls were taught posture and carriage; hair, skin, and nail care; manners and etiquette; clothing coordination; . . . physical fitness," table manners, telephone procedures, the importance of cleanliness, and so on. The recreation supervisor reports that in addition to the fun the girls had, the practical experience gained in behavior and appearance was an important step toward the goal of successful integration of the mentally retarded with normal young people.[25]

The social value of acquired recreation skills is further illustrated by a philanthropic project undertaken by the Debonaire School of Dance in Bakersfield, California. With the help of local high school and college volunteers, the dance school conducted weekly classes in social dancing for eighteen educable and trainable mentally retarded young adults. At first, the classes were conducted in the students' school setting, but later were moved to the dance studio ballroom. The director of the dance school reports:

> Mentally retarded children can be taught to dance, and through dancing many doors are opened socially and educationally. During the past four years our retarded students have become proficient in all of the modern social dance steps. . . . An integral part of the program has been instruction in the niceties of social etiquette—making introductions, escorting, sitting and standing properly, taking pride in personal grooming, thanking people graciously, and dressing appropriately for different social functions. The mentally retarded emulated the teenage assistants in matters of grooming, dress, and in the social amenities. Motor skill and dance ability developed to such an extent that observers could not distinguish most of the retarded students from their instructors.[26]

In addition to his efforts to bring about successful social integration of the retarded with the normal world, the recreator must also give consideration to the situations in which integration is neither feasible or sensible. For some retardates, especially the more seriously retarded, and in some places and times, social interaction only among themselves and segregated from the demands of the normal world is most satisfactory. In such cases, the therapeutic recreator should make every effort to provide recreation and social opportunities and experiences which are similar in type to the activities of normal persons in corresponding age groups. The activities should be modified to meet the retardate's ability to perform, but should be of a type and character appropriate to the chronological age of the retarded person. For instance, a sixteen-year-old boy, even though his mental age is six, should not have to learn songs based on nursery rhymes. In the vast range of music there are any number of songs that are simple enough musically for the retardate to learn but which still have the social and emotional appeal appropriate for a teenage boy. And so it is true with many other social and recreational activities. Because of the great variety of things to do which are recreative, the recreator can guide the retardate of any age to those activities which are simple, easily learned or readily modified, yet are appropriate for the retardate's degree of maturity.

Through deliberate skill training and counseling and guidance in the selection of recreation activities, the retarded person may have satisfying social experiences which will indeed enrich his life.

Notes, Chapter 3

1. John M. MacLachlan, "Cultural Factors in Health and Disease," *Patients, Physicians, and Illness*, E. Gartly Jaco, ed. (Glencoe, Ill.: The Free Press, 1958), p. 94.

2. *Ibid.*, p. 94.

3. *Ibid.*, p. 102. The relationship between such ritualistic addiction and the drug culture among some groups of young people in present-day Western societies might bear investigation.

4. Talcott Parsons, "Definitions of Health and Illness in the Light of American Values and Social Structure," *Ibid.*, p. 176.

5. Earl Lomon Koos, *The Health of Regionville*, (New York: Columbia University Press, 1954), pp. 39-42.

6. From *The Management of the Doctor-Patient Relationship* by Richard H. Blum. Copyright 1960 by McGraw-Hill Book Co. Used with permission of McGraw-Hill Book Co.

7. *Ibid.*, p. 7.

8. Stanley H. King, *Perceptions of Illness and Medical Practice* (New York: Russell Sage Foundation, 1962), p. 82.

9. Flanders Dunbar, *Mind and Body: Psychosomatic Medicine* (New York: Random House, 1947), p. 33.

10. Frances Upham, *A Dynamic Approach to Illness* (New York: Family Service Association of America, 1949), p. 179.

11. King, *op. cit.*, p. 93.

12. *Ibid.*, p. 108.

13. *Ibid.*, p. 93.

14. Julius A. Roth, "Ritual and Magic in the Control of Contagion," *American Sociological Review*, Vol. 22, No. 3 (June, 1957), pp. 310-314. Publication of the American Sociological Society.

15. Carl W. Sawyer, "The Psychology of the Sick," Address delivered before the Gray Ladies, Sawyer Sanitorium, Marion, Ohio [n.d.].

16. King, *op. cit.*, p. 355.

17. *Ibid.*, p. 208.

18. *Ibid.*, p. 341.

19. *Ibid.*

20. Robert W. White, *The Abnormal Personality* (New York: The Ronald Press Co., 1956), p. 578.

21. Chester T. Williams, "Recreation for the Blind: A Community Drama Project," *Therapeutic Recreation Journal*, Vol. III, No. 4, (Fourth Quarter, 1969), p. 20. A publication of the National Therapeutic Recreation Society.

22. *Ibid.*, p. 23.

23. Elliott M. Avedon and Frances B. Arje, *Socio-Recreative Programming for the Retarded* (New York: Bureau of Publications, Teachers College, Columbia University, 1964), p. 2. Avedon and Arje have presented a course of action to follow in socio-recreative programing designed to aid in the process of socialization, including prevention, support, and remediation for the socially independent retarded child, the semi-independent and the semi-dependent.

24. Lloyd M. Dunn, *Exceptional Children in the Schools* (New York: Holt, Rinehart and Winston, Inc., 1963), p. 93.

25. Lynn Brackey, "How Our Flowers Grow," *Challenge*, Vol. IV, No. 3 (January, 1969), p. 3. A publication of the American Association for Health, Physical Education, and Recreation.

26. Johnny Soiu, "Step Together Step," *Challenge*, Vol. IV. No. 3 (January, 1969), p. 5.

4 | Physical Potentials

Physical Condition—An Element of Health

HEALTH, ACCORDING TO Howard S. Hoyman, is not a static condition but a dynamic process with levels extending from zero health, or death, at one end of a continuum to optimal health at the other end. Health, Hoyman says, is optimal personal fitness for full, creative living. He further depicts personal fitness as a health triangle with three sides: physical fitness, mental health, and spiritual faith.[1] The President's Council on Youth Fitness also has indicated that fitness involves many aspects including the spiritual, mental, emotional, and social, as well as physical.[2] But it is the basic dimension of health that is physical fitness with which this chapter is concerned.

The quality of physical fitness has a number of characteristics. It involves sound organic functioning and the proper performance of body mechanisms. Physical fitness is characterized by good posture and carriage, good muscle tone and cardiovascular fitness. A fit person is well nourished but not fat. Fitness involves a motor condition characterized by flexibility, coordination, and strength:[3]

> A healthy person with optimal (not necessarily maximum) physical fitness can carry out his usual everyday tasks without undue fatigue and have enough reserve energy left over to enjoy his leisure; to meet emergencies such as an accident, illness, an operation, or a disaster; and to engage in activities requiring *reasonably* prolonged, vigorous physical effort when necessary or desired.[4]

How can one acquire and maintain a good physical condition? Although Wilkinson states, ". . . adequate rest, adequate diet, adequate exercise—that is all it takes,"[5] the American Medical Association has pointed out additional paths to fitness.[6] One is proper medical and dental care, including preventive measures such as periodic examinations and immunizations to protect against disease, as well as prompt treatment of illness or injury.

In answer to the question "How much exercise do you need?", the A.M.A. recommends:

1. Regular participation utilizing all body parts.
2. Vigorous enough to tax the power of your muscles.
3. Sustained enough to bring on healthful fatigue.

The purpose of such exercise is to improve the action of the heart, blood circulation and breathing function, step up muscle tone and help in weight control, develop skills which enhance enjoyment of physical activity, and give an overall feeling of zest and well-being.

Hoyman has pointed out that exercise alone is not the answer to physical fitness—that exercise is no panacea:

> But suitable exercise, taken regularly, with progressive over-loading is *one* of the essential factors in developing and maintaining physical fitness. Probably few health measures are so widely approved in theory and so often ignored in practice as the need for regular, suitable exercise. People who do take regular exercise, generally do so because it makes them feel better and they enjoy life more. The beneficial effects of regular exercise can only be "stored up" for a short time. The body grows stronger with proper use and weaker with disuse. Sporadic exercise does little good and, if too strenuous and sustained, may do serious harm, particularly to middle-aged and older people leading sedentary lives. However, probably more people have become ill, or aged and died prematurely, because of too little exercise in our sedentary culture, than have done so because of too much.[8]

The fact that exercise is an important element in physical fitness is presumably of some interest to readers of this book. Of perhaps greater interest are two further steps toward physical fitness which the AMA recommends. One is rest and relaxation. In addition to sleeping or just lying down, recommended ways to rest are "changing activities" and "participating in a hobby." By "rest" is meant "taking it easy." By "relaxation" is meant "doing what you like."

The other recommended path to physical fitness is "healthy play and recreation." This is to be discussed in some detail throughout this chapter.

General Values of Recreation in Physical Fitness

For an increasing number of people in a mechanized, automated society, life's daily tasks involve less and less in the way of physical activity. For such persons whose work, housekeeping, study, personal care and other necessary tasks require little expenditure of physical energy, opportunities for more or less vigorous activity have to be consciously sought. And for many people, some of the most palatable types of physical activity are found in recreation:

Recreation can make a conspicuous contribution to physical fitness by providing outlets for participation in interesting, vigorous physical activities. Participation in physical forms of recreation is particularly significant now because our present way of life with all its conveniences, comforts, and gadgets makes fewer and fewer physical demands upon the individual. The need for exercise, therefore, must be met through regular, planned participation in sustained, vigorous activity.

A part of one's total exercise needs can be met by participating in healthful, zestful recreation—both organized and informal. And the larger the proportion of exercise gained through such means, the better . . .[9]

John F. Kennedy, a great believer in the importance of physical fitness, stated, "I . . . believe that by drawing on our total recreational resources, all Americans can help to increase our physical fitness as individuals and as a nation."[10]

It is perhaps well to examine some of the qualities of recreation which constitute its uniqueness as a contributor to physical fitness. Most obvious, of course, is the fact that many of the things people do by choice in their leisure are by their nature physically active. All sports and athletics involve muscular and motor performance. The same muscular movements could, of course, be performed as pure exercise, but when they are combined and organized into formal patterns as they are in games, with set goals and an element of competition added, they become much more attractive and enjoyable. The excitement of competition, the thrill of winning are strong incentives to action. Running around the bases is more fun than running around the block. Physical activity in cooperation with others as it is in team sports is appealing to man as a social being. So it is that the elements of activities which characterize them as recreation act as strong motivation to embark on such activity and to continue beyond the point where such action, if undertaken only as exercise, would have become boring.

Although participation in physically active recreation pursuits at almost any level of competence can contribute to physical well-being, sustained interest and participation are most often dependent on acquiring a reasonably high degree of competence. Thus lifetime sports which can provide enjoyment over long periods of time and allow the participant to develop satisfactory skill are particularly valuable recreation activities.

Not all recreation calls for physical activity, however. Some recreation pursuits are decidedly sedentary in nature—reading, stamp collecting, needlework, and so on. Involvement in such interests is, of course, no substitute for physical exercise. But enthusiastic involvement in any recreation activity is the antithesis of listlessness and so can contribute to good physical condition. Might this not be called psychosomatic health? There is little doubt that one's mental attitude affects how one feels physically. The pleasure that recreation provides can have a decided effect:

When we are pleased, our blood circulates faster, our hearts pump more blood through our systems, our eyes shine, and we get a warm kind of glow. Whatever energy is developed expresses itself in smiles, joy, and laughter. We want to sing and move around. When we are displeased, when we are afraid, or when we hate, the reaction is just the opposite. We feel an emptiness in our stomachs; we are dejected and are left feeling miserable and alone. The by-products of displeasure can lead to physical and mental bankruptcy. The off-shoots of personal satisfaction and pleasure, which are the mainsprings of wholesome recreation, are more often the cathartic release to all around, substantial physical health and mental stability.[11]

The remarks above are obviously related to persons who are able-bodied and reasonably free from disease and illness. To speak of physical fitness in relation to the ill or disabled may seem a contradiction in terms, or it may seem to be the goal toward which all treatment is aimed. Yet attention on a disabled individual's physical condition, apart from his particular ailment, is not necessarily misplaced. Only the most seriously ill or the most severely injured find all of their body functions involved and impaired. For the vast majority of the handicapped population, maintenance of sound functioning of all parts of the body not involved in illness or injury takes on added importance. And those disabled persons whose difficulties are mental and emotional, rather than physical, surely have the same need for physical fitness as any of their non-disabled fellows.

If maintaining good physical condition in the general populace is a problem of national importance, it is often a greater problem in the lives of the ill or disabled. Those confined to a hospital or other institution, either temporarily or permanently, may find medical care, nutrition, and rest readily available. But opportunities for exercise and physical recreation, as well as the stimulation of work and hobby interests, may be greatly restricted. Too, motor movement may be difficult, awkward, and uncomfortable. Substitutions may need to be found for the normal movements of traditional exercises, to accommodate the disability of the individual. The possible ill effects, as well as beneficial effects, of physical activity on the ill or disabled person need to be weighed, not only by the individual himself, but also by the physician and various therapists, as well as the recreator working with the individual.

The values of recreation for maintaining physical fitness take on added meaning in the lives of the ill or disabled. The motivation for action to be found in recreation becomes especially important. There is considerable potential for extending the benefits of such treatment as physical therapy through the sustained involvement of recreational activity. Recreation activity can help in evaluating the potential of the patient's physical activity.

The following sections of this chapter deal more specifically with the contributions of recreation toward physical fitness as they are related to the different types of illness and disability. Consideration is also given to effective adaptations and modifications of some of the popular physical recreation activities to make participation in them feasible for persons with varying kinds of disabilities.

Physically Disabled and Medically Incapacitated

The therapeutic recreator's responsibility to the physically disabled or medically incapacitated person in realizing the physical potential of recreation lies in three major areas. The most obvious area is that of making adaptations for participation. Another is providing motivation for physical activity. The third is coordinating recreation activity with such treatment activities as physical therapy.

Adaptations

Persons who are prevented from participating in normal recreation activities because of their physical condition often are able to participate when adjustments are made in the means of getting about, in the facilities used in the activities, or in the rules of participation. Generally, it is best to avoid elaborate changes, and to make only those adjustments which prove to be most efficient. For this reason, it is important for the recreator to: (1) analyze the proposed recreation activity to determine the required physical movement, strength, endurance, sense perception, and so on; (2) determine what is the essence of the activity—what makes it fun; (3) know the specific disability of the participant; (4) determine what adaptations are most feasible for each participant to allow wholehearted participation without changing the basic character of the activity.

The game of spot billiards for the cerebral palsied illustrates an adaptation involving rules and equipment:

> Most members of the group showed enthusiasm and an ardent interest, although a few were unrealistic about their ability to play billiards. After carefully observing the participants, it was discovered that the cue sticks were much too long and heavy for the players, the game was difficult to play, and most participants needed assistance in making their shots.
>
> Accordingly, the game was modified to meet the abilities of the group. The modifications were: (1) shorter cue sticks with rubber tips; (2) spotting balls near the pockets to eliminate the break; and (3) assisting those severely handicapped in shooting.[12]

An example of adapting facilities to the play needs of young children in wheelchairs, braces, and on crutches is given by Richard Dattner in a model playground in New York City. Using sand and water as the main play materials, a well-defined play area was developed. The problem of getting sand and water into the joints of prosthetic devices was solved by building a trough high enough that the child could play in it while sitting in his chair, and not so low that sand or water could easily get into the prosthetic joints. The water trough is a continuous channel into which the child may drop things and follow them as they flow around the play area. The edge of the water channel is a handrail.[13]

Changing bodily position and methods of shooting are modifications that have been successful in archery for the multiply handicapped. In working with persons in wheelchairs and those who cannot control their hands or fingers for a normal bow pull, the instructor found that:

a few versatile and agile residents leaned over their chairs and shot with bows in a vertical position. . . . Many leaned slightly forward in their chairs and held bows in a horizontal rather than vertical position. . . those who have trouble controlling their hands and fingers and cannot pull the bow string with three fingers. . . . simply put the knock between the thumb and index finger, allowed the hand to rest upon their knee, extended the bow arm while leaning forward, and slowly moved the drawing hand back along the leg. They hit the target over 50 percent of the time.[14]

Canoeing became a feasible, enjoyable, and physically beneficial activity for three totally blind young adults when a fifty-mile canoe trip down the Goulburn River was organized so that one blind and one sighted person occupied each canoe.[15]

In some instances, adjustments can be made so that the disabled person can participate and compete in physical activities, games, and sports on an equal basis with able-bodied persons. This is particularly true when individual adjustments are made for the disabled participant, e.g., use of a prosthesis, or change in structure or the manipulation of equipment used by the disabled person. Paraplegics, for instance, sitting in wheelchairs have successfully competed with able-bodied persons in archery.

There are, however, a number of physical activities, particularly some team sports, which must be organized for participation by the disabled only, in order to retain their basic characteristics. For instance, paraplegics, quadriplegics, and amputees cannot play standard basketball with able-bodied players. But wheelchair basketball is a popular sport, specifically designed for competitive play by persons whose disability is in their means of getting about. The National Wheelchair Basketball Association has worked out rules and regulations for the game based on the wheelchair as the means of mobility rather than the player's own legs, yet preserving the essence and basic characteristics of standard basketball. According to T. J. Nugent, Director of the Division of Rehabilitation Education Services at the University of Illinois, national and international rules and standards have been set for competitive participation in a number of wheelchair games, for which the ultimate competition is in the Paralympics held often in conjunction with the International Olympics.

Therapeutic recreators and their clients need not aspire to such "Olympian heights" to adapt and organize sports and games for their own recreational purposes. Following the steps just indicated, any group of persons with like disabilities may adapt the rules and regulations of a number of games to suit themselves. The same principles apply to adapting physical activities for participation by those who are medically incapacitated. Adaptations for persons with cardiac or rheumatic fever conditions, for instance, are likely to be in regulating the activity to avoid long, sustained, vigorous, and rapid physical activity. A smaller playing area, doubles instead of singles in tennis, shorter periods, and similar adjustments are examples.

Motivation to Physical Activity

A person who is physically disabled or medically restricted is unlikely to experience the kind of joy in physical movement that is often spontaneously felt by normally healthy individuals. Fear of worsening one's condition, fear of injury, difficulty in movement, discomfort resulting from physical activity often act as restraints. Strong motivation beyond the sheer joy of movement is sometimes needed to entice the physically handicapped into any physical activity at all. Exercise for its own sake may not be highly motivating. But many recreation experiences, in which exercise is inherent, may be highly motivating because of some other qualities also inherent in them. For example, a two-hour walk may have little appeal to a blind person. But when it is a walk through the woods so laid out to give the blind person an opportunity to explore nature it is enjoyable exercise. Washington D.C.'s National Arboretum has a "Touch and See" nature trail which:

> uses to its best advantage the wood's interior where the sounds of man and machine are muted and forest life is easier to perceive. The crack of a twig, the whispering of fluttering leaves, the call of a bird, the damp smell of the fog or the warmth from the tree-filtered summer sun are amplified in the otherwise quiet and cool forest interior . . . the trail follows a winding course over undulating terrain . . . with features pointed out in braille and print at the 24 stations on either side of the trail. The visitor is led by a guide rope from one station to the next along one side of the trail and back along the other. . . . The winding path is as undisturbed as possible. Underbrush was cleared . . . the trail was built as narrow as possible but wide enough for two persons to walk abreast on the earthen pathway. . . . Features were chosen that were easy for a blind person to examine. For example, a large white oak beside the trail was chosen for its obvious saddle . . . the visitor is encouraged to "hug" the large trunk and estimate its size. . . . At the beginning of the [return] trail a felled tree provides a new experience. The visitor is encouraged to "climb" this tree, hand over hand, to sense the bark texture and the tree's large branches . . . the average time required for a blind person to make the round trip is one hour and 45 minutes. The time element is important. If the trail is too long the visitor will tire and lose interest.[16]

Recreational swimming can provide similar motivation:

> Swimming allows a handicapped child a kind of exercise and a freedom of movement he cannot enjoy out of water. In water, he becomes free of wheelchairs and all appliances . . . Being able to learn something new, to achieve something physical, brings new confidence. He can now join his family and friends in a favorite recreation. . . . The instructor . . . must remember not to seek perfection. The idea is to help the children to enjoy the water, to relax, to be free of all apparatus for a while. The style in which they learn to swim may be most unconventional. . . . Their goal is not to become Olympic swimmers, just to exercise and enjoy.[17]

As water gives support and freedom of movement to a physically disabled person, so does a trampoline give support and impetus for movement. Trampolining proved to be a new and exciting activity for orthopedically handicapped students:

> . . . Each child found himself in a new movement environment and with the assistance of the instructor each explored and experimented with different types of movement. . . . Many safely engaged in and accomplished movements they had never even tried before. Participation seemed to give many children the feeling of accomplishing something which normal brothers, sisters, or friends could not do or hadn't been given the opportunity to try.[18]

The opportunity to participate with family and able-bodied friends can be a powerful motivating force for physical activity. Such was the case in a project sponsored by the New York Easter Seal Home Service. Groups of physically disabled persons and their families were guests of the owners of a beach motel for a weekend just before and after the official summer season. With the help of local volunteers of the First Aid Squad and Fire Department, the captain of a fishing boat, a retail store owner, a miniature golf course owner, and other interested individuals, the disabled persons were able to participate with their families and other able-bodied friends in numerous activities associated with a seashore weekend.

> For parents and other family members, values in the Beach Haven weekend included, as was the case with patients, the opportunity for new experiences in a relaxed, permissive outdoor atmosphere. Beach Haven offered an opportunity for an outing as a family, a rare occurrence for many families in which a member is severely handicapped.[19]

Among the disabled who are most apprehensive concerning physical activity are those who have some abnormalities of the heart and/or blood vessels. According to the noted cardiologist, Wolffe, they tend to feel that physical activity—even within their limited capacity—is harmful. "They erroneously think of the heart in terms of a pocket battery. Usage, they believe, exhausts its power. This is far from the truth."[20] In promoting physical activity with cardiovascular patients, Wolffe has noted that in recreation the emphasis on play rather than display is advantageous. Competition and proving one's superiority are de-emphasized while the fun of group activity and the tonic of laughter act as enticements to participation.

Recreation can offer to aged patients with chronic brain syndrome an incentive for the limited physical exercise that is important for their well-being. At Kingsbridge House

> Various activities have been used to provide this exercise. Tambourines are played above the heads and circular movements of the instruments are made. Dancing with the hands to recorded music provides opportunities for bending and arm motions. Bowling, with an actual sized, light-weight plastic set, and sitting in a chair

so that wheelchair patients will not be handicapped, provides good bending exercise. . . . Ball playing is now used as a get-acquainted technique at the beginning of the program.[21]

The situations cited above are intended only as a few examples of the ways in which recreation can serve as a motivation to physical activity. They are in no way exhaustive of the possibilities.

Motivation to Activity for Treatment Purposes

It is perhaps inevitable that persons concerned with the treatment and rehabilitation of the ill or disabled will note the strong incentives to activity inherent in much that is play and recreation, and will want to direct that motivation toward specific activity that serves a frankly therapeutic purpose.

In treating obesity, for example, the fact that weight is determined by caloric intake and output together gives as much importance to activity as to diet. Yet obese patients experience considerable difficulty in following a program of exercise per se.

> Where the physician desires a specific caloric output in terms of activity, the recreator can work closely with the physical therapist and the patient to translate exercises into comparable recreative activities, such as bowling, swimming and walking, that are pleasurable and appropriate to the patient's situation in the outside world.
> "Snacking" due primarily to boredom and depression is a perennial evening problem. Thought should be given to finding activities for this time of the day that will help to alleviate precipitous eating. Neither frenetic activity and socialization every evening nor the opposite extreme of solitary T.V. watching are desirable, but finding stimulating new interest is essential.[22]

The use of toys and play to meet specific treatment objectives with crippled children has been given considerable attention. Studies carried on in various Easter Seal centers were specifically reported by the St. Louis Society:

> . . . Especially with preschool age children, motivation is essential in achieving desired results. Treatment per se is not always attractive to the young child and, if he is pushed beyond his capacity, it can produce negative results. On the other hand, when the child approaches his treatment with interest and enthusiasm, much more can be accomplished. . . .
> . . . The staff noticed that a toy built on a rocker platform helpd to stimulate bilateral hand activity. Children who needed bi-manual activity profited by stabilizing the rocker with their involved hand while they played. . . .
> . . . Balls seemed to have universal appeal for most children. Those who could not stand, sat in wheel chairs and played ball with the group. Different sized balls were required to fit individual needs of different children. Larger balls to some extent stimulated bi-lateral use of upper extremities when one extremity was involved. . . .
> . . . Bill, 12 years old, had undergone three operations in one leg. Throughout the

operations he made no complaints of pain or inability to use his leg. It was not un-till the casts were removed and the scars were made visible that he became so shocked he was afraid to try to walk. In beginning physical therapy, the therapist allowed Bill to throw darts while holding onto a table for support. When he became interested in the game, the therapist wisely busied herself so that Bill had to go after the darts himself. The game had sufficient fun to motivate him to walk and to some extent, forget the pain in his leg.

Walking to and from toys such as dart boards, horse shoes, quoits, and others in which parts must be retrieved by walking some distance, are of value in helping children think more conscientiously about correct walking posture and prescribed gait. Parading back and forth in front of a mirror is far less interesting to young children. . . .

. . . Colorful toys with movable parts proved to have a great deal of fascination. Teachers found that they offered an opportunity to develop motivation for bi-manual activity. . . .

. . . The hobby horse . . . helps in motivation and quickly develops balance which otherwise requires a longer period of time. . . .

. . . Light weight plastic interlocking blocks were found to be well adapted for use by children who had weak hands. . . .

. . . No one would argue with the fundamental principle that toys should be given to children for their primary purpose of fun, personal satisfaction and enjoyment. But other values are numerous, and it is logical that when properly used they can help a child accomplish other results. If this fundamental principle is kept in mind, there would seem to be no limitation of their possibilities in helping handicapped children realize objectives in treatment and training.[23]

Similarly, play activities have been used successfully in motivating the child with limb deficiency to learn and practice the use of his prosthesis. "Activities which require pinch with one hand and manipulation with the intact hand will emphasize to the child the advantage of a prosthesis. . . . A recreation program suitably coordinated with the occupational therapy program can be very effective in promoting the awareness that a hook terminal device is of important functional use and that the cosmetic hands serve them better in social situations."[24]

When recreation activities are used for specific physical treatment purposes, it is important that the recreator and the physical therapist cooperate fully. Such a cooperative program was introduced at Montefiore Hospital in Pittsburgh. A recreation program which could give good functional motor activities was used to support and supplement the physical therapy prescription program:

The physical therapist specified and taught the movements required of the patient. In consultation with the recreation therapist, she selected games for those movements and the recreation therapist conducted the games. . . . It was necessary for the physical therapist to devise adaptations of games both for functional purposes and for the limitations imposed by the patient's impairments. In turn the recreation therapist had to modify the structure of the game to suit the patient's handicap. . . .

. . . Without exception, the patient's progress was accelerated by the stimulation of and the motivation induced by the game contest or the game achievement. By adapting the game to the patient's progressive level of functioning, by modifying the self-aide devices and by raising the demands of the game performance, patients were kept continuously interested and challenged.[25]

Close cooperation with the physician is essential also when recreation activities are "prescribed" for testing and treatment purposes. This is especially true in working with cardiovascular disorders. At the Children's Rehabilitation Center at the University of Virginia, for instance:

For children with heart problems, the Recreational Therapy Cardiovascular Test Semi-Active exercise program is given daily with emphasis on pulse rate count. A medical doctor works closely with the recreation therapist to evaluate the cardiovascular effects.

This test of semi-active exercises for rheumatic fever patients is a conditioning agent as well as a method of evaluation.[26]

Physical effects of recreation activity on older persons with diseases of the cardiovascular system, as noted at the Valley Forge Medical Center and Heart Hospital, were cited in Chapter 2.[27]

Mentally Retarded

Because mental retardation represents a deficiency in cognitive learning, capacity for abstract reasoning, and most academic achievement, much effort on behalf of the mentally retarded has gone into finding means for remediation and compensation in these areas. Overlooked to some degree has been the potential for personal satisfaction and achievement on the part of the mentally retarded to be found in physical activity. Increasingly, however, attention has been given to the development of motor skills and physical fitness in the retardate, as a result of research findings which show that arrested mental development need not necessarily affect the ability to develop physically.

Since mentally retarded persons (at least those who are not multiply handicapped) have no particular physical disability, it might be assumed that no special consideration need be given to their physical activity and play—that they could easily be incorporated into activities with their normally intelligent peers. There are, however, several reasons why special consideration should be given to developing the full physical potential in recreation for the mentally retarded, several of which follow.

1. Most mentally retarded persons are deficient in physical development to some extent. They tend to be smaller in size and to have below normal eye-hand coordination as well as motor coordination and flexibility. Many have inferior sense perception—speech, sight, hearing—and lack normal vitality.
2. They do not spontaneously engage in physical activity or learn to play by association with others. They must be taught.

3. Many retarded persons are unnecessarily fearful of bodily harm which might result from physical activity.
4. As is true in all areas of their learning, they must be taught any physical activity step by step, involving a breakdown of the elements of the activity into finer components than is necessary with normal persons.
5. They must be motivated by the play or pleasure aspect of their physical activity. It is difficult for them to conceptualize a future reward and they see no reason for physical activity or exertion unless it gives immediate satisfaction and pleasure.
6. They should be offered selected activities and games that give opportunity for physical movement without requiring much in the way of reasoning out, or conceptual integration of skills.

Just as the physical therapist and the therapeutic recreator need to integrate and coordinate their efforts in working with the physically handicapped, so do the recreator and the physical educator become interdependent in working with the mentally retarded. The retardate cannot achieve the full physical potential of play and recreation without being consciously taught how to use his body. Nor will he use his body to its full potential unless the physical activity carries some incentive and motivation in the form of fun, pleasure, and play.

In providing and promoting opportunities for active play and physical recreation, recreators and others working with the mentally retarded might note the following considerations:

1. It is advisable to use fine degrees of progression in teaching skills. Julian Stein refers to this as the "developmental concept of motor activity," meaning the process of breaking down as far as necessary the components of specific activities so that they may be presented progressively and sequentially.[28]
2. It is advisable to minimize verbal instructions and to maximize demonstration.
3. Once the retarded child masters a skill, he likes to do it over and over. He is not bored by the repetition of his achievement. The recreator might well capitalize on this characteristic to promote healthy exercise.
4. When the retardate is learning something new, however, he is apt to perform best on the first few tries, then to tire easily and lose interest and attention. Frequent short attempts rather than sustained effort is indicated until the skill is mastered.
5. Successful activities include those with kinesthetic appeal, gross movement of a rhythmic nature, and tactile involvement.[29]
6. One cannot expect much transfer of learning from one activity to another. Nor is it advisable to depend too much on the retarded child's memory. Review, repetition, and rote are indicated.
7. The pleasure associated with the activity is especially important. The retardate's idea of what is fun may be different from the recreator's, however. Close observation of his reactions to types of movement and to the

elements of the game or play should be made and considered for suc-
ceeding programs.

8. Because retarded persons tend to lack imagination and initiative, it is
necessary to structure their recreation programs to a considerable degree to deliberately lead them into activity.

9. Retarded children experience more failure than success in almost all
phases of their daily living. Consequently, they require more than the
usual amount of encouragement and praise in order to maintain their
interest and effort—even in play.

10. Games or activities in which participants must wait for a turn, or are
eliminated, are usually unsuccessful with the retarded. It is best to keep
all participants involved in the activity in some way all the time.

11. The element of competition in games and sports needs to be handled
very carefully. For the retarded child, losing is equated with failure and
rejection. Competing against his previous record or against time is less
devastating than competing against someone else. In all games and
sports, there should be frequent opportunity for all participants to
"score" in some way.

Recreation and play activities which are adapted and presented in special
ways to provide the maximum physical benefit to retarded children may be illustrated in the following three examples.

A nature playground was developed in 1969 at Dixon State School for Retarded Children in northwestern Illinois:

> It is constructed of several natural objects, trees, rocks, sand, and grass. The play-
> ground is designed primarily to encourage retarded children and adults to develop
> coordination and physical skill through the stimulus of fun . . . several railroad ties
> [were] sunk in concrete and arranged side by side at different heights. The obvi-
> ous objective with this portion of the playground is to develop coordination. Trees
> are used throughout the playground for development of physical skills and tactile
> sensation.[30]

Of interest also is a playhouse which was revised so that the roof extends to
the floor. Children are able to climb from one side of the house to the other
over the roof.

The use of music and rhythm to motivate retarded and other handicapped
children into action that is physically beneficial and individually expressive has
been developed into a specific therapy technique by Ferris and Jennet
Robins.[31] In evaluating this technique, Frances Arje and Doris Berryman have
stated:

> The educational objective of Educational Rhythmics is to help children master
> everyday actions. The principle on which Educational Rhythmics is based is that
> every human being needs to experience what psychiatrist Paul Haun refers to as
> "Synchronization of efficiency, automation, rhythmicity, alternation and effort."
> The techniques of Educational Rhythmics allow for provision of a broad range of

opportunities for handicapped persons to experience synchronization at their own individual levels of motor and cognitive ability. The exercises follow a middle road between gymnastics, ballet, . . . and aesthetic expression.[32]

The approach is intended to promote a sense of physical harmony and internal equilibrium, and to include such motoric experiences as "muscle stretching, relaxing, balance, coordination of body movement, countermovement reaction, precision and speeding up of neuromuscular reaction patterns."[33]

A third example of recreation programing tailored to the capabilities of the mentally retarded and intended to promote physical activity is the Special Olympics. Sparked by the Kennedy Foundation and initiated in the Chicago Park District in 1968, this type of special event for mentally retarded youngsters has spread to many cities and districts throughout the country. The participating children are tested and carefully placed in the correct groups to ensure equal competition and a reasonable chance for success by each individual. The program includes such athletic events as the 50-yard dash, standing broad jump, high jump, softball throw, 440-yard relay and several swimming events. The pageantry and ritual characteristic of the traditional Olympics, which is included in the Special Olympics to whatever extent possible, serves as a special kind of excitement and added incentive for participation.

Mentally Ill and Emotionally Disturbed

Persons with some mental or emotional disturbance need to maintain a good physical condition, just as others do. And, as is true with the mentally healthy person, proper physical activity contributes substantially to the maintenance of physical health and fitness in the mentally ill person. His ability or willingness to recognize the importance of physical activity, and to pursue it on his own volition, however, is often seriously impaired. Thus, the management and treatment plans for mental illness and emotional disturbance are likely to make provision for physical activity using varying degrees of persuasion or coercion as may be necessary with each individual.

Mentally ill persons who are hospitalized may get a certain amount of physical activity through prescribed work. Work therapy has been considered to be an important part of the total treatment program, for instance, at Menninger Foundation. James Pratt has described this aspect of Adjunctive Therapies there, particularly the woodcutting program. "This activity does many worthwhile things for the patient; it gets him up and out to an activity early in the morning and there are all gradations of work possible in sawing, splitting, chopping, carrying, and stacking wood."[34] Other work is included in the program such as remodeling buildings, razing structures, planting trees, and cleaning walks.

In other treatment programs, prescribed exercise such as calisthenics, outdoor walks, and so on is included. But more often the best way to involve mentally and emotionally disturbed persons in beneficial physical activity is by means of recreation activity.

The values to the mentally ill of participation in active games and sports and other active outdoor adventures are not confined to maintaining or regaining good physical condition. Such other values are discussed elsewhere in appropriate chapters. But the discussion here is focused on the physical benefits of recreation and considerations for maximizing these benefits.

Persons who are disturbed to such a degree that their physical behavior becomes noticeably abnormal tend to be either hyperactive, or listless and inactive, or to alternate between the two extremes. The overly active person's expenditure of energy may be unfocused and uncontrolled, may be destructive to himself and others, and be continued to the point of exhaustion. It should be noted that emotionally disturbed persons, especially children, need more than just an opportunity to "blow off steam." Vigorous gross motor activity in itself may result in heightened excitability, confusion, hostility, and irritability rather than release of tension.[35] For such persons, the recreator's job is to encourage participation in recreational games and sports which provide formal structure, known acceptable limits for activity, and some immediate purpose and focus for their expenditure of energy. The acting-out child's recreation program requires very definite structure on which he can depend.

Mentally ill persons who are depressed, regressed, and/or withdrawn tend to be completely inactive if left alone. Persuading these persons to undertake any type of physical activity is often a serious problem. The recreator may require all his ingenuity to motivate or entice these patients into participation. The "voluntarily chosen" aspect of recreation is relatively meaningless with patients who are, in fact, incapable of making choices. Some of the other qualifications of recreation can be legitimately exploited, however, if the result is some arousal of interest and activity in the withdrawn patient.

Play activities which are instinctive or relate to happy childhood experiences are sometimes successful. Activity which gives immediate pleasure to the senses—dancing or moving to music; swimming or playing in water—is often effective. Patients can sometimes be persuaded to join in activities such as circle games in which the patient is closely supported socially and is not exposed to individual (and seemingly hostile) attention or competition.

With severely regressed patients, forcing reflex action is sometimes indicated. This technique is explained by Claudette Lefebvre in her work with adult psychiatric patients:

> To help a severely regressed person re-learn to selectively respond to stimuli, we may first have to reactivate some primary—or unconscious—reflex mechanisms. Grossly simplified, the following is one technique we might use: (a) the leader tosses the ball toward the pre-occupied person, in this instance Mrs. J; (b) at some point, an avoidance reflex will prompt her to move away or raise her hands; (c) the leader will continue to toss the ball, verbally encouraging Mrs. J. to catch it; (d) the procedure will be repeated until Mrs. J. consciously catches and tosses the ball back to the leader. When this selective response is evoked, the leader will be able to involve Mrs. J. in other recreational experiences.[36]

Being placed in certain "environments"—a trampoline rather than solid ground underfoot, water in a swimming pool—is almost certain to evoke some reflex action which the alert recreator can capture, encourage, develop, and help the patient to make highly pleasurable recreationally, and physically beneficial incidentally.

Motivating mentally ill or emotionally disturbed persons to physical activity often requires individual attention and treatment. The recreator should be alert to those things which seem to spark even the slightest interest in the patient. An animal, for instance, may be the patient's best contact with the real world. A spark of interest in ponies shown by a young autistic boy led to the fine recreative experience of riding horseback. In recalling the child's first lesson, his mother expresses her gratitude to and confidence in the volunteer instructor who was helping her child:

> Mr. Carpenter lifted Carlitos upon his prize horse, Blackjack, and he truly looked like a little prince. . . . Somehow it was not difficult to grasp the understanding that the more important role that Mr. Carpenter would be playing would be that of an inspirational force of encouragement, channeling Carlitos' energies in a constructive exercise. Hopefully, this "exercise" would succeed in awakening many of his dormant and heretofore latent faculties. . . . Hopefully, in the future more attention will be given to recreation (with an emphasis on horseback riding), as a means of restoring a broken body or spirit back to health.[37]

Notes, Chapter 4

1. Howard S. Hoyman, "Our Modern Concept of Health" (paper presented before the School Health and Public Health Education Sections, American Public Health Association, Detroit, Michigan, 1961), p. 3.

2. President's Council on Youth Fitness, *Physical Fitness, Elements in Recreation* (Washington, D.C.: United States Government Printing Office, 1962), p. 1.

3. Charles B. Wilkinson, "The Quality of Fitness," *Parks and Recreation* Vol. I, No. 2 (February, 1966), p. 149, publication of the National Recreation and Park Association.

4. Hoyman, *op. cit.*, p. 3.

5. Wilkinson, *op. cit.*, p. 149.

6. Department of Health Education, *Seven Paths to Fitness* (Chicago: American Medical Association, n.d.).

7. *Ibid.*

8. Hoyman, *op. cit.*, p. 5.

9. President's Council on Youth Fitness, *op. cit.*, p. iii.

10. *Ibid.*, foreword.

11. Charles K. Brightbill, *Man and Leisure* (Englewood Cliffs, N.J.: Prentice-Hall, Inc., 1961), p. 222.

12. Clarence T. Jones "Spot Billiards for the Cerebral Palsied," *Parks and Recreation* Vol. I, No. 2 (February, 1966), p. 159.

13. Richard Dattner, *Design for Play* (New York: Van Nostrand and Reinhold Co., 1969), p. 110.

14. Robert Peters, "Bullseye!" *Outlook*, Vol. 1, No. 4 (February, 1970), p. 3. publication of the American Association for Health, Physical Education, and Recreation.

15. Ralph Lightfoot, "Canoeing Builds Confidence in Blind Persons," *ICRH Newsletter*, Vol. 4, No. 3 (January and February, 1970), p. 1. publication of the Information Center, Outdoor Laboratory, Southern Illinois Univeristy.

16. Joseph M. Garvey, "Touch and See," *Parks and Recreation*, Vol. IV, No. 11 (November, 1969), p. 20.

17. Joe Streva, "How to Teach Handicapped Children to Swim," *Parks and Recreation*. Vol. I, No. 6 (June, 1966), p. 502.

18. Milton H. Pettit, "A Trampoline Program for the Orthopedically Handicapped," *Outlook*, Vol. 1, No. 2 (October, 1969), p. 3.

19. Margery McMullin and Margaret Clarke, "Weekends at the Seashore," *Parks and Recreation*, Vol. II, No. 6 (June, 1967), p. 41.

20. Joseph B. Wolffe, M.D., "Recreation, Medicine, and Humanities," *The Doctors and Recreation in the Hospital Setting*, Bulletin No. 30 (Raleigh, N.C.: The North Carolina Recreation Commission, 1962), p. 21.

21. Paula E. Gray, "Therapeutic Recreation Service for the Chronic Brain Syndrome Patient in a Home and Hospital for the Aged," *Recreation in Treatment Centers,* Vol. V. (September, 1966), p. 13. Publication of the National Therapeutic Recreation Society.

22. Caroline Weiss, "Obesity: Implications for Therapeutic Recreation Services," *Therapeutic Recreation Journal,* Vol. I, No. 2 (Fourth Quarter, 1967), p. 10. Publication of the National Therapeutic Recreation Society.

23. John H. Kniest, "There is More to Toys than Meets the Eye," *Crippled Child* (October, 1956), Publication of the National Society for Crippled Children and Adults.

24. Adell C. Carr, Liesel Friedman, and Chester A. Swinyard, "Essentials of a Recreation Program for Children with Limb Deformities," *Recreation for the Ill and Handicapped,* Vol. II, No. I (January, 1967), p. 5 Publication of the National Association of Recreational Therapists, Inc.

25. Edith H. Lipkind, "Recreation Therapy and Physical Therapy: A Blueprint for an Integrated Service," *Recreation in Treatment Centers,* Vol. II (September, 1963), p. 57-58.

26. Joseph Nee, "Rehabilitating Children with Birth Defects and Other Handicaps by Recreation Therapy," *Therapeutic Recreation Journal,* Vol. III, No. 2, (Second Quarter, 1969), p. 26.

27. Joseph B. Wolffe, "Recreation as Prophylactic and Therapeutic Measure in Diseases of the Cardiovascular System," *Recreation in Treatment Centers,* Vol. IV, (September, 1965), p. 30.

28. Julian U. Stein, "The Importance of Physical Activity for the Mentally Retarded," *Programing for the Mentally Retarded,* (report of a National Conference of the American Association for Health Physical Education and Recreation, Washington, D.C. 1968), p. 25-26.

29. Elizabeth M. Boggs, "Recreation in the Residential Setting—A Parent's Viewpoint," *Recreation in Treatment Centers,* Vol. III (September, 1964), p. 8.

30. "Nature Playground at Dixon," *ICRH Newsletter,* Vol. IV, No. 3 (January and February, 1970), p. 7.

31. Ferris and Jennet Robins, *Educational Rhythmics for Mentally Handicapped Children* (Zurich, Switzerland: Ra-Verlag Rapperswil S.G., 1963).

32. Frances Arje and Doris L. Berryman, "Educational Rhythmics Proving Its Worth," *ICRH Newsletter,* Vol. III, No. 15 (November, 1968), p. 2.

33. *Ibid.,* p. 2.

34. James F. Pratt, "Learning to Work and Play Again," *Recreation in Treatment Centers,* Vol. III (September, 1964). p. 19.

35. Hally B. W. Poindexter, "Status of Physical Education for the Emotionally Disturbed," *Physical Education and Recreation for Handicapped Children* (Washington, D.C.: Bureau of Education for the Handicapped, Department of Health, Education, and Welfare) p. 19.

36. Claudette B. Lefebvre, "Sports and Athletics in a 'Sheltered Community Center' Recreation Program for Short-Term Adult, Psychiatric Patients," *Recreation in Treatment Centers,* Vol. V (September, 1966), p. 28.

37. Marie Rita Perello, "Horseback Riding for the Handicapped," *ICRH Newsletter,* Vol. IV, No. 5 (May, 1970), p. 1.

5 | Avenues for Learning

"LEARN TO LIVE and live to learn. . . ." This epigram by the poet Bayard Taylor succinctly sums up the essence of the relationship between recreation and learning. Learning is a part of the human experience from birth to death. Indeed, viewed in its broadest sense, all of life is learning. Even during periods of unconsciousness, such as sleep, perceptual processes cannot be assumed to be at a standstill. Medical records support the assumption of possible perceptive, cognitive responses and activity among severely withdrawn, emotionally disturbed patients, autistic children, brain-damaged stroke victims, and even among many profoundly mentally retarded individuals. Thus, learning of some kind, or to some degree, may be seen to pervade all of life's experiences. Those that are recreational in nature offer some of the highest potential for learning. The self-motivation that carries one into recreation and the heightening of awareness and sensitivity that accompany pleasurable experience are cited as major factors in the potency of recreation as an avenue for learning. Recreative experience contains the incentive and the milieu for the learning process. Prominent among the propellants that lead one to seek recreation are the drive to know—curiosity—and the desire to explore the unknown, to seek new experience. In many instances, the terms "learning" or "educational" might be interchanged for "pleasurable" or "satisfying" to describe the primary objective of recreation. Probably more often than not the concepts involved are synonymous. What is truly recreational is also, cannot help being, educational.

However, as we have seen in Chapter 2, the term "recreation" is used to connote not only a life experience but also a service. "Education" is also used to indicate this dual connotation. As the concepts conveyed by the two terms in the sense of *experience* have been shown above to bear fundamental similarities, so education and recreation as areas of human service have close ties. This can be illustrated by looking at the basic objectives of the two fields. As Brightbill has so well stated, education, in addition to its primary purpose of discovering truth, seeks also to ". . . leave a larger personality in its wake . . ." and ". . . enhance the well-being of mankind."[1] No one would argue that at least the latter two of these objectives are also the *raison d'être* of recreation services.

Still another fundamental tie—often referred to but too little acted upon— exists between recreation and education as members of the family of human services. This is the whole matter of leisure education, of preparing people through purposeful educational planning, programs, and services for full living in an age when leisure is an integral and central fact of life for hundreds of thousands. Reciprocally, leisure living has much to offer the educational process. Brightbill, who in 1966 devoted an entire book to the topic of *Educating for Leisure-Centered Living,* reminds us that, "Learning involves observation, memorization, reasoning, and experiencing. Leisure can play a large role, especially in the last of these—experiencing."[2]

It is difficult to imagine any instance in which learning, at least in its broadest sense, is not an integral part or phase of the therapeutic recreation process. Ball sees recreation education as a step on a scale of experiences leading toward therapeutic recreation, which in turn may lead the individual into a full or true recreative experience. Berryman's adaptation of the double helix structure of the DNA molecule strongly implies that learning or educative processes are integral to all therapeutic recreation.[3] Moreover, the definition of therapeutic recreation proposed by the authors assumes that in the process of achieving or maximizing desired concomitant effects of recreative experience, objectives will include those that are fundamentally educative in nature. If, for example, therapeutic recreation services are purposefully directed toward developing the kinds of attitudes, knowledges, and skills that can make of recreation a potent force in promotive health, must not such aims encompass educational services and learning processes? If the major concern of therapeutic recreation in treatment centers is considered to be leisure, or recreation, habilitation or rehabilitation, could not the terminology "leisure education" or "leisure re-education" be considered as appropriate? Likewise, counseling and guidance may be described as being essentially educational services. Thus, the growing recognition of the therapeutic recreator's responsibility for leisure counseling indicates another area of close liaison between recreation and education.

Once again, the relationship is a two-way channel. We refer here to the possible contributions to cognitive functions and processes, or even to learning capacities that may be achieved through knowledgeable therapeutic recreation services. Although hard evidence is lacking to substantiate specific claims, modest beginnings of research in these areas are being attempted. Hypotheses related to such questions are being tested by therapeutic recreators participating in experimental projects with interdisciplinary teams of investigators, including special educators, behavioral scientists, physical educators, and others. Research in therapeutic recreation is the topic of a later chapter. It is appropriate to recognize here, however, that therapeutic recreators are collaborating increasingly with educators, special educators, and rehabilitation counselors not only in research projects, but in professional preparation, programs, and services.

The remainder of this chapter is devoted to exploring some of the potential educational benefits recreation holds and possible implications of the recreative experience in relation to the effects of various illnesses and disabilities. It is recognized that many, if not all of the values that come through recreation, such as those discussed in the other chapters of this part of the book, might quite correctly be considered aspects of learning. Thus in this chapter we attempt to call attention to some additional considerations concerning recreation-learning possibilities. The discussions in each section are intended to be illustrative or suggestive rather than exhaustive treatments of the topic.

Recreation—Learning—and the Mentally Retarded

In identifying learning as one of the major concomitant and potentially therapeutic values of recreative experience, a disabled group apt to be thought of first are the mentally retarded. This is logical since the primary effect of the disability has to do with learning capacity and processes.

The mentally retarded, who constitute approximately three percent of the population of the United States, vary along a wide range of personal attributes and abilities, as do any group of individuals. The characteristics they share as a group are those associated with the effect of the disability, defined by the American Association of Mental Deficiency as "subaverage general intellectual functioning which originates during the developmental period and is associated with impairment in adaptive behavior." Even within the classification of mental retardation as defined above, wide variation exists extending from the mildly (educable) retarded to the moderate or trainable group and on to the profoundly retarded who are the most severely disabled. Designations of the various degrees of retardation have been referred to also in Chapter 3. However, to define or refer to mental retardation in terms of descriptive classifications does not indicate the full extent of the possible disabling effects of the condition. As Avedon points out, "Depending upon the dimensions of his disability, a retarded person faces various degrees and intensities of physical, emotional, intellectual, social, and economic limitation."[4] Possibilities that recreation may offer in helping reduce some of these limitations are discussed in other chapters. We are concerned here with the question of what recreation may offer as a learning-enhancer.

The matter of motivation—of the incentive afforded by pleasurable experience—is considered to be perhaps the most basic, though admittedly imperfectly understood, element contributing to therapeutic benefits of recreation. It goes almost without saying that all the values to the individual that may come through recreation are conceivably enhanced by the stimulus afforded by anticipation of the involvement in pleasurable experience. Common as they may be to all recreative experiences, however, such motivational forces must not be overlooked in a discussion of recreation's contribution to the education of the mentally retarded. "It is mostly, if not only, in play that motivation to extend the self is most effectively sparked. Outside of play or pleasant experience, the retarded individual may use his powers, but very likely not all of his powers. In play there is a strong *élan* to stretch to new attainment, to launch into new activity, to attempt new contacts, to seek the mastery of new behavior."[5]

In the unlimited range of experiences it encompasses, recreation offers many possibilities for learning through various types of activity participation. Schools for the retarded which one of the authors has visited both in the United States and in various countries of Europe make wide use of games to teach many skills such as reading or recognizing traffic signs, telling time from clocks, recognizing relationships of form and color through puzzle solving. Singing and participation in other musical activity may help with memorization and coordination. Dramatic play may reinforce self-care habits or help in the development of speech skills.

Physical play has received particular attention for its beneficial effects in helping the mentally retarded child develop his capacities. Benoit, for example, claims that, "In physical play . . . the probability is great that the utmost or true absolute learning potential of the individual is activated."[6] The National Association for Retarded Children says that, "Mental development, like physical development, is promoted by the right kind of activity and stimulation, and retarded when it is lacking. Indeed, the two tend to interact. In this process the years of early childhood, when the nervous system is maturing and language developing, are certainly very critical."[7] There is even some research evidence of improvements in measured intelligence of retarded children through participation in planned programs of physical fitness type activities. Both Oliver in 1958 and Corder in 1965 found significant gains in IQ among groups of educable mentally retarded boys, ages 12-15, who participated daily for several weeks in progressive and systematic programs.[8] Taylor found enough evidence of intellectual progress among subjects in a limited experimental study of developmental dance with ten educable mentally handicapped girls to warrant a recommendation for further studies in this area.[9]

The general climate or milieu in which recreation occurs may be particularly conducive to learning for the mentally retarded. The happy atmosphere, the verbally or non-verbally communicated acceptance and understanding, the emphasis on capacities and individual worth, the opportunities for successful effort, the freedom and lack of pressure—in short, the kind of characteristics the recreator seeks to infuse into the recreation situation—can be of great importance in freeing the mentally retarded child to function to the fullest extent of his capacities.

Among the variety of community or institutional settings in which recreation services are offered for the mentally retarded, none provides a better opportunity for maximizing the environmental potential then does recreation camping. The increase in both day and residential camping for the retarded has been marked in recent years. Interest has been spurred and action sponsored by local public park and recreation agencies; voluntary or non-profit organizations such as the Kennedy Foundation, National Association for Retarded Children, American Association on Mental Deficiency, and by local chapters of various organizations including the Girl and Boy Scouts, YMCA, YWCA, Jewish Community Centers, and others; by various agencies of the state and federal government; and by the National Recreation and Park Association and the American Association for Health, Physical Education, and Recreation. William Freeberg is experienced in recreation camping and research with the mentally retarded. While he is cognizant of the difficulties in retaining the recreational elements of a camping experience when it is structured and designed for therapeutic and educational objectives, Freeberg nevertheless sees in camping more opportunities for educational and recreational experiences than in any other type of program. He has proposed four basic objectives for a well planned and organized camp program for the retarded, pointing out that the degree of achievement may be, for most individuals, related to the degree of retardation. The objectives are to:

"1. Assist the retarded by giving them learning experiences which will help them adapt to community life and community services.
2. Assist the retarded by giving them learning experiences that will help them adjust better to family life.
3. Assist the retarded by giving them learning experiences that will develop them socially and physically for a more enjoyable life and as a necessary preparation for vocational training.
4. Assist the retarded by giving them learning experiences that will help develop skills and hobbies which will enable them to use their leisure constructively."[10]

After reviewing recent studies on physical fitness with the retarded in camp situations,[11] Freeberg also made this observation:

> The overall conclusion of this study [Bateman, 1965] is that retarded children, like all children, learn what they are taught. This is not meant as a truism in any sense, but as the most important single guideline in planning a camp program for mentally retarded. The first step must be [to] determine with great precision what is to be taught in camp, and only then to plan the activities which will best achieve these specific goals. This is actually a reversal of the usual procedure of planning activities and then asking what the children might learn from them.[12]

Another dimension of the significance of recreative experience as a major avenue for learning for the retarded, as for all people, is its life-pervasiveness. Formal schooling is confined for most people to anywhere from an eight- or ten-year minimum to an upper limit of seventeen or eighteen years—or portions thereof—during childhood, adolescence, and young adulthood. Continuing into adulthood, work may bring additional opportunities for both incidental and planned learning experiences. However, one of the marked aspects of the technological revolution of the twentieth century, as we all know, has been the unprecedented reduction both in the individual's working years and in the amount of time he spends on the job daily, weekly, and annually during those years. For the ill or disabled, the time allotted to work will, in all probability, be much less than for others. Play or recreation, on the other hand, is an integral part of life experience from infancy throughout the individual's life span. Thus opportunities for learning through play and recreation are coextensive with life itself.

The importance of experiences in the pre-school years both for preventing retardation that may stem from social or emotional deprivation and for promoting the child's capacities has received considerable emphasis. According to a brochure distributed by the Kennedy Foundation (*Recreation for the Mentally Retarded: What You should Know: What You Can Do*) it has been estimated that the IQ of some children may be raised or lowered by as much as thirty points through experiences in the first two or three years of life. Exposure and encouragement of children from early infancy to play related to such developmental processes as reaching, grasping, crawling, etc., are of utmost importance. Colorful, attention-attracting toys; adult encouragement or even assistance with the infant's movements until he attempts to move on his own volition; use of rhythmic activities; toys such as push-pull types and large blocks that stimulate physical activity, and those that provide additional experiences along with physical activity such as bells, drums, tambourines, and finger-paints—these are some of the many play-learning aids and exposures that can be introduced as the child advances from infancy through early childhood. Opportunities to participate with other members of the family and with his peers in play and social experiences are important to the retarded child's developmental processes. Providing a wide range of opportunities for play experiences; encouraging, assisting, and supervising the retarded child's play without overprotecting him—these are the essential roles of the parent or adult working with the pre-school retarded child.[13]

For the school-age retarded child, much of the learning process will continue to be enhanced by play-adapted equipment and curricular content, as well as by the use of recreation leadership methods and approaches on the part of the teacher.

Reciprocally, methods of special educators and the findings of recent experimental studies in behavioral research may be of particular value to the recreator in helping the mentally retarded learn the physical and social skills necessary to happy play and satisfying recreation. For example, Anthony G. Linford and Claudine Y. Jeanrenaud have proposed an interesting "Systematic Language Structure for Teaching Recreative Skills to the Mentally Retarded." Observing how attempted verbal communication with a retarded child may be blocked by excessive, confusing stimuli and by jumbled words and concepts unfamiliar to the retardate, Linford and Jeanrenaud devised a task analysis of levels of recreative responding both as a model or guide for the teaching of play skills and for use as an evaluative instrument. Essentially the teaching guide and evaluative instrument are based on an analysis of various levels of verbal control or behavioral response. These are identified as: (1) imitative, and (2) receptive language. Progress from an initial non-verbal imitative level to a second stage in which the child responds imitatively to a verbal command of "Do this" is described as being quite easily and quickly effected with the use of behavior modification techniques. The teaching sequence as recommended is then:

> Therapist's Statement: "Do this. Kick." (Therapist demonstrates.) "Kick." (Fade out the "do this" but maintain demonstration.) "Kick." (No demonstration. Therapist indicates object to be kicked by pointing.)
> At this point the child can respond to a verb at a receptive level. The next stage is to move to verb-object (noun) connections. . . . Take an object that the child is very familiar with, e.g., a ball, and pair the verb with the noun.
> "Kick ball." (No indications other than the verbal command.)
> Finally, . . . try to generalize the verb to a number of objects.
> "Kick ball."
> "Kick beanbag."
> "Kick balloon."
> When you reach this level you have established a pivotal language base . . . "kick" being the pivot to which many nouns can be attached.[14]

On the basis of concepts such as those indicated in the preceding discussion, recreative experiences of the individual may be seen as the hub or central force for much of the retardate's learning in the social, sensory-motor, cognitive domains. Major enhancers of the learning process inherent to recreation include the motive force of pleasurable experience—both anticipated and realized; the positive atmosphere or environment of emphasis on capacity; and the opportunities for participatory-experiential involvement in motor activity, social and object relationships. Therapeutic recreation services directed toward maximizing these potential avenues to learning may be offered, according to the individual's developmental stage or degree of disability, at the preventive or promotive (primary), supportive or reinforcing (secondary), or remedial-rehabilitative (tertiary) level.

Recreative Learning Related to Other Conditions

Much that has been said about the learning potential of recreative experiences for the mentally retarded can be applied in relation to the effects of other disabling conditions or illnesses. The incentive that pleasurable experience offers needs no further elaboration as an important force in the learning process, although methods and techniques employed by the recreator or teacher to motivate learning through play may need to be adapted to the specific effects of the disability and to the capacities of the individual. For example, it is apparent that certain types of games, game materials, and play equipment, as well as leadership techniques, such as some referred to above in relation to the mentally re-tarded, may properly be used as aids toward cognitive development goals with other children who are experiencing learning difficulties, even though the etiology of the problem differs. However, for the disabled person who is men-tally alert, for example an orthopedically disabled child with no mental incapac-ity, the use of such games and techniques as inducements to learning might be inappropriate. Nevertheless, play-appealing, recreative encouragement of learning is widely used in many aspects of the teaching-learning process with all people.

Likewise, the necessity of physical activity to the individual's total growth—including his mental capacities—is a universal life requirement. For all people, then, regardless of life condition, play and recreation can be seen as providing major opportunities for physical activity and thus for development of mental, along with other capacities. The value of recreative experience for strengthen-ing or maintaining the individual's mental capacities through pleasurable physical activity could thus be cited in relation to possible effects of any num-ber of disabling conditions.

Applications to the effects of various types of illnesses and disabilities could also be made concerning the potential for learning processes inherent in what was alluded to above as the recreational climate or environment. And the fact that recreation is a life-continuous force lends to its significance as an avenue of learning for people of all ages and with varying disabilities and capacities.

As previously recognized, also, much of the educational value of recreation for people affected by various health impairments has to do with such major goals as the development or strengthening of the individual's social or physical condition or with his capacities for self-realization and self-identity—all topics of other chapters in this section.

In the discussion that follows, therefore, repetition has been avoided. Instead, concentration is upon a few illustrative situations and points that will suggest to the reader additional learning-recreation links that may be of particular bene-fit in relation to the effects of different illnesses or disabling conditions.

For the person who has a permanent physical disability, habilitation or re-habilitation should encompass more than training in the functional activities of daily living and vocational preparation. Much emphasis should be placed upon education or re-education for leisure. This implies not only training and devel-opment in skills, or even the addition to such training of a variety of exposures and opportunities for practicing and using such skills in recreation pursuits, but also, and more basic, helping the disabled person develop attitudes that will enable him to value the leisure that is sure to be a large time factor in his life as an opportunity for full, rich living rather than approaching it as an empty, dreaded wasteland. Leisure-recreation counseling services and programs un-fortunately are almost non-existent. There are indications, however, of growing recognition of the importance of and need for leisure counseling in the total re-habilitation effort. Articles on the topic by leading therapeutic recreators have appeared in recent issues of professional journals.[15] There is also reason to believe that curriculums in therapeutic recreation will include more in the areas of guidance and counseling in the future.[16] It is of some significance to this discussion, too, to note that in the latter half of the 1960's the Vocational Rehabilitation Administration of the United States Department of Health, Education, and Welfare changed its designation to the Rehabilitation Services Administration, thereby indicating a broadening of the concept of rehabilitation from the traditional limitation to a vocational focus. Even prior to its change of title, however, the then VRA in 1963 became the first federal agency to accord recreation recognition as an important field of human service through the awarding of funds to six colleges and universities for graduate traineeships and to five for teaching grants in therapeutic recreation.[17]

The need for leisure education as a part of recreation counseling in the rehabilitation process is, of course, by no means limited to the permanently physically disabled. Any birth defect or congenital condition which has the effect of limiting the child's play-learning exposures and experiences heightens the need for helping the individual to learn to play. The recreator's counseling responsibilities in these instances will be to the parents and other adults concerned with the child's care. Indeed, because of the effects of the disability, it is obvious that recreation-leisure counseling will always be in the nature of an indirect service for those who are severely mentally retarded. This will be true also for other individuals whose mental capacities are affected for either an extended or temporary period by the nature of the illness or disability, as for example the psychotic patient who is in a stage of either severe withdrawal or hallucination and hyperactivity.

For those people—youth and adults—who will have permanent disabilities as a result of illness or injury, leisure rehabilitation and counseling services directly to the individual involved or indirectly through those caring for him—or in many cases, both—are indicated as a major service to be offered by the therapeutic recreator. Needs for such services in many, if not most, instances will extend beyond the treatment center and the period of hospitalization to the community and for as long as the individual may continue to need some educational-counseling-supportive guidance or assistance toward the goal of full, rich leisure experiences in his total life pattern. In such situations the recreator must be particularly sensitive to the need to avoid the development of a dependency relationship. The goal of leisure rehabilitation and recreation counseling, like all recreation services, is to help the individual achieve the fullest possible measure of independence in his recreative uses of leisure.

There are many avenues for learning through recreation and they are by no means one-way streets. Learning and communication cannot be unilateral processes. Thus much of the awareness and knowledge necessary for developing leisure and recreation services to meet the needs and capacities of the ill or disabled must be gained, either incidentally or through consciously planned or programmed efforts, from those who experience the effects of the condition. An outstanding example of an educational program for just such purposes is offered by physically disabled students who attend the University of Illinois. Sponsored by the Recreation and Athletics Department of the University's

Division of Rehabilitation-Education Services, the renowned Gizz Kids—disabled student athletes—each year participate in many competitive and demonstration events on and off campus. The teams, including their cheerleaders who are also in wheelchairs, travel to all parts of the United States and have appeared in countries of Africa, Europe, the Far and Middle East. In line with the philosophy of the Division and its Director, Timothy J. Nugent, one of the major objectives of these activities is to educate people everywhere—special groups, members of the health and helping professions, the general public—concerning the needs and capacities of the disabled. For the disabled college students the enrichment that participation in the program brings to their education can hardly be overestimated.

Some of the methods, techniques, and equipment used in the education-recreation process with people who have visual or auditory disabilities must be specifically designed or adapted to their needs and capacities. It is self-evident that the braille system of printing or writing and talking or recorded books for the visually impaired and hearing aids for the hard of hearing are of major importance for their users in all areas of living, including recreation and learning. Much needs to be done to develop and scientifically test the effects of materials and equipment that might enhance learning and recreation for those with sensory disabilities. Possibilities for the enhancement of learning for blind children through a specially designed outdoor play area are suggested in the following excerpt from an article describing the program of the Children's Division of the Harris County Lighthouse for the Blind in Houston, Texas. The playscape described below was designed by a commercial playground equipment corporation.

> Among the most well-known of the outdoor environments in which the children play, is a specially designed series of coordinated forms called a Playscape. This planned play environment . . . is composed of stationary Playforms which are closely integrated to create a setting for imaginative, fantasy games.
>
> In day-to-day use, the Playscape is entered by our blind children and "converted" into an unlimited number of stages in which they enact physical games of a social order. Although they are visually impaired, the youngsters can feel their way into the various shapes and forms of the Playscape and construct such fantasies as "Playing House," "Follow the Leader" or "Train Trip," with group participation.
>
> In the process, the children are exercising their motor and perceptual faculties, are developing their coordination, and are fundamentally "playing" in much the same way as do their normal counterparts. The rich content of their fantasy games also serves as an emotional and mental stimulant, . . .
>
> A chief advantage of play within this type of environment is the various levels of challenge that it offers all children. Since blind children with aggravating handicaps are uniquely different, they require play opportunities in which they can respectively determine their own game tasks. It is important that they are able to do so because game play, particularly for the blind, must be success-oriented and confidence building.[18]

The hard-of-hearing child may exhibit problem behavior resulting from the constant strain of trying to understand and the frustration of frequent failure.

Fatigue is increased for children whose difficulty in communication demands more than the usual concentration, effort, and attention. Intervention in this work-study pattern with judiciously timed and programmed periods of relaxing recreation might be expected to enhance the learning process by helping to maintain a healthy physical balance and positive mental attitude.[19]

Concepts of recreation as being not only supportive to learning but as the basis or foundation for a special education program were exemplified in an experimental school which one of the authors was privileged to visit in the Netherlands. In this new model facility, experimental teaching methods and research were being conducted with children whose learning difficulties stemmed from developmental problems. Emotional difficulties which the children might display in conduct problem, acting out behaviors were cited as being indicative of secondary rather than primary neuroses; nor were the learning problems related to deficient mental capacity. These children were not considered to be mentally retarded. The school's director, Dr. Wilha Bladergroen, laid great stress upon the importance of play in developing movement coordination and visual, auditory, tactile integration as prerequisites to learning the skills involved in reading, writing, arithmetic, and other educational subject areas.

After the evaluation of each child according to developmental tests administered upon his admission, the following sequence was indicated to exemplify the approach to the child's education:

1. Instructing and helping the child learn to play.
2. Correcting faulty eye functioning and other problems as needed.
3. Reading instruction.

Progression for the child in his class provided for movement through the following stages:

First—all play.

Second—Seventy-five percent play/twenty-five percent work (formal class instruction and study).

Third—Fifty percent play/fifty percent work.

Fourth—Twenty-five percent play/seventy-five percent work.

Fifth—Class time all devoted to work with play periods separate from class time.

Physical facilities were carefully designed in harmony with the philosophy and principles upon which the program functioned. One of the first concerns was for the need of children who come to this school to have opportunities to relax. Accordingly, much attention was given to acoustical materials and provisions. Classrooms were large and well lighted. The study area had desks for the students and teacher. The rest of the room was a large play area with various types of art, music, and other equipment available. Grassy outside areas were accessible from classrooms. There were no black top or cement surfaces. A large sandbox was in one area and the director indicated that more provisions for sand and water play were desired. In the gymnasium, where activity could be observed through a one-way mirror, various types of gymnastic and adapted equipment were used in the motor-space perception instruction.[20]

A different approach linking recreation with a required training or educational program is suggested by Brightbill's description of a neuropsychiatric center, also in the Netherlands. Here, in a community-like environment, a required cultural skills program was at the heart of an important phase of the total treatment program which also included both work therapy and recreation. Brightbill described it thus:

> What was the core of this effort? Well, aside from all of the other standard forms of treatment, the central theme matched the approach to the problem of leisure in a progressive and modern community. It was a three-way approach to full living and personality development: First there was the work therapy. This was work, not for the purpose of job training or retraining, but rather productive activity for thera-peutic purposes. . . . Then at the opposite end of the line was the recreation program in which participation was, of course, voluntary. The real "meat," however, . . . was not in the prescribed work, or the optional recreation, but rather in what was in be-tween. And what is, or should be, between work and play, or working and living? Of course! Preparing for work and preparing for leisure, or what this hospital preferred to call its required cultural skills program! This program was divided into four areas: (1) movement (including sports, games, exercise and dance . . .), (2) the graphic and plastic arts, (3) the theater (or . . . drama . . .), and (4) music. Each patient, each day was required to participate in all four phases of the program. If there was any area of omission it might have been in Nature Education. But even this was evident in much of the work therapy program. There is no way that I can adequately describe the beneficial influence of these programs upon the patients. It was quite remark-able![21]

For older people, generally, there is recognition among recreators of needs not only to increase the amount and availability of leisure opportunities, but also to improve greatly their quality. An "adult education" approach might have something to offer in providing more appropriate and stimulating recrea-tion services and programs for these people. It is all too common, particularly with elderly patients in hospitals and nursing homes, and with aged, infirm people in communities, to find patronizing attitudes expressed by staff and childish, sterile recreation activity programs. Some evidence of a progressive trend is indicated in a report by a Task Force on Recreation, Group Work and Leisure-Time Needs in Westchester County, New York. Indications were found in some of the larger centers in the county of a trend toward more meaningful programs for the aged population, including " . . . self-government, adult educa-tion classes, and service projects."[22] Even for those elderly people who sustain cerebrovascular accidents or strokes, most of whom will not be feasible candi-dates for vocational rehabilitation, recreation may enter into partnership with speech and physical therapy in the process of re-education toward goals of helping the individual to retain or regain maximum use of his remaining capac-ities. The Director of Recreation at the Mary Manning Walsh Home in New York included in a list of recommended objectives for recreation programs serving chronic brain syndrome patients ". . . the exercising of existing mental capac-ities by requiring the patient to problem solve and think for himself."[23]

The need for seeking ways of maximizing the potential concomitant values of recreative experience is probably nowhere more urgent today than among the economically and socially disadvantaged both in the congested, deteriorating cores of our urban centers and in the depressed rural areas of some regions of our country. Tensions among the races, gaps between the generations, divisions between social and economic groups, alarming increases of crime and delinquency bring into sharp focus critical needs that call for the marshaling of all resources that can offer positive contributions toward helping solve or alleviate the problems. If one of the basic areas of need has to do with communicating, sharing, learning about, understanding life-styles and value systems among the various populations and individuals, then recreation should have much to offer as an avenue for harmonious, pleasurable communication, sharing, and learning.

Notes, Chapter 5

1. Charles K. Brightbill, *Educating for Leisure-Centered Living* (Harrisburg, Pa.: The Stackpole Company, 1966), p. 42.

2. *Ibid.*, p. 46.

3. See Chapter 2, pp. 41-42.

4. E. M. Avedon, *Recreation and Mental Retardation* (Arlington, Va.: United States Department of Health, Education, and Welfare, Public Health Service, Division of Chronic Diseases, Mental Retardation Branch, Public Health Service Publication No. 1512 [June, 1966]), pp. 1-2.

5. E. Paul Benoit, "Extending the Mind Through the Body," in *Activity Programs for the Mentally Retarded*, reprinted from the American Association for Health, Physical Education, and Recreation, *Journal of Health, Physical Education, Recreation*, Vol. 37 No. 4 (April, 1966), p. 29.

6. *Ibid.*

7. *Facts on Mental Retardation* (New York: National Association for Retarded Children, Inc., n.d.), p. 7.

8. Julian U. Stein and Roy Pangle, "What Research Says About Psychomotor Function of the Retarded," in *Activity Programs for the Mentally Retarded, op. cit.*, p. 38.

9. Lucile N. Taylor, "Developmental Dance in the Education of the Educable Mentally Handicapped Child" (unpublished Masters thesis, University of Illinois, 1964).

10. William Freeberg, "Recreational Camping for the Retarded," *Recreation in Treatment Centers*, Vol. V. (September, 1966), pp. 8-9.

11. Studies reviewed were:
Barbara Bateman, "A Pilot Study of Mentally Retarded Children Attending Summer Day Camps." Two research projects. (Unpublished, Washington, D.C.: The Joseph P. Kennedy, Jr. Foundation, 1965 and 1966.)
Frank J. Hayden. "Physical Fitness and Camp Shriver." Research project. (Unpublished, Washington, D.C.: The Joseph P. Kennedy, Jr. Foundation, 1967.)

12. William Freeberg, "Research-Recreational Camping for All Handicapped," in *Physical Education and Recreation: Proceedings of a Study Conference on Research and Demonstration Needs* (Washington, D.C.: American Association for Health, Physical Education, and Recreation, and NRPA in cooperation with the Bureau of Education for the Handicapped, United States Department of Health, Education, and Welfare, 1969), pp. 41-42.

13. Additional ideas such as the above and suggestions for recreation services and program models can be found in Avedon, *Recreation and Mental Retardation, op. cit., passim*, and in Elliott M. Avedon and Frances B. Arje, *Socio-Recreative Programming for the Retarded* (New York: Bureau of Publications, Teachers College, Columbia University, 1964), *passim.*

14. Anthony G. Linford and Claudine Y. Jeanrenaud, "A Systematic Language Structure for Teaching Recreative Skills to the Mentally Retarded," *Therapeutic Recreation Journal*, Vol. III, No. 1 (First Quarter, 1969), pp. 8-11. Publication of the National Therapeutic Recreation Society.

15. See Sidney H. Acuff, "Recreation Counseling as an Aspect of Programming for the Short Term Psychiatric Patient," *Recreation in Treatment Centers*, Vol. V, (September, 1966), pp. 5-7; Fred Humphrey, "Recreation Counseling for the Institutional Dischargee," in *Therapeutic Recreation Dialogues with Doctors*, Bulletin No. 41 (Raleigh, North Carolina: The North Carolina Recreation Commission, 1968), pp. 62-68, and Gerald S. O'Morrow, "Expanding Recreation Services—Recreation Counseling," *Recreation in Treatment Centers*, Vol. VI, (September, 1969), pp. 1-3.

16. In its April, 1968, revised draft (unpublished) of Standards and Evaluative Criteria, the National Recreation Accreditation Project recommends that general education requirements for all students in the recreation and parks curriculum include course work in the psychology of the learning process. Standards recommended for undergraduate students electing an emphasis in therapeutic recreation also specify a requirement for course work to include study of guidance and counseling. See Chapter 8 for further discussion of the National Recreation Accreditation Project.

l7. H. Douglass Sessoms, "The Impact of the RSA Recreation Trainee Program, 1963-1968," *Therapeutic Recreation Journal*, Vol. IV, No. 1 (First Quarter, 1970), p. 23.

18. Mrs. Page Lawson, "Play . . . A Way to Help Realize the Potential of Sightless Children," *Therapeutic Recreation Journal*, Vol. III, No. 2 (Second Quarter, 1969), p. 32.

19. "Focus on the Hard of Hearing Child," reprint from *Michigan's Health* (February, 1961), pp. 12b-13c.

20. Conference with Dr. Wilha Bladergroen and observations at experimental school directed by Bladergroen, Groningen, Netherlands, May 3, 1966.

21. Charles K. Brightbill, "Recreation for the Ill and Handicapped: A Recreator's Responsibility," *Recreation in Treatment Centers*, Vol. I (September, 1962), pp. 8-9.

22. Rudolph H. Shelton, "Recreation for the Handicapped and Aging: the Need in Westchester County, New York," *Therapeutic Recreation Journal*, Vol. II, No. 3 (Third Quarter, 1968), p. 11.

23. John Skinner, "Recreation Programming for Patients Possessing the Chronic Brain Syndromes Associated with Cerebral Arteriosclerosis," *Recreation in Treatment Centers*, Vol. V (September, 1966), p. 35.

6 | Opportunities for Self-Realization

THE ETHICAL THEORY on which much of American culture is based assigns high value to man as an individual being and to his right to realize or fulfill himself to the extent of his capabilities. In presenting this chapter, the authors assume that self-realization is indeed a splendid goal, and that persons who are ill or disabled have the same right to seek this goal as anyone else.

The recreator who works with the ill or disabled needs to have some understanding of the obstacles which illness and disability often put in the way of achieving self-realization. Further, the recreator should know how recreation may serve as an avenue toward self-realization.

Several concepts are involved in the idea of self-realization. These concepts are discussed below, particularly as they relate to therapeutic recreation.

Self-Awareness

Self-realization begins with the fact of "being"—with the recognition of oneself as an individual, an entity. Human characteristics are so complex that no two individuals are alike. Those qualities of behavior, emotional tendencies, habit patterns, character traits, attitudes, and so on which characterize an individual, considered collectively, make up his personality, and each individual has a distinct and different personality.

Awareness of one's own individuality normally begins early as the little child discovers his own body and its functions. The effect of body-image on one's self-concept continues to be important, as Menninger points out. "As the child grows older, his sense of personal worth and well-being is closely related to the skills and prowess of his own body in play with his contemporaries."[1] The child, and the adult as well, whose body or body function is other than normal because of disease, illness, birth defect, or injury, may develop a distorted self-concept, based disproportionately on body-image. He is painfully aware of his uniqueness because of the attention that has necessarily been focused on his body functions and disabilities. With a distorted self-image, the "self" of which he is so aware is scarcely one which he feels is capable of being developed in any positive way.

The disabled person's uncertainty about himself is often reinforced by the attitudes of those around him and by the norms of society. Thus his self-awareness may tend to be limited to his body and its dysfunction, with little recognition of the many other facets that make up his individual personality, his true self.

The loss of independence occasioned by illness, by disability, and especially by hospitalization too often carries with it a loss of identity as a person. And dependency is the antithesis of self-realization.

Another group of people with whom therapeutic recreation is concerned—the aging—may also fall victim to a sense of loss of identity. In many cases this is caused not by dependency or hospitalization but by the loss of family and family responsibilities which had previously given them assurance of who they were.

Faulty or inadequate self-concept is at the very core of some mental illness. The causes for serious distortion of the patient's self-image, as well as a distorted concept of his environment, may be many and varied. But whatever the cause, the process of regaining mental health involves achieving a realistic view of oneself, a self-awareness based on fact.

The inability or refusal to recognize one's true self is a characteristic not only of the hospitalized mentally ill, but of many people in the general population. Martin refers to this as "self-alienation" and indicates that in "everyday life . . . self-alienation is the most prevalent form of maladaptation. . . ."[2] About "self" and "self-alienation," Martin states:

> Regarding the concept of "self", I have in mind the following: the real, essential, natural "self", as distinct from some image of the "self": . . . This would be the "self" that is naturally evolving toward greater and greater awareness of wholeness and uniqueness; in other words, the "self" that Kierkegaard had in mind when he spoke of life helping us to "become what we really are."
> I think of self-alienation as an unconscious dissociative process involving denial of, escape from, or deadening of those inner conflicting feelings, wishes, and impulses which are expressions of the true self. . . .[3]

Martin cites a number of cultural patterns which he believes play a dynamic role in the etiology and perpetuation of self-alienation. One or two of these have particular significance for the therapeutic recreator in that the effects of these patterns may be heightened in the lives of disabled persons.

One cultural pattern Martin calls the *frictionless pattern*. Healthy, interpersonal friction in the forms of physical conflict, competitive games, and mind-contact interplay is "one principal means of differentiating the self from the not-self."[4] But the interference of misunderstanding parents and the taboo imposed by a work culture on all "horsing around" as a waste of time have created a *frictionless pattern*. Add to this the over-protection of the ill or disabled child —and adult too—based on the supposition that conflict or competition of any kind is unfair or may be harmful, and the disabled person is further handicapped by the denial of an essential means for gaining a sense of uniqueness and identity, for strengthening self-awareness.

Another pattern that has special significance here Martin calls the *compulsive pattern*. In the American way of life, the work culture has tended to create an outer compulsion to work. The person who is freed from this outer compulsion, that is, who has acquired leisure because of advanced technology, perhaps, is too often unable to be truly free. This compulsive pattern impels him to set up a subjectively imposed compulsion. Rather than recognizing the strength and authority of his own inner self, he depends on some outer authority, albeit perhaps a contrived one. The person whose leisure is forced upon him by illness or disability is even less likely to forego some outer authority and to recognize his own autonomy.

"Like any crutch or protection provided by nature, self-alienation *per se* retards growth but does not necessarily endanger it. The real danger arises from its unconscious perpetuation by the culture and by the individual himself."[5] Surely if the disabled person is to be assisted in seeking the goal of self-realization, such assistance should include efforts toward the avoidance of self-alienation and toward the recognition and awareness of the true, unique, and individual self and all its possibilities for fulfillment.

It would perhaps be shortsighted to suggest that leisure provides the only or best opportunity for self-awareness. Yet leisure is an essential condition in the process of self-awareness and self-development. The relaxed freedom of self-chosen activity in unobligated time provides a good frame of reference for seeing oneself as one truly is.

The recreator who understands the true nature of leisure and who is skilled in leisure activities is in an excellent position to assist the disabled person in removing obstacles which prevent a valid self-concept. For instance, a recreator working with physically disabled persons is able to analyze the movements required in various competitive sports, to adapt them to the abilities of the individual, to analyze the factors in the game which contribute to healthy competition, and under these conditions to provide disabled clients with the opportunity for the healthy, interpersonal friction mentioned above.

While the mentally retarded child has difficulty developing an acceptable self-concept in an atmosphere which stresses academic and mental development, in the leisure world of play he can be aided by the recreator in gaining awareness of himself through carefully selected recreation activities which he can successfully experience.

The impersonality of an institution such as a hospital, which tends to deprive the patient of his normal identity, can be counteracted by the recreator whose interest is in the patient as a person and a personality, and whose business is, in part at least, the preservation of the healthy personality. Restoration of the healthy personality is, of course, the aim of psychotherapy and the business of all therapists working with the mentally ill. But it is perhaps in the area of mental illness that leisure activity has been used most effectively in the treatment process. The non-compulsive, unhurried, and non-restrictive qualities of most leisure activity can create an atmosphere in which the patient dares look at his true self and eventually like what he sees.

Self-Expression

Another integral part of self-realization is self-expression. It is necessary for each individual not only to have self-awareness (to develop a genuine and real concept of himself) but also to be able in some way to show this self to others. It may be relatively easy to demonstrate one's identity based on the roles one plays—husband, teacher, musician, student, neighbor, etc.—but self-expression involving the complex components of one's personality is more difficult. Although one's true self includes how one feels, self-expression is more than just expression of a single emotion or isolated feeling. Laughter, tears, angry screams, table pounding are easily recognized expressions of feelings. Susanne Langer refers to these as symptomatic expressions of feeling which indicate that the individual "has an emotion, a pain, or other personal experience, perhaps also giving us a clue to the general kind of experience it is—pleasant or unpleasant, violent or mild—but not setting that piece of inward life objectively before us so we may understand its intricacy, its rhythms and shifts of total experience."[6]

Expression of the "inward life" Langer refers to is not always easy and is often made more difficult for handicapped persons because the vehicles for such self-expression are limited for the crippled child or the aged infirm. Work, or vocational accomplishment, as a means of expression is ruled out for many disabled persons. Expression by means of verbal communication can be frustrating for the mentally retarded, the deaf, and the mentally ill. For the emotionally disturbed child, self-expression may take forms that are unacceptable to those around him—in "acting out" behavior.

The therapeutic recreator should recognize that the best possibilities for self-expression for the disabled individual often lie in his leisure life. Two vehicles for self-expression that are particularly within the province of recreation are discussed here. One is art in all its forms, the fine arts as well as the performing arts. The other is sports.

The role of art as a non-verbal means of expression is well accepted. Participation in art activity gives the individual an opportunity to objectify his self-concept, his feelings, emotions, and attitudes; to fix them in form for others to recognize and perhaps feel too. The form may be that of color and line in painting, of shape, texture, and mass in sculpture, of rhythm, tone, harmony in music, and so on.

The recreator who is truly interested in assisting the disabled person's efforts toward self-expression will not stop with the mere provision of art materials. The paint brush in hand or the guitar on the lap does not necessarily elicit self-expression. This is merely the first of several stages leading up to the possibility of self-expression, according to a theory described by Jeanrenaud.[7] Fixed patterns of behavior have been observed in children's free play when they are presented with novel objects or new situations, and can readily be seen in the individual's approach to art activity. The first stage is that of wonder, Jeanrenaud states, and is resolved either by acceptance or rejection of the object or situation. If it is accepted, stage two involves exploration. The individual becomes acquainted with the properties and possibilities of the new object or situation and masters the techniques of its use. Play follows in the third stage. The pleasurable properties of the object or situation serve as a stimulus to the individual for repetitive activity. When the stimulating properties have been exhausted, the individual in stage four can distort the physical reality through fantasy and creativity. Not until this stage is reached is the person really able to express himself as an individual.

In considering art activity, then, as a vehicle for self-expression, the recreator may need to lend assistance to the disabled person in mastering the techniques of the chosen medium and providing possibilities for exhaustive "play," so that he may reach the expressive stage. The kind of special assistance needed will, of course, depend on the characteristics of the person's disability. It may range from the slow step-by-step teaching of colors and shapes to the retarded child, to the adjustment of the mechanism of a potter's wheel so that it can be operated by a paraplegic. Each person is to be considered individually. Self-expression is seldom a group function.

The kinship between art and sport as vehicles for self-expression may be a bit obscure at first glance. However, the performer's body itself, as in drama and particularly in dance, provides an acceptable bridge. Expression by means of body movement finds its highest form in artistic dance, no doubt. But since artistic dance is not within everyone's capabilities, other forms of body movement found in a variety of sports—diving, swimming, skating, running, tennis, archery, fencing, and so on—can be effective means of expression. Ernst Jokl comments on this in referring to the progression of a trend toward restriction of freedom of self-projection. "Outside of sport," he says, "the range within which workers can move about without restraint and project their personality has become steadily decreasing. . . . Sport offers possibility for display of the self which life otherwise does not render feasible."[8]

As some individuals may find self-expression in the objectification of feeling in art activity, so others may find self-expression in the exteriorization of feeling in sports activity. Similarly, the stage at which sport may be expressive comes after some acquisition of skill. The recreator's responsibility to the disabled person lies in following the principles of adaptation that apply to other areas of functioning. Fortunately, considerable work has been done in devising the most effective techniques for helping persons with physical disabilities to acquire sports skills. In some cases this involves compensatory use of unaffected parts of the body, as in swimming for persons with paralyzed lower limbs. In other cases, the motions involved in the sport are modified, as in wheelchair fencing. Or the adaptation may involve an appropriate system of non-auditory signals, as in competition sports for the deaf. Effective methods for teaching sport skills to the mentally retarded are described in a number of publications and films prepared by agencies specifically concerned with mental retardation.

One of the tasks of the therapeutic recreator may well be to help the disabled or ill person to find the means for self-expression which will most appropriately fit his abilities and personality. Recognizing that individualization is the very essence of self-expression, he will avoid making assumptions such as that all blind persons find self-expression in music, or that the mentally retarded are capable only of pattern work in art. There may be several avenues open for each disabled person and the recreator should use his knowledge and skills in exploring these avenues with the person.

Self-Respect

A characteristic of the healthy personality is the need to feel that, as an individual, one has a place in the universe. This involves a sense of independence, and an opportunity to manifest the positive, rather than the negative, aspects of one's personality. It involves the need to feel that one has value and can make a contribution to society, and to feel that this contribution is recognized. Meeting these needs leads to self-respect, an important component of self-realization.

In the lives of the ill and disabled, there seem to be many things which can potentially contribute to loss of self-esteem, self-confidence, and individual dignity. One is the necessary dependence on others that disabled persons usually have for various aspects of daily functioning. Dependency, allowed to become exaggerated, erodes self-confidence and dignity. The restrictions on the freedom to choose where to go, what to do, and so on, particularly in institutional living as discussed in Chapter 3, are not conducive to a feeling of much self-respect. Acute awareness of his physical or mental "differentness" caused by his illness or disability tends to contribute to a loss of self-confidence, particularly social confidence.

It has been stated by many observers of life in a technological society that a sense of personal value cannot always be gained through the work one does. If this is true for the healthy able-bodied individual, how much more so for the disabled person. Gainful employment of any kind may be out of the question. Or one's disability may restrict him to kinds of work which are anything but self-fulfilling. Or through prejudice and misunderstanding on the part of employers, he may be prohibited from performing those work tasks which might bring satisfaction and self-esteem.

For the disabled person, as well as his able-bodied counterpart, who finds difficulty in gaining a sense of personal value in the work-a-day world, the world of leisure assumes considerable importance in providing opportunities for gaining such a sense of value. He may, for instance, find himself a contributor in any of a number of voluntary efforts. A fine example of this is found in Delta Sigma Omicron, which is a fraternal organization composed of physically disabled persons. The functions of DSO are manifold, including social and recreational aims, sponsorship of an excellent athletic program, and, of particular importance here, service to others. The substantial contributions in funds to charitable organizations that DSO has made from proceeds from their wheelchair athletic events, exhibitions and demonstrations, etc., gives a boost to all members' personal sense of value.

Another example is found in the Foster Grandparent program in operation in certain schools for mentally retarded children. Older people past their prime as economically productive persons are enlisted to assist with the care and training of mentally retarded children. Their ability to give love, attention, and the benefits of a lifetime's good experiences to these little children whose needs are great is a satisfying source of service, the recognition of which contributes to their sense of dignity and value. This kind of service in reverse is illustrated by a special project undertaken by a group of Campfire Girls in a day school for mentally retarded children. The Campfire Girls, all trainable mentally retarded, regularly visit the elderly residents of a local nursing home, giving what they have to offer—attention, affection, youth, and a blissful unawareness of the old folks' incapacities.

A Red Cross recreation worker describes another way in which recreation activity helps to shore up the faltering self-confidence and self-respect of traumatically injured patients in a military hospital:

> We first started involving community groups and organizations in our recreation planning 2 years ago, when there was an influx of burn patients as a result of the Vietnam conflict. The patients were, for the most part, young men in their late teens and early twenties. When a choral group from a local college requested to entertain on the wards, we had a conference with the charge nurse and received approval to bring the girls to the ward. The patients were so appreciative that the recreator decided to plan for participation by more community groups and received approval and support from the medical staff to develop this program. When volunteers came to the ward, the recreator interpreted the ward situation and encouraged them to be themselves around the men. The patients responded so well that it was apparent that contact with these individuals in a social situation was playing a vital role in helping the patients acquire social confidence. . . . It is our conclusion that the recreation program is an important factor in the gaining of social confidence by these severely limited patients, especially when cosmetic disfigurement is involved. The study was made during a typical three-week period in which the patients were brought into regular contact with individuals from community groups and organizations and encouraged to participate in diversional activities.[9]

Other avenues that recreation and leisure offer for achieving self-respect and eventual self-realization are discussed more fully in the next two sections.

Mastery and Achievement

Recognition of one's individuality, of one's right to be and to express oneself is essential, of course, but eventually it is what is done by the individual that brings self-realization. Writing about all men, not just the ill and disabled, Brightbill says: "So much can be done *with* us and *for* us, but in the end it is that which is done *by* us that helps us realize our deepest satisfaction. . . . It is the joy of mastery that we love. It is the feeling of accomplishment, of having conquered the obstacles and come through to victory, that we need so desperately. . . ."[10]

A sense of mastery, a feeling of accomplishment, visible achievement, successful experience, all are human needs and are needs of the disabled as well as the able-bodied. Brightbill further points out that these needs are not always met—even for the able-bodied—in school or on the job. "If the opportunity for achievement and mastery is to be preserved, for many people, it will have to be not during their *work* time but during their *free* time."[11] How much more true this often is for those who are ill or disabled. Many disabled people have free time in abundance. As has been pointed out previously, jobs open to disabled persons are often singularly lacking in features which might provide a satisfying sense of achievement. Normal school requirements may be such that just keeping up with his contemporaries is viewed as an achievement on the part of the disabled child. But the disabled person needs to feel that he is capable of some achievement unrelated to his disability, if he is to reach true self-realization. For these reasons the world of leisure, of recreation, provides a fertile field for exploring the possibilities of mastery and achievement.

Berton Kaplan suggests, in fact, that certain recreation experiences might be classified as mastery type:

> It would seem possible that certain recreation opportunities could provide a patient with some experiences which contribute to the development of an inner sense of personal mastery. For example, the learning of a new game could help a person with a mastering type corrective experience. In this regard, a patient may learn to paint and consequently learn to begin to master alien feelings. To perform well in a new recreational role, and to be rewarded accordingly, could contribute to feelings of self confidence, along with other aspects of the therapeutic regime. Surely, in children's games we see the learning of recreation roles performed in part with the intent of developing certain mastery type skills, whether over body coordination, ability at team play, role performance, etc.[12]

Perhaps one of the best types of recreation experience to provide opportunities for mastery, particularly mastery of the environment, is camping. Nowadays opportunities are available for camping experiences at almost any degree of ruggedness. These range from day camp in a city park to primitive camping in the deep forest. Thus the ill or disabled, whatever their limits of strength or type of disability, should be able to participate in a camping experience which will permit them to gain mastery over the environment to the extent of their ability. To catch a fish, to build a fire, to dig a trench around one's tent, to learn to swim, to follow a trail, to sleep in the open, all may be masterful accomplishments. The therapeutic recreator's responsibility is to see that these experiences are made possible—that barriers to such experiences for the disabled are eliminated.

Another kind of mastery experience is found in art activity, mentioned previously. In one respect this might be thought of as mastery over materials, in another as symbolic mastery of reality. Shaping a piece of clay to one's will, controlling the vibrations of a violin string to produce a desired musical tone, combining colors of paint into meaningful symbolic forms on canvas all represent a satisfying kind of mastery and achievement.

Gaining mastery over one's handicaps, particularly physical handicaps, commands a large share of the disabled person's attention and time. In no way is this confined to leisure time; in fact this may constitute his chief work. Yet recreation activity may provide the incentive, the immediate purpose for this difficult work. For instance, the game that he wants to play right now rather than the job he may get in the future will provide the stronger motivation to the young boy for gaining mastery over his body coordination. The recreator keeps such incentives continuously on tap and further, through play, provides a means for the patient to practice and reinforce the gains he has made toward mastery of his handicaps.

Haun has attested to the importance of recreation in the lives of those for whom the degree of handicap is such that economic self-sufficiency is, from all practical standpoints, impossible:

> To the individual who cannot work, rhythmic alternation with play is possible. He must somehow get from avocational pursuits both sets of values that other men find in their serious work and in their elective recreational activities—self-respect as well as fun; a sense of meaningful accomplishment as well as the pleasure of following one's own preferences; the sober respect of one's fellows as well as their friendly companionship in a transitory interest.[13]

For those whose illness or disability is temporary, the enforced leisure of such a period of illness or convalescence provides opportunity to explore areas of interest and to develop skills and abilities in those areas—opportunities that perhaps would not be available without an enforced "time out." One of the authors recalls, for instance, the interest in journalism and the writing talent that was developed by a patient during her long months of recovery from tuberculosis, when she took on the job of editing the hospital newspaper—a function of the hospital's recreation department.

The wide variety of activity and the unrestrained enthusiasms that make up recreation offer opportunities for successful achievement on many levels of ability. Successful accomplishment in leisure activity need not be related to economic success. The nature, then, of recreation activity is such that one is allowed to try one's hand at whatever seems intriguing—to fail, perhaps, but without disastrous results—and to go on to something else. Failure in recreation is not ruinous, but success is particularly satisfying because it stems from genuine interest and enthusiasm rather than from economic pressure.

The will to succeed can circumvent disability, as is dramatically illustrated in the achievements described by Jokl:

> Harold Connolly, who had suffered a birth injury which caused his left arm to remain withered, broke the world record in the hammer throw. The Hungarian crack pistol shot, Karoly Takasc, lost his dominant right lower arm in an accident, but won gold medals at the 1948 and 1952 Olympic Games holding the weapon in his left hand. The Danish equestrienne Lis Hartel, whose muscular power remained critically reduced after an attack of poliomyelitis, proved herself the best woman rider in the Olympic dressage contests in Finland in 1952, and in Sweden in 1956.
>
> The human brain can use any part of the motor system to convert abstractions into concrete movements. This fact was alluded to by the 18th-century German poet Gotthold Ephraim Lessing, who wrote in his drama *Emilia Galotti* that "Raphael would have become an immortal painter even if he had been born without arms."[14]

Creative Expression

"The opportunity for releasing our physical and emotional energies in creative, expressive ways must be preserved," says Brightbill. "Through such experiences we develop an immensely satisfying sense of power, sense of mastery, and sense of achievement."[15] If, as the psychologists say, creativity provides one basic yardstick of the measure of man, it is indeed an important component of self-realization.

The therapeutic recreator's interest in establishing a milieu for creativity for those he serves is reinforced by the findings of psychiatry which indicate that among the characteristics of neurotic illness are the disturbance of recreative functions and the serious disturbance of creative activity.

Martin has discussed at some length what he considers to be the creative process:

> ... the whole creative process ... follows a rhythmic pattern. (1) There is a phase of conscious struggle and effort; this is followed by (2) a recreative or leisure phase, relaxation of conscious efforts, abandonment of logical work and reason, a period of "leaving it alone." At some time during this phase, the "peak experience" (creative insight) occurs (3) and this, in turn, is followed by (4) a period of conscious effort to improve and refine what emerged during the creative flash.[16]

Martin emphasizes the importance of the leisure phase of this process, and speaks of a "psychological and cultural resistance to the whole subject of leisure, relaxation, and recreation ... it is in overlooking and denying the function of true leisure at all phases and levels of intellectual life that our creativity is being impaired and nullified. It is by the compulsive glorification of work, to the exclusion of all leisure, that we create so much sterility, whether that work be artistic, intellectual, scientific, or physical."[17]

Creative activity may occur in various realms as indicated above. But creative expression that takes form in beauty or results in esthetic experience is indeed an achievement which may contribute immeasurably to self-realization. To quote Brightbill once more: "To create beauty is a joyous and satisfying experience. But to create beauty and share it, too, is the zenith of personal accomplishment...."[18]

One is inclined to think of the artist only as the creator of beauty and of the art object—the picture, the song, the poem—as the result of creative activity. Yet the re-creation of artistic work by means of esthetic perception, appreciation, and performance is, in itself, creative activity. In fact it is often true that the act of creation is not complete until it is re-created. For example, the symphony, originated in the composer's mind and recorded on paper by means of musical symbols, requires the performing orchestra to bring it to life.

Re-creation as well as creation of beauty are found in the esthetic experience. And on examination one finds that what the estheticians describe as the esthetic experience and what the philosophers of recreation describe as the recreative experience bear striking resemblance. In many definitions of recreation, the idea is present that the experience has no end beyond itself, that its value is contained within itself. This is perhaps what Arnstine refers to as "terminal" in his first condition for the esthetic experience. He says that the experience is taken to be valuable on its own account, that it is intrinsically valuable. His second condition for the esthetic experience, however, narrows the experience in that it requires the "appearance of affect cued by perception of a formal pattern within the occasion for the experience."[19] One would hesitate to say that this is always true or necessary in the recreative experience. Affects or emotions are without doubt present in the recreative experience—in fact, Romney says that recreation is a matter of emotions rather than motions[20]—but they may not be aroused by the perception of formal elements. But perhaps sometimes they are. Perhaps it is the perception of the integrated elements of a competitive game, the form of movement in athletic endeavors, as well as the more obvious perception of form in the arts, that arouse pleasurable emotions in a recreative experience. Jokl observes that, "The esthetic implications of the acts that engender beauty in sport are fundamentally the same as the acts that engender beauty in music and on the stage."[21]

The art activity of patients, particularly psychiatric patients, has been pressed into service as a diagnostic tool for the psychiatrist and as a therapeutic agent for the patient. This is possible because of the great potential that creative expression has for specific achievement, for reaching certain goals, and for revealing the true self. It is therapeutic use of a process engaged in by everyday people in their efforts toward self-realization, but a process which is intensified and more carefully scrutinized.

Maximum Development

The human characteristic with which this chapter is concerned is the continual striving to develop one's inherent potentials, to maximize one's value. Raymond McCall refers to this as "invested self-expression" and discusses it as a principle of human motivation:

Behind and sustaining all or virtually all particular human motives there is an élan to maximize; not merely to maintain life—though that of course is basic to the enterprise of maximization—but to live it as fully as possible, to develop one's capacities, extend and deepen experience, exercise one's powers in the highest; in a word to achieve for one's self the greatest possible self-enrichment, psychologically speaking.

. . . .

Man looks for the maximum of self-realization . . . and in virtue of his ability to transcend the present, he looks for the perdurance of the good possessed as well as for its increase.[22]

The "best possible" is not the same for everyone, nor are the avenues for attainment open equally for everyone. Haun speaks of the "tillable acreage" that each individual has, and of the scanty holding that may be the lot of the ill and disabled. But no one should stifle the disabled person in his striving to develop his full potential, whatever it may be, by whatever avenues are open to him.

Because the world of leisure and recreation can provide a "permanently fertile ground for self-realization"[23] in everyone's life, and especially in the lives of the disabled, the therapeutic recreator has a responsibility to help his disabled clients take maximum advantage of that world. This responsibility may include also helping the disabled person to establish for himself a practical and achievable set of goals. In McCall's discussion, he further states that "the ultimate goal of the maximum possible is the same for all, or at least for most, but the penultimate goals are amazingly diverse."[24] The recreator may help the disabled person to survey his own "tillable acreage" by means of the testing of reality that is possible in play and recreation. Putting aside from consideration those areas in which there is no prospect of being productive, they may then build on the known strengths of the disabled one, and happily exploit to the fullest what *is* there.

The recreator must be very careful not to short-change those whose only avenue for self-realization is in leisure activity or recreation. The limited physical strength, or motor ability, or intellectual functioning, or mental lucidity which they have for discretionary use should not be dissipated in meaningless activity. Rather, each individual should be provided with every opportunity to invest his efforts in activities which can make some contribution to maximizing his value, to fulfilling his potential. Self-realization is, of course, a "self" function, but the ill or disabled person who is likely to find many obstacles in the process can use some help along the way.

Notes, Chapter 6

1. Karl A. Menninger, "Psychiatric Aspects of Physical Disability" (Vocational Rehabilitation Administration, Psychological Aspects of Physical Disability, Washington, D.C., Vocational Rehabilitation Administration, 1953), p. 11.

2. Alexander Reid Martin, "Self Alienation and the Loss of Leisure," *American Journal of Psychoanalysis*, Vol. XXI, No. 2 (1961), p. 156. This and the following three quotations from Dr. Martin's article are reprinted with permission of *The American Journal of Psychoanalysis*.

3. *Ibid.*, p. 157.

4. *Ibid.*, p. 158.

5. *Ibid.*, p. 156.

6. Susanne K. Langer, "Expressiveness and Symbolism," Melvin Rader, Ed., *A Modern Book of Esthetics*, 3rd Edition, New York: Holt, Rinehart and Winston, 1962, p. 254.

7. Claudine Jeanrenaud, "The Application of a Play Orienting Theory to Aesthetic Therapy in a Hospital Setting" (unpublished paper, 1969).

8. Ernst Jokl, *Medical Sociology and Cultural Anthropology of Sport and Physical Education* (Springfield, Ill.: Charles C. Thomas, Pub., 1964), p. 16.

9. Jane Curtis Oswalt, "Recreation Program Studies," *Intercom*, Vol. XXIV, No. 1 (July-September, 1970), pp. 5, 7. Published by the American National Red Cross.

10. Charles K. Brightbill, *Man and Leisure* (Englewood Cliffs, N. J.: Prentice-Hall, Inc., 1961) p. 168.

11. *Ibid.*, p. 169.

12. Berton H. Kaplan, "Critique" *Recreation's Contribution to the Patient* (Raleigh, N.C.: The North Carolina Recreation Commission, 1963), p. 24.

13. Paul Haun, *Recreation: A Medical Viewpoint* (New York: Teachers College Press, 1965), p. 76.

14. Jokl, *op. cit.*, p. 32.

15. Brightbill, *op. cit.*, p. 169.

16. Alexander Reid Martin, "Leisure and the Creative Process," *The Hanover Forum*, Vol. VI, No. 1, p. 13. Talk given at Hanover College (Indiana) Convocation, April 9, 1959.

17. *Ibid.*, p. 16.

18. Brightbill, *op. cit.*, p. 131.

19. Donald Arnstine, "Shaping the Emotions," *Journal of Aesthetic Education*, Inaugural Issue (Spring, 1966), p. 50.

20. G. Ott Romney, *Off the Job Living* (New York: A. S. Barnes & Co., 1945), p. 14.

21. Jokl, *op. cit.*, p. 17.

22. Raymond J. McCall, "Invested Self Expression: A Principle of Human Motivation," *Psychological Review*, Vol. 70, No. 4 (July, 1963), p. 302.

23. Brightbill, *op. cit.*, p. 171.

24. McCall, *op. cit.*, p. 131

7 | Integrative Possibilities

TO CONSIDER THE integrative possibilities of recreation requires an understanding of one of the most fundamental aspects of the nature of recreative experience. For recreation is an indivisible, whole phenomenon of human experience. The wholeness of recreation is at once its constant attribute and a dynamic element in life's integrative processes and patterns. Recreation is something that is not only experienced by the whole person—the total physical, emotional self—but recreative experiences are, themselves, pathways to integration of the individual as a total being in a time-space continuum and as an entity in a larger social order. Paradoxically, although this unity or wholeness may have offered the greatest resistance to analyzing and applying recreation as a therapeutic agent, yet it may be seen that it is precisely in this aspect of the recreative experience that there resides the greatest therapeutic potential on both the individual and societal levels.

Self-Integrative Potential

As recreation is an individual experience, so its integrative potential is basically and primarily related to the self. Self-integrative implications of recreative experience are a continuing thread interwoven through the discussions of preceding chapters. Indeed, concepts of self-realization, as presented in Chapter 6, and of self-integration are inseparably linked. Thus it is necessary only to refer to and emphasize further what has been previously said or implied concerning self-integrative aspects of recreation.

More than thirty years ago, James Plant, who was Director of the Essex County, New Jersey, Juvenile Clinic, saw recreation as an integrating experience ". . . because it follows the rhythm of the individual." In contrast to a machine that imposes its own rhythm on the person, recreation like "a tool in one's hand—a chisel, a plane, or whatever else—is an extension of the individual."[1]

Haun sees the integrative nature of recreation as the prime requisite of its identity and basic explanation of its outcome as a satisfying, enjoyable experience. "It is," he says, ". . . the exact synchronization of instinctual drive, motivation, feeling tone, idealized goal, performance capacity, and social acceptance into a unified, intrinsically coherent product that marks the genuinely satisfactory human act. . . ." And speaking more specifically of play, Haun continues:

> . . . we inevitably find that play is characterized by that kind of smooth and coherent synchronization we have called facility. Skipping rope seems entirely effortless, hide-and-seek has the balance and rhythm of classical ballet, a good-natured wrestling match the ordered spontaneity of a sculptured frieze. Nor are efficiency, automation, rhythmicity, alternation, and apparent lack of effort present only in their objective, perceptually evident forms. There is at the same time complete instinctual, emotional, intellectual, and social coherence. We see an integrated, total interaction of the living organism with all relevant aspects of its environment. We see an authentic miracle of life in complete accord with matter.

The hallmark of this phenomenon is enjoyment. In a beautifully stated summary of this thesis, Haun defines re-creative play as:

> . . . man's sovereign opportunity to tap life's deepest currents; to have again and again the vital experience of integration in which all his levers and gears and shafts and wheels mesh in perfect synchronization with the world of people and of matter; to feel again and again the happy power of facility where impulse, performance, and result blend uninterruptedly into a unified whole.[2]

Another aspect of the self-integrative value of recreation is deserving of emphasis here also because of its impact in the lives of those who are ill or disabled. Certainly among the cluster of experiences that attend being or becoming ill or disabled, recreation occupies a unique place. Where illness disrupts and shatters lives, recreation puts them together; where pain or handicap tends to narrow or pinpoint attention, recreation broadens perspective; and in the treatment process, recreation services are addressed to the individual as a total being in contrast to the specificity of most forms of treatment.

Leisure—Life-Integrated Continuum

Not only are play and recreation an integral part of the individual's total life span; how one uses his leisure is integrated with his total life practices. The unity of life's experiences is emphasized by health educator, Hoyman. Addressing a conference on recreation for the chronically ill in the community setting, Hoyman presented "An Ecologic Model of Health, Disease, Longevity." He expressed conviction that recreation has much to contribute in the ecologic, interdisciplinary approach to the goal of public health in prolonging ". . . the health span and useful life of humans, not to turn people into 'human vegetables' or to put them in the deep freeze." Implications for leisure life practices can be readily associated with Hoyman's description of an evolving model of health which he says:

> . . . is being decisively shaped by the current movements in human ecology and epidemiology. Human ecology utilizes holistic models based on a unitive view of man as an open-system engaged in reciprocal dynamic transactions with his total environment. Man is viewed as a self-regulating, self-renewing, self-actualizing organism, capable of inhibiting his impulses in satisfying his needs as related to his ideals, values and goals.[3]

Recreative expression as a way of life, a pattern of leisure living, develops in a reciprocal, symbiotic relationship with all of the forces that shape and develop attitudes, values, habits, including those conditioning, shaping effects caused by the presence or the lack of certain resources and opportunities. Recreation, in varying forms, amounts, and quality, is a life-continuous form of experience and expression. It is integrally related to all other facets of life's circumstances and experiences, either as the receptor and reflector of such influences or as their shaper and molder. Thus recreation may be seen both as being integrated with total life patterns and as being in itself one of life's integrating forces. This basic connection between the way the individual handles his leisure and the way he copes with his life was recognized by the American Psychiatric Association when it organized a permanent committee to work directly with leisure agencies throughout the country. As Martin puts it:

> . . . we have found that the way you spend leisure hours—what you do and how you feel about them—has a close connection with what you do with your life as a whole: how you function as a person and a parent, what kind of employer or employee you are, what kind of wife or husband, friend or neighbor.[4]

Integration of Therapeutic Recreation Services

Recreation entered the treatment center when it was recognized as an indispensable element of life, needed by people during periods of enforced, as well as true leisure. The problem of how recreation relates to, or can be integrated with, medical treatment has received much attention. As indicated in Chapter 2, concepts have ranged from very general to more or less specific patterns of recreation-treatment (or therapy) relationships. Whether recreation services were developed in the general context of medical approval or on the basis of more specifically prescribed guidelines, therapeutic recreation took its place along with other services in those special communities—hospitals, institutions, treatment centers—which are, by the very nature of their mission, more highly integrated than is the general community.

On another level of relationships, the integration of recreation with other adjunctive or ancillary services is of key importance in the medical setting. Although this is not unlike the need for community recreation to form viable working relationships with other human services including education, urban planning, and the like, the treatment situation necessarily brings therapeutic recreation into close daily contact with occupational therapy, physical therapy, and social services. Needs for effectively relating such services in the total treatment pattern for the patient have been apparent for some time. The establishment of such "umbrella" departments as activity therapy services may be seen as attempts to bring together various ancillary programs into administrative relationship. The unit system, in its various interpretations and applications, as a form of treatment substructure within a larger institutional complex, has as a major purpose enhancing the possibilities for effectively integrated interdisciplinary programs.[5] Coordination and integration are involved in the comprehensive concept of milieu therapy.

Various proposals and methods have been advanced for integrating recreation with other services, both in general and specific terms. An example in the latter category can be found in the plan for an integrated recreation-physical therapy service at Montefiore Hospital in Pittsburgh. In the organizational scheme as charted in this plan, the recreation department would occupy a central role in its responsibility for translating the remedial exercises and rehabilitative activities prescribed through the occupational and physical therapy departments into opportunities in which patients would be motivated to participate for recreative purposes. As envisioned by Lipkind:

> The services of these three professions will be integrated, not on the basis of a "craft union," but on the principle of how best they can be coordinated for the benefit of the patient. The training and experience of occupational and physical therapists can be used in the development of self-aide devices and in the adaptation of game equipment. Together these specialists can function practically with the recreation therapist who is trained to conduct recreational programs and to evaluate the patient's emotional needs and his response to a selected activity.[6]

Realization of the integrative possibilities recreation offers in the clinical setting requires that the therapeutic recreator have a basic and sound philosophical orientation and understanding of his professional identity and responsibilities. Such understanding is essential to the effective development of logical relationships and integrated services. Furthermore, "The role of the various disciplines must be defined on the basis of their specific objectives and methods rather than the media used."[7] Demarcation of the boundaries between occupational therapy and therapeutic recreation as arts and crafts on the one hand and active games and sports on the other is as specious as the implication that in community leisure programs cultural activities and recreation are separate entities.

Increasing concern for relating recreation services in the treatment center to those in the larger community and for developing community-based leisure opportunities for ill or handicapped residents may seem to be only a continuation of former tendencies of therapeutic recreators to follow along in the wake of the medical profession's leadership. And in part this may be true. The growing medical emphasis in recent years, particularly in the field of mental health, on community-related or -based treatment is well known. However, among recreators, whether employed in hospitals, institutions, or community agencies, the fundamental rationale both for strengthening links between treatment-centered and community leisure services and for developing community-based recreation services for ill or disabled people stems from the concept of recreation as a life-continuous force. Increasingly recreators are recognizing that there is more implied than even the relatively long accepted concept that recreation is needed and experienced by all people regardless of their condition or station in life. Understanding of leisure experiences and recreative expression as continuing life patterns underscores comprehensions of the unifying, integrating nature and potential of recreation and underlines the rationale for offering leisure services in related, continuing patterns designed to add to the unity and wholeness of the ill or disabled person as an individually and socially integrated being.

An example of an institutional program that stresses integration of services and treatment patterns can be found in The Children's Village at Dobbs Ferry, New York, an educational, research, experimental residential center offering comprehensive treatment for emotionally disturbed, culturally deprived, character-disordered boys. Emphasis placed on integrative concepts and approaches is expressed in a statement of the philosophy of the department and in descriptions of its staffing and program policies. Illustrative of this focus are the following excerpts from the statement on "Philosophy," "Staff," and "Integration with other Departments":

> Traditionally, institutions have conducted recreation and leisure time programs as part of the cottage or school functions. Since children in institutions generally return to a community living experience, it is becoming increasingly important for institutions to prepare them for leisure time experiences in community centers, Y.M.C.A.'s, Y.M.H.A.'s, Boys' Clubs, and other community agencies providing recreation programs. The Children's Village is pioneering in this endeavor throug⸱ the establishment of a department devoted to the organized recreation and leisure time needs of emotionally disturbed boys. This department is called the Recreational Services Department.

. . . .

> Various types of staff personalities are needed to meet the needs of different types

of emotionally disturbed boys. No single professional discipline has all the answers to recreation and leisure time problems of our boys, so it is necessary to integrate the efforts of several disciplines within the department to provide the staff services necessary to carry out departmental goals and objectives.

. . . .

. . . at the Children's Village . . . effort [is made] to unify and integrate all disciplines engaged in the residential treatment of emotionally disturbed boys so that they work as cooperative and productive members of the residential treatment team. Such an interdisciplinary approach requires communication, coordination, interpretation and proper assessment of dynamic needs of children under care at all times. It further encompasses services to each individual boy and his family on a continuing basis through the three major stages of treatment, i.e., pre-care, in-care and continued-care. Implicit in such a program is the recognition of a clear definition of each member's role on the team, clarity of department function and responsibility, and the willingness of all participating persons to adapt themselves to such a team approach. The Recreational Services Department takes its place along with other departments of the Children's Village as a member of the residential treatment team. Integration with other departments takes place on the administrative, supervisory and practitioner levels on both a formal and informal basis.[8]

Four challenges were articulated by William Hollister to a group of therapeutic recreators at a workshop on community recreation services for the ill or disabled. The charges, listed below, succinctly summarize some of the issues critical to the provision of comprehensive, integrated, continuing therapeutic recreation services. The recreators were asked to examine:

How well are we preparing patients for using Recreation as an intricate [sic] part of their post-hospital living?

How well are we getting our ideas about Recreation, as being beneficial and therapeutic, built into discharge planning?

How about our professional responsibility outside the hospital—how well are we developing recreational resources for the after-care of our patients?

Are we truly going to follow the pattern of developing systems of care or are we going to keep our past images of pigeon holes of care?[9]

The "systems of care" concept suggests leisure counseling as a type of service through which integrative potentials of recreation may be enhanced. With the development of this area of recreation services and with a broadening of rehabilitation concepts beyond the traditional focus only on vocational aspects, leisure rehabilitation—or habilitation—is taking its place as an essential component of the rehabilitative process in serving total, integrated life needs of the patient or client.

One of the movements away from institutional treatment is represented in the establishment of community mental health centers. In these settings, according to E. Mansell Pattison, clinical evidence shows the inappropriateness of "typical middle class psychotherapeutic methods." The need is for activities to "be structured and conducted according to the cultural mores of the population to be served." Recreation offers a natural channel for effecting such relationships on an expressive level. Pattison sees important implications and roles for the adjunctive therapies, including therapeutic recreation, in the community mental health center:

> ... the community mental health model of a social system offers a very viable model for the adjunctive therapies. I see the adjunctive therapists as being in a strategic position to develop theories and techniques for a continuum of human interactional experiences in the therapeutic setting that replicate natural social experiences.[10]

In bringing therapeutic recreation services into general community programs, consideration must still be given to questions concerning the extent of need for specialized or separate programs for the ill or disabled and the degree to which they can be drawn into general community recreation patterns. Again, a continuum (not necessarily a straight line) rather than a dichotomy is the appropriate concept. Many ill or disabled people will progress—and it is the duty of the recreator to aid and encourage them to do so—from needs for specialized leisure provisions to totally undifferentiated recreation pursuits. Supportive programs are frequently needed, for instance, to help people recently discharged from psychiatric institutions through the early stages of their postdischarge reorientation to community living. Some disabled people may be expected always to require special consideration for some aspect of their leisure living, such as constant alertness to the elimination of physical facility barriers for those who are confined to wheelchairs. In a few instances, special provisions may be necessary for ill or disabled persons to have any opportunity at all for recreative experiences. Such an individual might be one who is homebound and immobile. In such a situation the recreator should seek every means of helping to minimize the separation and isolation of the individual through such efforts as maximizing opportunities for secondary associations in the sharing of recreative experiences when primary, face-to-face associations may be limited or difficult to arrange. Findings of a national study reported in 1970 on "Availability and Utilization of Recreation Resources for Chronically Ill and Disabled Children and Youth in the United States" led to recommendations for continuing and increasing attention to several issues pertinent to the foregoing discussion, including " . . . architectural barriers and methods of removing or minimizing them; . . . criteria for development of segregated and integrated recreation services for disabled children and youth; . . . and development of methods of programming for children and youth with visual and auditory disabilities in relation to both segregated and integrated services."[11]

Examples of Integrative Potentials of Recreation in Relation to Various Specific Conditions

It is patently impossible, as the authors pointed out in the introduction to Part II, either to consider social, physiological, or psychological aspects of life as discrete entities, or to compartmentalize recreative experience according to any one of its many possible accompanying effects. In harmony with these views and with the concepts of the integrative nature and potential of recreation, the subject of this chapter logically follows discussions in the preceding chapters of various types of benefits possible through recreation. For to focus on the integrating nature of recreation brings us full circle once again to the whole human being and the experience we call recreation in which such possible concomitant benefits as those previously identified—social, physical, educational, self-realization—blend in a unified whole.

Integrative potentials of recreation are thus apparent in much of what has already been said about the effects of various illnesses and disabling conditions upon the individual's needs and capacities for realizing benefits of recreative experience. This in no way denies the importance of considering variations that may be achieved in the mix of social, physical, educational, or other effects through the types of activities participated in or the way participation may be structured. We can agree without elaboration that some pursuits are solitary, others social in nature; that either competition or cooperation may be emphasized by the type of activity as well as by leadership goals and methods; or that skilled application of specific techniques by knowledgeable leaders may enhance the learning opportunities of recreation for the participant. Our aim in the following paragraphs is to cite some additional examples which emphasize consideration of various dimensions and potentials of leisure and recreation as integrating forces in relation to specific conditions. Even here it must be noted, however, that in most instances the ideas and suggestions could be applied or adapted with some modification to needs and capacities of people affected by other conditions or illnesses as well as those indicated below and should be considered as only indicative of some of the needed awarenesses and possible approaches for realizing health-enhancing integrative potentials of recreation.

Mental Health and Mental Illness

The primary concern in all health areas, including mental health, is for the maintenance of health and prevention of illness. This requires constant vigilance and concerted effort to remedy conditions that may lead to health problems or breakdowns.

Mental illness in its various manifestations is characteristically disintegrative both etiologically and pathologically. Thus recreation's potential as a major life integrating force is particularly significant in relation to mental health and illness.

There are opportunities and needs for recreators to play major roles in preventive community mental health efforts. Both individually and as members of interdisciplinary mental health teams, recreators are called upon to exercise their responsibilities as the only professional persons primarily concerned with all aspects of leisure and its uses. In situations indicative of possible mental health problems, investigation and knowledge of the quality of leisure, of the context in which it occurs, the ways in which it is used, and the resources available for leisure purposes are essential for prompt, constructive or remedial action to strengthen the possibilities for recreation to contribute to life patterns that are meaningfully integrated and harmoniously synchronized rather than frustrating, fragmented, or divisive.

In the crowded, economically depressed, racially segregated, chaotic inner city or in the suburban environment that presents on the surface, at least, the appearance of middle class stability, questions must be asked about how leisure and its uses relate to problems ranging from gang battles, riots, and near anarchy to alienation of the young, moral bankruptcy, and cultural revolution. How much of the discretionary time available to youths and adults is desired, true leisure in contrast to enforced leisure resulting from lack of work opportunities necessary to meet life neccessities? What is the nature of the physical environment for children's play and adult leisure hours? What is the housing situation? The family life pattern—how stable or insecure? What are the ethnic and cultural characteristics of the population? What is the quality of the schools and the status of leisure education as well as vocational preparation? What are the health problems and characteristics of the people and how available are health services and medical care? What public, private or voluntary, and commercial leisure agencies are there in the community and what resources do they provide in terms of leadership, programs, services, facilities, etc? To what extent do educational and leisure programs, including mass media entertainment such as television and movies, motivate people to seek enriching, fulfilling leisure experiences, or add to their sense of frustration and alienation by arousing and playing upon unattainable desires and goals? Information related to questions such as these must be sought in order to understand how leisure and its uses relate to or are integrated with the total life conditions of the people to be served, what changes are necessary in leisure patterns and provisions, and how the individual may be helped toward the wholeness and unity of mental health through the maximizing of the integrative value potential of recreation.

If the recreator is to contribute effectively in the area of primary or preventive mental health services, it is apparent that he must function as an integral member of an interdisciplinary group including medical people, psychologists, social workers, educators, and perhaps also anthropologists, urban planners, and others. Therapeutic recreators who are members of the local public recreation staff are in a key position to serve in a liaison capacity and to provide the vital link in the resources-referral chain between general recreation and other professionals or interdisciplinary groups.

Agencies such as Boys' Clubs have played key roles in projects designed to develop constructive and remedial health, education, and leisure programs and services with hard-to-reach youth. One of the authors was privileged to observe the program of one such agency in a particularly troubled area of one of the nation's largest cities. A tour of the agency's facilities revealed a lack of power tools and other similar equipment that might generally be expected to appeal to boys in the age groups served by the agency. The Director's explanation concerning the omission of this type of equipment illustrates the importance of understanding the whole context within which leisure services and programs are offered. In this instance, a negative attitude that had developed among the predominantly black and poor residents of this section of the city toward shop and manual arts types of activities was attributed to the public school's "two track" system—one college preparatory, the other vocational and terminal. According to the Director, the youth in the area looked upon their placement in the vocational education program as practically automatic and a "put down." Extension of activities related to this school program into leisure programs was considered undesirable in this case.

For the individual who must be hospitalized for psychiatric treatment there are numerous ways in which the integrating benefits of recreation may be maximized. Emphasis in the therapeutic recreation process or services of any of the concomitant values of recreative experience according to assessments of the patient's needs and capacities can be considered as having the ultimate purpose of helping to build or rebuild a total—that is healthy—personality. A major responsibility of the therapeutic recreator is the relating of the patient's in-hospital recreation exposures and experiences to his pre- and post-hospitalization leisure life. This may be in the direction either of changing previous undesirable patterns or of supporting or reinforcing the continuation, renewal, or extension of established recreation interests of the individual. Involvement of the therapeutic recreator may extend from participation in in-take conferences and obtaining of leisure case histories; through discharge planning including intermediate programs such as transitional care, halfway houses, and the like; to follow-up with appropriate individuals or agencies in the community to which the former patient returns. With growing recognition of the health implications encompassed in the continuum concept of leisure and recreation, recreators are being charged with increasing their efforts to find ways of strengthening the effectiveness of relationships between recreation programs and services in treatment centers and communities.

Disabled Children

Many kinds of disabling conditions have the effect of separating children from association with their families and non-disabled peers to a much greater degree than is either necessary or desirable. A major aim for all disciplines concerned with disabled children is thus to strengthen capacities and to emphasize opportunities for them to participate as fully as possible in normal educational, play, and family life situations. In an address to the National Recreation Congress in 1965 Maynard C. Reynolds, Director of the Department of Special Education at the University of Minnesota, outlined a ". . . full range . . . continuum or battery of administrative arrangements for special education of children . . ." along with the underlying principles.[12] These principles and the special education model as described by Reynolds suggest many parallels and possible applications to the development of recreation services along a continuum providing for varying degrees of specialization and integration in relation to the capacities of the disabled child.

The order or direction indicated both in the listing of principles and the description of special education provisions is from integrated and non-specialized to separate and specialized. This order contrasts to that of ". . . services by welfare, correction and medical authorities [which] tend to be centered first on the most extreme problems and grow toward services to the moderately deviant persons."[13] Application of the following principles to recreation requires only substitution of professional terminology:

> 1. . . . handicapped children ought to be educated in situations as close to the normal pattern of school and home life as possible.
> 2. . . . youngsters are always placed tentatively and temporarily . . . children are moved . . . towards specialized services in the continuum only so far as vitally necessary and removed for return back toward normal school and home life as soon as feasible. Evaluation is continuous and placement is fluid.
> 3. . . . specialized services ought to be provided as early in life as possible and then discontinued when specialized treatment effects have been maximized.
> 4. . . . school systems [are] developing their special education programs in the order . . . [of] first . . . strengthening regular classroom resources to deal with handicapped children, . . . next . . . [bringing] in specialists such as psychologists and social workers to consult with regular classroom teachers. Then we see movement to programs which are extensions . . . to more highly specialized program levels.[14]

In the chart that follows, the range or continuum of special education provisions for disabled children as described by Reynolds is represented in the column on the left. This is paralleled on the right with a column for recreation services and provisions. In the center column some examples are indicated of kinds of disabling conditions that might be found among children who participate in the programs. It is evident that special education and recreation have much in common in the continuum thus represented. However, it also seems clear that recreation services may have a greater potential than does special education for lessening the degree of separation from home and community life even when the child must be placed in a special school or residential institution.[15]

The Aging

The proportion of elderly people in the population of the United States is increasing. For most of these people, life is leisure-centered whether by their own choosing or for reasons of poor health or compulsory retirement. The meaning and effects of the abrupt changes in focus and balance of living that retirement brings are of concern to recreators, sociologists, medical people, and others, as well as to the elderly, themselves. Along with health, housing, and economic condition, leisure is a major force in the lives of these people with potential for disintegrating emptiness or for full and satisfying living.

Needs to extend and raise the quality of recreation services to older resi-

CONTINUUM OR RANGE OF SERVICES

Special Education ◄———————	Child's ————————►	Recreation
	Disabling Condition	

Enrollment in regular classes	Disability has ◄—— minor effect ——►	Participation in general program and services
Basic enrollment in regular class plus consultation by teacher with specialists in related fields	Some degree of problem evidenced by effect of disability	Participation in general program plus consultation by recreator with therapeutic recreator and specialists in related fields.
Enrollment in regular class for basic instruction in most subjects plus specialized instruction one period daily or several weekly periods	Example: child with speech or hearing problems	Participation in general program plus special planning and supportive services by the recreator
Enrollment in regular class with part of each day spent in "resource room" programs	Examples: child with learning disabilities; blind child	Participation in most of the general program plus special programs, services, and facilities provided in the recreation center, camp, or other locations
Part-time special class	Example: child with behavior or conduct problems	Structured special programs in conjunction with special class plus participation in general programs
Full-time special day classes	Example: TMR child	Special "sheltered" programs for this group plus inclusion in community events
Special day school (increasing separation from normal or ordinary school and home environments to more separate and specialized programs)	Example: physically handicapped child	Special programs and services at the school plus emphasis on arrangements for participation in general program to as great extent as possible
Residential school (complete separation of child from his home situation and from ordinary school situations)	Example: Moderately to severely retarded child	Full therapeutic recreation program and services in institution with strong liaison that both brings leisure programs and services from community to institution, and provides opportunities for children to go from institution to participate in community programs

dents of communities and institutions across the country are apparent. Advancement in this respect requires continuing efforts to improve the present levels of knowledge and preparation in gerontological aspects of leisure and recreation.

A study recently reported has particular import in relation to matters with which this chapter is concerned. Subjects of the study were 322 retired men who had migrated from the Midwest to retirement communities in Arizona. Among the findings of importance to the present discussion are the following:

> The pre- and post-retirement activity levels of the respondents evidenced continuity. Persons who were the most active in formal groups in their home communities tended also to be those who were the most involved in recreational activities in the retirement community setting. Less than half . . . of those with no pre-retirement participation . . . were now involved regularly in two or more recreational activities. Conversely, twice as many of those with earlier patterns of non-participation were currently inactive.
>
> The prominent pattern for these migrants was to disengage from formal groups in their home towns and to engage in the social life of their current communities through increased and new participation in leisure activities. Both continuity and discontinuity, therefore, characterized their social patterns: continuity in their overall level of activity but discontinuity in the specific nature of their involvement in the social structure.[16]

The investigators caution that various characteristics of the population of the retirement communities included in the study—high socio-economic level, favorable orientation to leisure (in contrast to older people from other segments of the population who may be imbued with the work ethic), etc.—must be considered in applying the findings. Nevertheless, the evidence as reported in this study is indicative of the potential that leisure and recreation may hold as central integrating forces in the lives of older people and the need for recreators who work with the aging to be cognizant of the whole context and pattern of their leisure-life continuum of attitudes, habits, and practices.[17]

It would be possible to continue citing examples of the integrative nature and potential benefits of recreation in the lives of people affected by a great variety of types of illnesses or disabling conditions. However, such a discussion would grow to voluminous proportions beyond the scope of this chapter. The intention thus has been to indicate concepts of the integrative values of recreation as: (1) a synchronized, unified, whole experience of the individual; (2) a continuing life force; and (3) an area of service that is integrally related to the total life conditions and patterns of the individual. If the reader is stimulated to make further applications, investigations, and refinement of the ideas presented here, the purpose of the authors will be served.

Notes, Chapter 7

1. James S. Plant, "Recreation and the Social Integration of the Individual," *Recreation*, Vol, 31, No. 6 (September, 1937), p. 340. Publication of the National Recreation Association.

2. Paul Haun, *Recreation: A Medical Viewpoint*. Elliott M. Avedon and Frances B. Arje, comps. and eds. (New York: Teachers College Press, 1965), pp. 36, 37, 38. Reprinted with permission.

3. H. S. Hoyman, "An Ecologic Model of Health, Disease, Longevity," (unpublished paper), p. 3.

4. Alexander Reid Martin, "Are You a Weekend Neurotic?" reprinted from *This Week* magazine, (June 10, 1956), for the American Psychiatric Association's Committee on Leisure Time and its Uses, n.p.

5. See Chapter 9 for discussion of these and other patterns for delivery of services.

6. Edith Lipkind, "Recreation Therapy and Physical Therapy: a Blueprint for an Integrated Service," *Recreation in Treatment Centers*, Vol. II (September, 1963), p. 59.

7. Albert L. Meuli, "An Organizational Complex," *Recreation in Treatment Centers*, Vol. II (September, 1963), p. 17.

8. "The Children's Village, Dobbs Ferry, New York, Recreational Services Department" (unpublished paper), pp. 1, 2, 4.

9. William Hollister, M.D., "Community Services and Recreation for the Ill and Disabled," in *Recreation: Proof of Its Value in Research and Application*, Bulletin No. 38 (Raleigh, N.C.: The North Carolina Recreation Commission [August, 1966]), pp. 32, 33, 34.

10. E. Mansell Pattison, M.D., "The Relationship of the Adjunctive and Therapeutic Recreation Services to Community Mental Health Programs," *Therapeutic Recreation Journal*, Vol. III, No. 1 (First Quarter, 1969), pp. 22, 24.

11. John E. Silson, M. Joan Davis, William E. Knott, Frances B. Arje, and Doris L. Berryman. "Availability and Utilization of Recreation Resources for Chronically Ill and Disabled Children and Youth in the United States," *Therapeutic Recreation Journal*, Vol. IV, No. 4 (Fourth Quarter, 1970), pp. 36-37.

12. Maynard C. Reynolds, "Recreation's Contribution to Education of the Handicapped"(Address presented at the National Recreation Congress, October 6, 1965), pp. 3-6.

13. *Ibid.*

14. *Ibid.*, pp. 4-5.

15. *Ibid.*, pp. 3-4.

16. Gordon Bultena and Vivian Wood, "Leisure Orientation and Recreational Activities of Retirement Community Residents," *Journal of Leisure Research*, Vol. II, No. 1 (Winter, 1970), pp. 3, 11. Publication of the National Recreation and Park Association. A footnote on p. 3 indicates that "This analysis is part of a larger study of post-retirement migration supported by the Administration on Aging, U.S. Department of Health, Education, and Welfare."

17. *Ibid.*, pp. 5, 13-14.

Part III | PROFESSIONAL MATTERS

8 | The Therapeutic Recreator

IN RECREATION, AS in all professional fields, the quality of programs and services depends to a large extent upon the caliber of the professional leadership. The therapeutic recreator has a particularly sensitive role in serving the leisure needs and interests of those who are ill or disabled. The extent to which recreative experience enhances the therapeutic process may, in large measure, be dependent upon the therapeutic recreator's ability to activate various concomitant benefits of recreation as he guides, assists, or intervenes in leisure behaviors. Thus, our first concern in a discussion of various professional matters in the development and delivery of therapeutic recreation programs and services is with the therapeutic recreator himself.[1]

Needs for Therapeutic Recreation Personnel

Therapeutic recreators are among the most recent additions to the professional personnel of treatment centers. Although they are beginning to make their appearance on the staffs of a few public and voluntary community recreation agencies, the number so employed was still minimal at the opening of the 1970's. It has not been easy for therapeutic recreators to establish themselves as essential members of the professional team either in the institution or in the community agency. Among the reasons for this may be cited lack of understanding on the part of administrators of the basic nature of recreation as an essential form of human experience and expression and of its integral relationships to health; narrow conceptions of the role and functions of the therapeutic recreator; and, in some instances, confusion concerning the identity of and relationships between the therapeutic recreator and other professionals such as occupational therapists. Such conditions, along with the fact that the number of individuals educationally prepared and experienced in therapeutic recreation has failed to keep pace with increasing numbers of positions available, have resulted in employment in some cases of unqualified people. This in turn often contributes to the perpetuation of misconceptions concerning the nature and the scope of the therapeutic recreator's professional role.

Nevertheless, the increase in demand for therapeutic recreators that began with the World War II surge in the employment of people as recreators in hospitals has continued. Various types of settings and agencies in which therapeutic recreators are employed are described in Chapter 9.

A recent manpower supply and demand analysis found that:

> There are not enough qualified leaders to fill positions presently available in the recreation and park field, and the gap in manpower supply and demand will continue to widen for many years to come.
> . . . .
> The need for qualified personnel to provide recreation services which contribute to the recovery or adjustment of individuals with varying types and degrees of illness, disability, or special social problems is no less acute.[2]

The team for this National Recreation and Park Association study used three methods in projecting figures: ". . . (1) status quo (based upon recreation personnel to population ratio trends); (2) judgment (based upon trends in expenditures for parks and recreation); and (3) target (based upon trends in expenditures adjusted for anticipated individual increases in productivity)." The study team believed that the target projection was the most realistic of the three methods. The following tables summarize the findings.[3]

Table 1   Estimated Numbers of New Therapeutic Recreation Service
Personnel Needed by 1980*

YEAR	PROJECTION METHOD		
	STATUS QUO	TARGET	JUDGMENT
1970	1,609	3,963	6,103
1975	3,020	10,938	10,753
1980	3,003	18,786	29,218

*The following assumptions underlie the figures in Tables 1, 2 and 3: an attrition rate of three percent per year was assumed; and new entrants to the field of therapeutic recreation were estimated to total approximately four percent of all graduates from degree-granting institutions; two percent from community colleges; and two percent from bachelors, masters, and doctoral programs.

Table 2 Projected Estimates of Need for Therapeutic Recreation Service Personnel Requiring Two Years of College Training

	STATUS QUO			TARGET			JUDGMENT		
YEAR	Supply	Demand	Deficit Need	Supply	Demand	Deficit Need	Supply	Demand	Deficit Need
1970	4,239	4,859	- 620	4,239	5,809	-1,566	4,239	6,665	- 2,426
1975	4,102	5,203	-1,101	4,102	8,385	-4,283	4,102	10,320	- 6,218
1980	4,685	5,590	- 905	4,685	11,933	-7,248	4,685	16,125	-11,440

Table 3 Projected Estimates of Need for Therapeutic Recreation Service Personnel Requiring Four or More Years of College Training

	STATUS QUO			TARGET			JUDGMENT		
YEAR	Supply	Demand	Deficit Need	Supply	Demand	Deficit Need	Supply	Demand	Deficit Need
1970	6,243	7,232	- 989	6,243	8,640	- 2,397	6,243	9,925	- 3,677
1975	5,825	7,744	-1,919	5,825	12,480	- 6,655	5,825	15,360	- 4,535
1980	6,222	8,320	-2,098	6,222	17,760	-11,538	6,222	24,000	-17,778

Startling as these figures may seem, they are presented as conservative estimates of therapeutic recreation manpower deficits since they do not:

> . . . take into account the expected additional increases for personnel trained in therapeutic recreation service who will be needed to fill newly created positions in institutions, day care centers, hospitals and other programs serving as part of a treatment team for persons who for medical or social reasons are unable to participate in normal community recreation activities."[4]

These quantitative data, however, give only a general idea of total needs for therapeutic recreation personnel. The following sections indicate the range of roles and functions required of therapeutic recreators in various positions and qualifications considered necessary for assuming such responsibilities.

Roles of Therapeutic Recreators

The basic professional roles, responsibilities, and functions of therapeutic recreators are those that are generally common to all recreators regardless of area of specialization or setting. Patterns of staff organization that provide for administrative, supervisory, and leadership levels and the responsibilities characteristic of each of these levels are generic to all kinds of business and professional endeavors. Moreover, as Brightbill pointed out, the essential tasks of the recreator, therapeutic or general, are:

... shaping the environment and motivating the individual toward developing certain attitudes, and hence appreciations, interests, and values; helping the individual acquire and sharpen certain skills; helping to create opportunities for the participant so that he may use his leisure in his innate desire to express himself through non-work activities—all aimed at expediting personal satisfaction and enjoyment which might contribute to the growth and development of personality rather than its disintegration; to help the individual attain balance and inner stability.[5]

Nevertheless, some modifications of function are occasioned by the general context within which the services are offered. This is true even in the broad, general areas of responsibility such as administration. In the treatment setting, for example, the role of the therapeutic recreation administrator may vary from that of his counterpart in a public agency to the extent that the former functions within and through the total, and often complex, administrative structure and hierarchy of the hospital or institution, whereas the public recreation and park executive is directly responsible to the policy making body that governs the programs and services he administers. Relative emphasis or balance of various types of functions and responsibilities may also vary. The therapeutic recreator may be less directly involved in some aspects of total financial administration than is the administrator of a public recreation and park agency. On the other hand, although public information and education is a major ongoing responsibility of all professional recreation personnel, the therapeutic recreator may be required to devote particular emphasis to educational, interpretative efforts in representing and advancing the leisure interests and needs of ill or disabled people.

The nature and mission of the treatment center and even its geographic location, as well as the characteristics of the population served, may affect both the nature and balance of supervisory responsibilities of therapeutic recreators. For example, one of the authors, in examining the role of the American Red Cross supervisor in military hospital recreation programs, found that:

> The Red Cross Recreation Supervisor has perhaps a unique relationship with members of her staff. This relationship is not likely to be found in business, industry, school settings, or many other agencies. The circumstances of the job make for uniqueness.
>
> . . . Many . . . staff members are young, inexperienced girls, recently out of college. They are away from home . . . , on their own for the first time. They are assigned to a locality not necessarily of their own choosing, perhaps even overseas. They are in a military atmosphere quite unfamiliar to most of them. They are dealing with people of many more varied backgrounds than they have ever before encountered. All these things present problems of a personal nature, quite apart from their job performance, which they demand help in resolving. An understanding supervisor is the one to whom they most often go for help. So whether she likes it or not, the supervisor-counselor has a dual role.[6]

Another factor adding to the prominence of the supervisory role in therapeutic recreation is the extensive use of volunteer services in supplementing and increasing recreation opportunities and resources for ill or disabled people. The effectiveness of the volunteer is largely dependent upon the quality of the professional supervision and guidance he is given. The selection, screening, training, supervision, coordination, and evaluation of volunteers constitute major responsibilities for many therapeutic recreators and for most are important aspects of their total duties.

Therapeutic recreation, like any area of professional services or specialization, must have its educators and researchers. Again, descriptions of the basic roles and functions within these roles would not vary from one field to another. Therapeutic recreation education and research efforts must, of course, be directed toward the leisure life concerns of the ill or disabled. This will be a major influence upon curriculum development and content, research problems identified and undertaken and the methods used in their solution.

Expansion in the range and scope of recognized needs for therapeutic recreation services has been accompanied by a growing awareness of needs to develop or emphasize additional roles for therapeutic recreators. Included among these roles are the more or less familiar categories of counselor and consultant as well as a category tentatively referred to as "master clinician," and another incorporating functions considered appropriate to an aide, assistant, or technician classification. While once again the functions generic to these roles are not unique to any given discipline, there are applications and needed emphases that are particularly pertinent to therapeutic recreation.

Recreation counseling was instituted as a patient service as early as 1957 in the Psychiatric Service of the Veterans Administration Hospital at Kansas City, Missouri.[7] A description of this pioneering program suggests some of the kinds of objectives, guidelines, and results that might be applied or adapted to other therapeutic recreation counseling programs.

The provision of patient recreation counseling at the Kansas City VA Hospital stemmed basically from the mission of the Psychiatric Service to return the patient to his home community within a relatively short time, i.e., within a few months. This led to essential concern for ensuring, insofar as possible, that the environment to which the patient was returned would be ". . . calculated to foster recuperative processes" begun during the period of hospitalization. Expectations that recreation counseling might contribute to such aims were based upon the staff's:

> . . . experience that with sustained psychiatric treatment in the hospital environment withdrawn patients have come to participate with apparent enjoyment in social-recreation activities. Contact with patients who have required rehospitalization here or at near-by psychiatric centers indicated that some tend to lapse into solitary ways on discharge and thus set the stage for reactivation of old pathological patterns of behavior. Our observation suggested that in several of these cases, specific guidance in this area—living through the non-working hours—was indicated.[8]

The Recreation Counseling Program which was instituted was a cooperative, interdisciplinary effort carried out by the hospital's Neuropsychiatric Service and Special Services and by the city's Recreation Department. The objective ". . . to help patients maintain the level of social contact reached while hospitalized and to guide them in the use of their leisure time." Both group and individual counseling were available to the patients. Techniques used in individual counseling were ". . . similar to those of the counseling psychologist with social satisfaction rather than job satisfaction the goal."[9] Experience with 150 to 200 patients in counseling groups showed the following results:

1. Strengthening of existing affiliations: patients have indicated renewed interest in church activities and have reported reactivation of memberships in lodges and clubs. Several have begun to think in terms of recreational activity that involves the whole family.
2. Formation of new ties: Contacts made while in the hospital have been maintained. Some patients of retirement age have profited from introduction to social groups in their age range. Several have become involved in planning a program of activity to take up the slack caused by retirement. The authors feel that formal counseling such as described in this paper may prove particularly effective with the large numbers of older patients currently in psychiatric hospitals.
3. Knowledge of recreational facilities and of how they can be used: Learning how to avail themselves of facilities and thinking in terms of such outlets have been of general value. The counselors also were amazed at the social, recreational and educational opportunities that existed in the community. Some patients have looked into the social-recreational opportunities in communities distant from the hospital, and the city recreation department is helpful in this area.
4. Mobilizing community resources: Not the least of the results of this program is the involvement of individuals and groups in the community in mental health problems. The program demonstrated that large segments of the population are willing to help if called upon and can be relied on to further rehabilitation processes when given some professional guidance.[10]

The basic role of the therapeutic recreator in the counseling situation has been described by Sidney Acuff as being ". . . more that of the resource person than the skills instructor."[11] Fred Humphrey stresses the need to enlarge concepts of recreation counseling services and programs to provide for the use of non-verbal as well as the more traditional verbal communicative techniques and processes.[12] In any event, it is apparent that therapeutic recreators have unique opportunities in leisure or recreation counseling roles to contribute to the habilitative or rehabilitative process, and to serve the ill or disabled as liaison-resource persons in strengthening the continuity of health-supportive leisure life patterns. That these services are as yet largely undeveloped should not be considered indicative of the potential importance recreation counseling may assume as a major professional role of the therapeutic recreator. Gerald O'Morrow, in fact, reported that data collected for a 1968 study indicated greater than expected expansion of recreation counseling services in relation to pre-discharge planning with psychiatric patients.[13]

Another role which therapeutic recreators are being increasingly asked to assume is that of consultant. Some agencies, such as the American National Red Cross and the National Easter Seal Society for Crippled Children and Adults, have for some years employed recreation consultants on an area or nationwide basis to strengthen, develop, and upgrade the quality of their agencies' recreation staffs, programs, and services.

A newer and potentially more extensive area of need for therapeutic recreation consultants is emerging. One of the major forces influencing this development is the increase in extended care facilities (nursing homes and convalescent hospitals) along with stipulations for licensure of these facilities to provide Medicare services. Recreation for patients, under the category of "Patient Activities," was written into federal regulations as a condition for Medicare participation. However, the standards for recreation as set forth in the Medicare regulations were minimal, vague, and confusing. This resulted, as Jean Tague pointed out, in recreation situations in ECFs in which:

1. Any person, regardless of experience and/or professional training, may plan and direct the patient recreation program. In many cases, this person is the administrator's wife, a patient's daughter or a volunteer.
2. Almost any type of activity is acceptable to the licensing agency. For example, television, magazines, volunteers and friendly visitors, (that nice lady from the church who visits the patients once a month) may comprise the total patient recreation program in an ECF.
3. The acceptable numbers of activities available to the patients each week is left to the individual interpretation of the field representative of the local licensing agency.
4. In many instances, the licensing agency accepts the "word" of the administrator that a patient recreation program does indeed exist in his facility.[14]

It is obvious that professionally qualified therapeutic recreators are the key to remedying such situations in ECFs. Yet the increase in numbers of nursing homes and convalescent centers along with the present and predicted shortages in therapeutic recreation personnel, as cited in the manpower study referred to earlier, make impractical any suggestion that all ECFs be required, or even expected, to employ degreed therapeutic recreators in full time face-to-face leadership roles. A more realistic suggestion for helping to alleviate the problem would be to place increasing emphasis on developing, organizing, and providing consultative services by qualified therapeutic recreators to given numbers of ECFs. The Medical Section of the California Parks and Recreation Society developed and published "Guidelines for the Therapeutic Recreation Service Consultant in Convalescent Hospitals, Nursing Homes, and Mental Facilities for the Aged." Major types of responsibilities as detailed in the "Guidelines" include the following "Areas of Consultation for Therapeutic Recreation":
A. Administrative Consultation
   1. Establish contact with administrator.
   2. Develop effective contractual agreements.
   3. Establish staffing patterns, professional and non-professional.
   4. Determine policies for records and reports.
   5. Advise on utilization of space and equipment.

    6. Establish budget for the recreation program.

    7. Coordinate recreation program with the Dietary and Housekeeping Departments (with approval of administration).

    8. Advise on new developments including research and legislation.

B. Program Consultation

    1. Recreation programs developed to meet the need and interests of patients.

    2. Implementation of specific activity programs.

    3. Advise on community resources, sources of volunteers, equipment and supplies and other resource materials.

    4. Periodic review for potential revision of program.

C. In-service Training and Continued Education Consultation

    1. In-service training for nursing staff.

    2. In-service training for other staff and health care consultants.

    3. In-service training for Recreation Leader.[15]

Additional important responsibilities of the therapeutic recreation consultant are included in the "Guidelines" as "Areas of Coordination with Multidisciplinary Consultants for the Purpose of Recreation Planning." These are:

A. Other Patient Care Consultants

    1. Director of Nurses.

    2. Restorative Services [occupational, physical, and speech therapy].

    3. Social Services.

B. Consultants to the State and Local Government Agency Administering the Medicare Program and/or Local or State Programs for Health and Mental Health.

C. Professional Organizations, State Board of Professional Standards, Universities and other Educational Institutions.

D. Community Resources.[16]

An innovative program for providing consultative services of a somewhat different type was initiated by the Activity Therapy staff of a state psychiatric hospital. Dubbing themselves "circuit riders," teams composed of members of other disciplines and patients as well as activity therapists offered consultation and training in activity skills to personnel in sheltered care facilities and special schools in nearby communities. Upon request, the hospital "circuit riders" went to the agencies to conduct training sessions that varied from one-time, half-day programs to a six-week series of classes. Patients participated in the "circuit riding" through demonstrations of various activities and responses. Consideration was also reportedly being given to training individual patients to act as assistants to the activity therapists. Thus, not only were staffs of the agencies helped in learning skills but participating patients gained the experience of helping others. The Activity Therapy Director noted that the "circuit riding" program helped in ". . . strengthening the relationship between the Hospital and health related agencies in the community, and . . . aiding groundwork for other mutually helpful projects between agencies."[17]

A comprehensive survey of agencies providing recreation services for the ill or disabled in Kentucky was conducted by one of the authors in 1969. Data collected from nursing homes and extended care facilities included in the study indicated

> . . . a trend toward the emergence of the consultant in therapeutic recreation services, to serve a number of nursing homes within a manageable geographic area. Indeed, many of the respondents indicated a need and desire to share the services of a therapeutic recreation specialist with other nursing homes or small community hospitals. This newly emerging occupational role should also be fully exploited.[18]

Furthermore, as pointed out in a report of the Kentucky study, development of therapeutic recreation consultants may be seen as being not only related, but basic to sound and practical use of personnel resources—aides and attendants— already within the staffing patterns of nursing homes. Large numbers of such personnel, as well as volunteers, might be served through district or regional training sessions organized and directed by a therapeutic recreation consultant. Thus, the University of Kentucky recreation faculty concluded that they have responsibility ". . . (1) to include in the recreation curriculum the ingredients necessary for preparing the kind of consultant mentioned above, and (2) to act as a catalyst for the initiation and implementation of short-term or in-service training programs for nursing home personnel."[19]

It is apparent that one of the major responsibilities of the therapeutic recreation consultant has to do with training and helping personnel who may have had limited, if any, professional preparation in therapeutic recreation. This may be seen as indicative of a change or development in the concept of the role that these people—variously classified as attendants, aides, assistants, technicians, and the like—may play in the total spectrum involved in the provision of therapeutic recreation services. In fact, attitudes have changed from rejection or condemnation of assigning recreation responsibilities to individuals lacking either baccalaureate degrees or experience in therapeutic recreation to recognition of the potential of this group as an important resource in helping fulfill needs for therapeutic recreation services. Recruitment of such personnel is being encouraged.

Several factors are bringing emphasis to the role of the therapeutic recreation assistant, aide, or technician. Shortages of educationally prepared personnel, rapid expansion of medical care facilities and programs such as the nursing home-extended care situation described above, escalating costs of medical care, and limitations of financial resources all are—and promise to remain for the foreseeable future—key factors. A more positive force, however, has been the rapid expansion of junior or community colleges. In 1968 Ball noted that the growth of the two-year college and the proliferating demand for recreators in an increasing variety of situations was effecting a major change in the training of recreation personnel for direct leadership roles. Both the roles and the training for them are in need of clarification. Progress in this direction has begun with studies funded by the Office of Education, such as that conducted by the National Recreation and Park Association to develop guidelines for recreation major programs in junior colleges. Others have been undertaken by university staffs, notably a series at New York University directed toward analyzing tasks and identifying competencies needed by recreation aides in extended care facilities.[20] Inclusion of the categories of Therapeutic Recreation Assistant and Therapeutic Recreation Technician in the 1970 revision of the National Therapeutic Recreation Society Standards for Registration provided further evidence of the growing recognition being accorded these roles.

Among the emerging roles of therapeutic recreators is one tentatively referred to as "master therapeutic recreation clinician." Very little has been done to analyze or describe this role. However, it would appear that progress toward effecting and refining therapeutic processes possible through recreative experiences will require individuals with advanced skills and educational preparation to engage in research studies and their application. This will call for a type of sophisticated face-to-face leadership as well as ability to demonstrate and teach others leadership methods and techniques shown through research to be effective in achieving desired results. Such a role is, in fact, in contrast to the traditional concept of direct leadership that is increasingly, and correctly, being assigned to assistants and aides.

These new and emerging concepts of professional roles in therapeutic recreation are in harmony with new developments in career ladder concepts. It has long been recognized that the single-line progression from leader to supervisor to administrator is inadequate both in offering many individuals opportunities to advance in directions calculated to develop and use their particular talents and abilities and in attaining the best possible fit between needs for and exercise of such abilities. Thus, individuals with various combinations of skills, experience, and types of training or educational preparation may find several career "ladders" or paths open at entry levels. Moreover, flexibility is being increasingly urged both in opportunities for on-the-job development and in training and educational programs to allow for cross-overs from one career path or ladder to another, as well as for progression within each one. The person whose particular talents and skills can be most effectively expressed in direct leadership capacities will thus not be limited to advancement along a line leading only to administrative positions. In fact, a more appropriate metaphor to apply might be that of a career "lattice" rather than "ladder," with advancement and cross-overs possible from entry or beginning level positions in clerical and maintenance categories, as well as program leadership. On the basis of the analysis of data collected for a study conducted at New York University concerning the "Development of Educational Programs for New Careers in Recreation Services for the Disabled," a three-dimensional career lattice was suggested ". . . to provide vertical, horizontal and diagonal mobility. . . ." The diagram that follows was developed as a representation or model of such a career lattice concept.[21]

It is appropriate to point out, also, that just as provisions for entry and advancement levels must be broadened and made more flexible, so graduate-level preparation and professional practice must expand from singularly conceived objectives and opportunities to provide for a wider range of top-level career options. Doctoral programs, for example, should provide alternative patterns for those who wish to pursue high-level administrative career objectives, college teaching, or research.

Qualifications and Professional Identity

Having indicated something of the needs for therapeutic recreation personnel and having identified various types of services they will be expected to provide, the discussion turns to such key questions as: Who can provide the needed services? What kinds of qualifications are needed? What types of educational preparation and professional identity are indicated?

Qualities

Consideration of the qualifications for any professional role begins with the individual himself—with that blend of personal qualities or attributes deemed basic to preparation for and performance of the kinds of services, functions, or responsibilities that will be expected and required of him. Qualities desirable in the recreation student or professional person have been frequently discussed and listed. It is generally recognized that the qualities so identified are by and large those that are not only desired and needed in any field of human service, but are attributes admired in anyone in any situation, professional or personal. Nevertheless, it has been stated that:

> . . . because the field which he [the recreator] hopes to represent is as broad and as deep as human behavior itself, and because the franchise of free choice in leisure must be preserved, these qualities are demanded to a higher degree than in some fields and summon attributes which further human understanding, social perception and democratic action. Among the more important of these are:
> —creative imagination, disciplined with common sense
> —intellectual capacity, stimulated by intellectual curiosity
> —initiative and resourcefulness bolstered by energy and diligence
> —personableness and personal confidence tempered with humility
> —breadth of vision strengthened by depth of human understanding
> —aesthetic sense coupled with functional appreciation
> —professional commitment minus a provincial outlook
> —courage, conviction and determination balanced with sensitivity and consideration
> —critical insight buttressed by an ability to think, analyze and decide
> —unified sense of direction backed up with principles and standards but with capacity to adapt, adjust and change
> Underlying all his [the recreator's] work must be a recognition and deep appreciation of self-determination in the strengthening of individual integrity. Finally, he must have a personal philosophy of life, based on sound moral and ethical concepts. . . .[22]

Haun urged that, "Every second of the time that can realistically be spent in training recreation workers, . . . [be] devoted to refining their own highly spe-

A Suggested Working Model for a Career Lattice

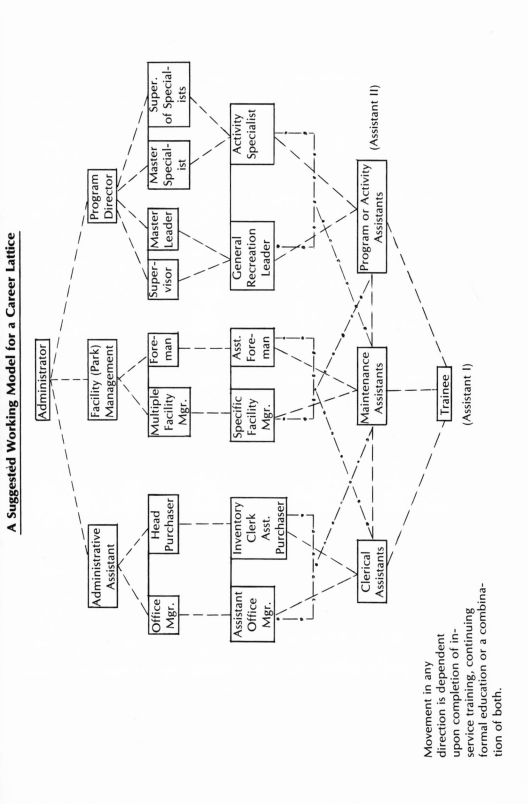

Movement in any direction is dependent upon completion of in-service training, continuing formal education or a combination of both.

Administrator

Administrative Assistant

Program Director

Facility (Park) Management

Head Purchaser

Office Mgr.

Super- of Special- ists

Master Special- ist

Master Leader

Super- visor

Fore- man

Multiple Facility Mgr.

Inventory Clerk Asst. Purchaser

Assistant Office Mgr.

Asst. Fore- man

Specific Facility Mgr.

Activity Specialist

General Recreation Leader

Program or Activity Assistants (Assistant II)

Maintenance Assistants

Clerical Assistants

Trainee (Assistant I)

cialized skill: *the skill of helping people meet their human need to have fun."*
In Haun's view, recreators must be:

> . . . unusual individuals to start with, possessing an innate optimism that is not
> dampened by an unhappy environment or undermined by identification with spe-
> cious goals. They must be unusually healthy people, so secure in their own esteem, so
> in love with life, that they cannot avoid sharing their interest and their job with all
> the world. They must like people, all kinds of people, even those who appear to be
> selfish, or unmannerly, or hostile. Always giving of themselves to others, they must
> not, they cannot, fall into the trap of emotional bookkeeping and know frustration
> when they do not receive in kind. They need a great store of tact and graciousness,
> a humility which contains nothing of servility but much of the deep respect for
> human dignity so nobly characterized in the life and thought of an Albert Schweit-
> zer.[23]

Some of the qualities important to all recreators have particular significance
for those who serve the ill or disabled. One of these is sensitivity—not the
inward-directed, thin-skinned, easily offended variety, but the outward-directed
perceptive awareness that senses how others may feel or react in or to a given
situation. The importance of such a quality is obvious for the therapeutic recreator who serves a "captive audience" of patients who cannot come and go at
will and whose leisure is itself abnormal in the sense that it is an enforced situation. Sensitivity of this kind is akin to empathy—the ability to "feel with" another, to understand and be genuinely concerned without either overwhelming
the other's identity or losing one's own, to provide the kind of support that helps
the person along the way from dependence to independent recreative experiences.

Haun's observations concerning the need for recreators to be healthy have
particular import for therapeutic recreators. Lest there be any misunderstanding, a disabled person, particularly one who may be physically disabled,
can be as qualified from the standpoint of health for serving as a therapeutic
recreator as a non-disabled person. In some instances, the very fact of having
experienced a disability may increase one's empathy quotient. However, serving the recreation needs of ill or disabled people demands mental and emotional
balance and maturity, and physical stamina.

The therapeutic recreator serves people at times when they are apt to be in a
more dependent, and therefore more vulnerable state than is normal. Moreover, like other professional staff working with the ill or disabled, information
and knowledge of a confidential, sometimes intimate nature often comes to the
therapeutic recreator. Such circumstances demand a high degree of personal
and professional integrity on his part.

Many of these qualities—part of the complex amalgam of each individual's
personal traits and abilities—are admittedly difficult to assess and nurture.
Nevertheless, it is a primary concern and responsibility of the profession at
large and of its educational arm to develop and strengthen such attributes
among its personnel.

Training and Education

Preparation and development of professional recreators, including therapeutic recreators, involves various kinds and levels of training and educational programs. These may be thought of broadly in terms of pre-entry preparation and continuing education.

Pre-entry qualification for therapeutic recreation positions has been linked basically to the criterion of a baccalaureate degree, preferably with a major in recreation which might be further strengthened by an orientation to, or an "option" in, therapeutic recreation. Graduate-level academic preparation has been considered the necessary requisite for specialization in therapeutic recreation with individuals either pursuing a master's degree as a pre-entry professional preparation or as a continuation of formal education after having had experience in the field.

It has become apparent, however, that a broader range of criteria is needed to relate qualifications more realistically to the various types of duties and positions that exist in the field as well as to the sources of supply of needed manpower. These qualifications involve both pre-entry preparation which is primarily academic in nature, and continuing education, including various types of on-the-job staff development opportunities, resumption of academic study, combined work-study programs, special institutes and other training programs, and the like. Changes have been, and are occurring in concepts of the level of academic preparation needed to perform certain types of functions with the range extending all the way from high school graduation or equivalency to the doctoral degree. However, it was not until the late 1960's and early 1970's that some systematic study was beginning to be directed toward attempts to define therapeutic recreation job functions and the related competencies as a basis for development of curricular guidelines. Reference has been made to such studies conducted, or in progress at New York University. Similarly, the planning phase of a study at the University of Kentucky to develop a master's degree program in therapeutic recreation included a comprehensive state-wide survey of the status of therapeutic recreation services and personnel. This was followed by "... extensive job analysis procedures ... to determine the role-performance and specific responsibilities of presently employed therapeutic recreation service personnel." This analysis of actual or desired job functions contributed to the identification and selection of knowledges and competencies necessary to the holder of a master's degree in therapeutic recreation in the performance of his responsibilities. The following outline indicates the broad categories of knowledges and competencies proposed as guides for curricular development at the University of Kentucky:[24]

History, Philosophy, Interpretation
   A. Knowledge
        1. Knowledge of the basic philosophical foundations of leisure and recreation.

2. Knowledge of the special philosophical focus of therapeutic recreation.
3. Knowledge of the history and development of therapeutic recreation.
4. Knowledge of the role of therapeutic recreation in education, treatment, and rehabilitation.
5. Knowledge of current issues and trends and their implications for therapeutic recreation services.

B. Competencies
1. Ability to relate historical to contemporary events.
2. Ability to communicate philosophy and show how recreation experiences relate to the therapeutic process.
3. Ability to interpret importance of recreation to individuals and society and the role of therapeutic recreation services in meeting their needs.
4. Ability to reconcile the philosophy, policies, and procedures of therapeutic recreation service with those of institutions in which it occurs.

Programing
C. Knowledge
1. Knowledge of the basic elements of program activities as means to promote individual expression, improve interpersonal relations, and provide interaction for the ill and disabled.
2. Knowledge of the dynamics of leadership.
3. Knowledge of the principles of group dynamics.
4. Knowledge of the nature and etiology of disability and illness and its psychological, physiological, and sociological impact and effect on the individual's ability to engage in recreation activity.
5. Knowledge of basic clinical treatment patterns for each type of illness and disability.

D. Competencies
1. Basic skills in all recreation interest areas.
2. Ability to plan, organize, and implement recreation programs for patients or clients.
3. Ability to adapt recreation program opportunities to special needs of individuals with disabilities.
4. Ability to prescribe and evaluate therapeutic recreation service on an individual and group basis.
5. Ability to perform the functions of advanced leadership, and group dynamics processes.

Community and Interdisciplinary Relationships
E. Knowledge
1. Knowledge of the roles and interrelationships of medical and rehabilitation disciplines.
2. Knowledge of administrative systems and services of agencies and institutions in the community.
3. Knowledge of the interdisciplinary aspects of therapeutic recreation services.

F. Competencies
1. Ability to coordinate therapeutic recreation services with other re-habilitation-education services.
2. Ability to make and maintain liaisons with community resources.
3. Ability to structure community relationships to help achieve goals of therapeutic recreation, and to initiate involvement in community organization processes.
4. Ability to identify and eliminate the societal barriers which prevent participation of the patient or client.

Counseling and Consultation
G. Knowledge
1. Knowledge of the principles of guidance and counseling.
2. Knowledge of processes and techniques needed to serve as a consultant.
3. Knowledge of community, institutional, and agency resources, services, and means of assisting clients or patients to attain optimal recreation and leisure functioning.
H. Competencies
1. Ability to counsel the patient or client in relation to his personal and social recreation and leisure concerns within the framework of existing physical and social environments.
2. Ability to counsel and advise staff regarding professional goals and growth.
3. Ability to render consultation services and direct assistance to other agencies initiating, expanding, or evaluating recreation services for the ill or disabled.

Administration and Supervision
I. Knowledge
1. Knowledge of the basic principles of recreation programing, supervision, and administration.
2. Knowledge of the settings in which therapeutic recreation occurs.
3. Knowledge of hospital and institutional administrative patterns and functions.
4. Knowledge of basic business procedures.
J. Competencies
1. Ability to plan, schedule, coordinate, and evaluate program activities.
2. Ability to apply administration and supervision principles and procedures for recruitment, training, and use of personnel.
3. Ability to apply administration and supervision methods and practices in the integration of recreation services with other agency or community rehabilitation services.

Research, Evaluation, Dissemination
K. Knowledge
1. Knowledge of the contribution and role of research in therapeutic recreation functioning.

2. Knowledge of the principles and techniques of scientific investigation.
3. Knowledge of the methods for retrieving and disseminating professional information.

L. Competencies
1. Ability to use the scientific method in acquiring knowledge and solving problems in therapeutic recreation.
2. Ability to interpret and use knowledge and insights gained through research in therapeutic recreation and related fields.
3. Ability to develop evaluative criteria re therapeutic recreation settings, programs, services.
4. Ability to write or otherwise make scholarly presentations of the results of scientific investigation.

Education and Training
M. Knowledge
1. Knowledge of curriculum development.
2. Knowledge of educational systems in which professional preparation takes place.
3. Knowledge of adult education methods.
4. Knowledge of the reciprocal relationships between therapeutic recreation personnel and that of other disciplines.

N. Competencies
1. Ability to identify training or educational needs of staff personnel and/or students.
2. Ability to retrieve, organize, and impart knowledge.
3. Ability to marshal the educational resources of the institution and community, including personnel from related disciplines, for the benefit of students and staff personnel.

Projects such as those described above have been necessitated in part because there has been no accreditation to date of college and university curricula in recreation and because there is considerable variation in these rapidly expanding educational programs. Proposals developed by the National Recreation Accreditation Project in the 1960's were still awaiting implementation in the early 1970's, due largely to jurisdictional problems. Some apprehension has also been expressed by recreation educators concerning the inhibiting effect that accreditation might exert on the experimentation and creativity needed for the development of a new and as yet inadequately defined professional program. However, awareness among recreation educators of the recommendations of the national committee who have worked on the Accreditation Project can be assumed to have had some influence upon recent curricular developments.

As far as therapeutic recreation educational programs are concerned, standards recommended by the Accreditation Project are in agreement with the concept that undergraduate preparation in this area should consist of an orientation which the student may elect to add to his basic general education and professional preparation as a recreation major. Emphasis is on additional areas of knowledge to be acquired through general education with only an orientation to therapeutic recreation as an addition to the professional recreation education curriculum. The program emphasis in therapeutic recreation includes the following as recommended additions to the undergraduate recreation curriculum:

General Education:
 Knowledge of man's anthropological antecedents, his sociocultural development, and his societal involvements.
 Knowledge of . . . [human] anatomy and physiology. . . .
 Knowledge of the kinds and degrees of physical, mental, and emotional disability and concomitant effects on the individual.
 Knowledge of group dynamics and social psychology.
 Understanding the principles and techniques in guidance and counseling.
Professional Education:
 Knowledge of medical terminology, general knowledge of administrative structure of treatment and custodial institutions and interrelationships among the various disciplines within the institution; knowledge of the implications of the physical and emotional limitations imposed by illnesses and handicaps in relation to recreational activity.
 Interpretation: At the undergraduate level, this competency should be considered as an orientation to therapeutic recreation, rather than a depth study which comes at the graduate level. It may be met through knowledge obtained from field work and general course work.[25]

Specialization in therapeutic recreation at the master's level is recommended by the Recreation Accreditation Project through the addition to the basic core of understandings of the historical, philosophical, and social bases of recreation, and of competencies in research, the following types of knowledges and competencies. Again, it will be noted that many of these, as listed below, cut across various areas of specialization in the recreation field, although some are more specific to therapeutic recreation:

 Understanding of the nature of activity.
 Knowledge and understanding of programing principles and development.
 Knowledge and understanding in depth of a program field, setting, or concern. [e.g., delinquency, aging, mental illness, physical disability, etc.]
 Ability to work with handicapped people in the community setting which involves a depth of understanding of community organization and program coordination, as well as of handicapped people and their physical and psychological problems.
 Ability to relate theory to practice.
 . . . Internships and intensive clinical experiences are recommended.
 Ability to design, develop, and administer programs to meet special needs of ill and handicapped people with respect to unusual areas and equipment requirements and other special problems posed by atypical health conditions.
 An understanding of special administrative aspects peculiar to particular settings.
 An understanding of the principles and procedures related to planning, development, design, and maintenance of recreation areas and facilities.
 An understanding of principles of supervision of personnel.

An understanding of the dynamics of human growth and development, with specific reference to needs, interests, and problems of age groupings.

An awareness of social forces as they relate to recreation and parks.

An understanding of the behavior of people in group settings and activity.

An understanding of the disciplines involved in treatment and rehabilitation settings. Studies should emphasize philosophy, roles, functions, and goals of other therapeutic disciplines and the importance of coordination.

Understanding of the nature and implications of illness and handicaps from physiological, psychological, and sociological viewpoints. Clinical observations and studies should include mental illness, mental retardation, and physical disability, with additional depth study in special career interests, such as:

Mental retardation—special education concepts, neurological implications, rehabilitation techniques.

Physical disability—physical medicine and rehabilitative techniques.

Mental illness—psychiatric specialization such as child mental illness, geriatrics, alcoholism, and drug addiction.[26]

Recommendations concerning doctoral programs had been stated only in general terms when the 1968 revision of the National Recreation Education Project was written. Emphasis, as might be expected, was placed on a core of research competencies and upon breadth of understanding of the total field of recreation, accompanied by depth of insight into meaning and effects of leisure in the lives of people and the world in which they live. With respect to special areas of emphasis, such as therapeutic recreation, the document states only that:

It is recognized that the areas of emphasis set forth in master's degree program present many more competencies than can be achieved at the master's level. Doctoral programs should go into more breadth and depth in the area of emphasis of the candidate's choice. Special sequences of work should be recommended for those interested in being researchers, recreation analysts, educators, top-level executives, recreation planners, programmers interested in depth study of social implications, etc. The availability of such sequences at an institution should be solely dependent upon the resources of the institution.[27]

From the above it is apparent that the proposals of the Accreditation Project are already in need of updating and upgrading. Although it is conceded that standards such as these always represent minimum requirements, recreation curriculums in many institutions of higher learning now exceed the accreditation recommendations. Furthermore, such new factors as the rapidly developing phenomenon of junior or community college recreation curriculums must be recognized not only in terms of guidelines and standards needed for their development but also in relation to the impact they have on other types and levels of educational and professional preparation programs. (Indeed revision of the accreditation standards is in progress as this book goes to press.)

Professional Identity

Professional identity is important to the individual practitioner, to the profession he represents, and to the people or constituency he professes to serve. The object is to protect and upgrade the quality of professional services by assuring that those offering the services are qualified to accept and discharge such responsibilities.

Professional identity is achieved in several ways. Basically, it is the integrity of the person, himself, and the quality of the services he renders that mark an individual as a professional. Experience can be an important factor in developing and refining an individual's professional performance and thus his professional identity. In those fields that have achieved professional status, training and educational preparation programs are developed and become important criteria for assessing and identifying a person's professional qualifications. Another mark of the professional person is his affiliation and active participation with societies and associations aimed at betterment of the field of service.

Some of the factors related to professional identity for therapeutic recreators —personal qualities and educational preparation for the field—have been discussed above. Opportunities to achieve identity through professional affiliation are available to therapeutic recreators in many states as well as nationally. In keeping with the philosophy expressed earlier and reflected throughout this book, the identity of therapeutic recreators is first and basically with the total field of recreation services and then with that part of the profession that addresses its services to a particular or special part of the total population, the ill or disabled. Thus, therapeutic recreators should be active participants in the affairs of their state recreation and park societies or associations as well as with therapeutic recreation branches or sections where these exist within the state. Usually, as is true of the national organization, such state special-interest sections are organic parts of the larger state park and recreation organization. Nationally, membership in the National Recreation and Park Association is open to all who are concerned with any of the areas of the total field. It is by virtue of membership in the large organization that one may then affiliate with the branch or branches that represent his particular areas of interest. For therapeutic recreators, the National Therapeutic Recreation Society offers the major opportunity to become involved and identified with their special-interest area on a national level.

It is through the efforts of persons in such professional association that an important means of identifying qualified therapeutic recreators was developed and is administered. The development of a plan for national voluntary registration of therapeutic recreators was included in the historical account in Chapter 1. In 1966, the newly formed National Therapeutic Recreation Society assured continuance of this plan by assuming responsibility for its administration. In 1969, the Society adopted an updated and expanded revision of the original standards. The new five-level plan which replaces the original three-level plan reflects some of the developments noted earlier with respect to entry level positions, qualifications, and enlarging concepts of roles and functions performed by therapeutic recreators. A complete description of the standards and information regarding voluntary registration through the National Therapeutic Recreation Society are included in the Appendix. Thus it is necessary to note here only that the earlier provision for two "professional" categories—leader and supervisor-administrator—plus a "sub-professional" level—aide—has been expanded to serve both the individual professional person and the field more realistically and beneficially. The current plan provides for registration of those employed in the field on the basis of qualifications of experience and education that extend from combinations of no college study but experience or training under qualified supervision through two-year college programs, baccalaureate, and master's level preparation. Various combinations of experience and academic preparation provide flexibility in applying the registration standards to those who have earned baccalaureate or master's degrees in fields other than recreation or therapeutic recreation. Yet, in spite of the inclusiveness and flexibility that characterize the revised Voluntary Registration Standards, only 297 therapeutic recreators appeared on the national registry in 1970![28]

It is obvious that effort must be directed toward encouraging persons qualified at all levels to enter the field and identify themselves with the profession. This effort should be helped by the evidences of present and anticipated needs, the expanding variety of professional roles and functions for therapeutic recreators, and the increasing numbers, quality, and flexibility of educational programs.

Notes, Chapter 8

1. In this chapter we are concerned with professional personnel in therapeutic recreation. Volunteers are discussed in Chapter 10.

2. Peter J. Verhoven, "Needed: 18,000 Therapeutic Recreation Service Personnel by 1980—," *Therapeutic Recreation Journal*, Vol. III, No. 1 (First Quarter, 1969), pp. 4, 5.

3. *Ibid.*, pp. 5-6, 7.

4. *Ibid.*, p. 7.

5. C. K. Brightbill, unpublished notes.

6. Martha Peters, "Counseling in Relation to the Red Cross Recreation Supervisor" (unpublished paper), p. 1.

7. William E. Olson, M.D., and John B. McCormack, M.D., "Recreational Counseling in the Psychiatric Service of a General Hospital," reprinted from *The Journal of Nervous and Mental Disease*, Vol. 125, No. 2 (April-June, 1957), p. 237.

8. *Ibid.*

9. *Ibid.*, p. 238.

10. *Ibid.*, p. 239.

11. Sidney H. Acuff, "Recreational Counseling as an Aspect of Programming for the Short Term Psychiatric Patient," *Recreation in Treatment Centers*, Vol. V (September, 1966), p. 5.

12. Fred Humphrey, "Recreation Counseling for the Institutional Dischargee," *Therapeutic Recreation Dialogues with Doctors*, Bulletin No. 4 (Raleigh, N. C.: The North Carolina Recreation Commission, 1968), p. 64.

13. Gerald S. O'Morrow, "Expanding Recreation Services—Recreation Counseling," *Recreation in Treatment Centers*, Vol. VI (September, 1969), p. 3.

14. Jean R. Tague, "The Status of Therapeutic Recreation in Extended Care Facilities: A Challenge and An Opportunity," *Therapeutic Recreation Journal*, Vol. IV, No. 3 (Third Quarter, 1970), pp. 13-14.

15. Janet Brownlee, ed., *et al.*, "Guidelines for the Therapeutic Recreation Service Consultant in Nursing Homes, Convalescent Hospitals and Mental Facilities for the Aged," *Therapeutic Recreation Journal*. Vol. IV. No. 3 (Third Quarter, 1970), pp. 26-30.

16. *Ibid.*, pp. 31-32.

17. Louis Lehmann, "How Recreation Activities are Promoted by 'Circuit Riders' in Nursing Homes and Other Facilities," *Therapeutic Recreation Journal*, Vol. II, No. 1 (First Quarter, 1968), pp. 34-36.

18. Martha Peters and Peter J. Verhoven, Jr., "A Study of Therapeutic Recreation Services in Kentucky Nursing Homes," *Therapeutic Recreation Journal*, Vol. IV, No. 4 (Fourth Quarter, 1970), pp. 19-22.

19. *Ibid.*, p. 22.

20. Edith L. Ball, "Academic Preparation for Therapeutic Recreation Personnel," *Therapeutic Recreation Journal*, Vol. II, No. 4 (Fourth Quarter, 1968), pp. 16, 19.

21. Doris L. Berryman, "Development of Educational Programs for New Careers in Recreation Services for the Disabled" (United States Department of Health, Education, and Welfare, Office of Education, Bureau of Research, March 1, 1971), pp. 8, 9. See Appendix for job descriptions related to positions indicated on "career lattice."

22. "Statement of Policy and Position," Department of Recreation and Park Administration, University of Illinois (unpublished paper), p. 7.

23. Paul Haun, *Recreation: A Medical Viewpoint* (New York: Teachers College Press, 1965), p. 91. Reprinted with permission.

24. Peter J. Verhoven, Jr., Project Director, "Prototype Grant Proposal," Curriculum in Recreation and Parks, University of Kentucky (November 24, 1970), pp. 1, 7-12. Project partially supported under a grant from the Office of Education, Bureau of Education for the Handicapped. See Appendix for a complete description of the University of Kentucky prototype program for a Master's degree curriculum in therapeutic recreation.

25. National Recreation Education Accreditation Project, "Standards and Evaluative Criteria," unpublished report, sponsored by the Federation of Organizations for Recreation, Revision, (April, 1968, [n.p.]). Dr. Betty van der Smissen, Chairman of the Project, notes that this draft was intended for temporary use with additional work expected to continue on some segments, including the graduate program.

26. *Ibid.*

27. *Ibid.*

28. "NTRS Registry," *Therapeutic Recreation Journal*, Vol. IV, No. 1 (First Quarter, 1970). p. 31.

9 | Provision of Services

Settings

EXAMPLES CAN BE found of the provision of specialized recreation services to people in almost all stages of illness and disability. Therapeutic recreation can be a part of the lives of persons soon after the onset or the recognition of an illness or disability, and continue through the processes of hospitalization, convalescence, rehabilitation, and return to the home and community.

Therapeutic recreation services are being increasingly extended to reach people in a wide variety of diagnostic groups. From a modest beginning in military and veterans hospitals and in state-supported mental hospitals, the therapeutic recreation specialization now is concerned with such diverse groups as drug addicts, the mentally retarded, lepers, the aged, the culturally deprived, as well as the more conventionally ill and disabled. Furthermore, therapeutic recreation services are no longer confined within the walls of institutions but are offered increasingly in the mainstream of community life.

For the most part, however, organized recreation services for the ill and disabled are found where such people are concentrated for care and treatment. These treatment centers include hospitals, nursing homes, special schools, clinics, rehabilitation centers, halfway houses, and sheltered care centers and workshops. There are few entirely independent recreation programs for the ill and disabled. Most programs operate within the administrative structure of an institution or agency whose concern is with the needs of the whole person, including his recreation needs but not excluding other needs. Thus the organizational patterns and administrative structure of therapeutic recreation services may differ somewhat from those of recreation services provided for the general population. A therapeutic recreation program depends to some extent on: (1) the administrative pattern of the hospital or agency within which it operates; (2) the kinds of patients or clients to be served; (3) the financial structure of the agency or institution; (4) other services similar to recreation which the hospital or agency provides; and (5) overall orientation of the hospital or agency to the treatment aspects of recreation.

Hospitals may be classified in a number of ways, the most common being by clinical treatment specialty, and by ownership and control. For the purpose of locating recreation services within the administrative structures, the prevalent types of hospitals will be briefly discussed in terms of ownership and control.

Federal Hospitals

The various divisions of government, i.e., federal, state, and local, control and operate many hospitals. The Veterans Administration, a federal agency, operates some 160 hospitals throughout the United States to serve the veterans of the Armed Forces. These hospitals range in capacity from approximately 100 to 2000 beds, with an average capacity of about 800. Until recent years, a number of the VA hospitals treated predominantly one type of disability, e.g., mental illness, tuberculosis, and so on. The tendency now, however, is for each hospital to offer a full range of treatment by having general medical and surgical, pulmonary disease, and psychiatric units.[1]

Recreation is one of the professional services provided patients in VA hospitals. It is one of the modalities that make up a broader service designated as Physical Medicine and Rehabilitation Service. This is one of several professional services responsible to the Chief of Staff, who in turn is responsible to the Hospital Director.

VA hospital recreation programs generally have both a treatment program and a diversional or voluntary program. "Recreation therapy" may be prescribed for the patients individually, the prescription indicating that the patient is to participate in specific group activities at specific times. Patients may participate on a voluntary basis in a general recreation program during times they are not assigned to treatment or work schedules.

Another type of federal hospital is that operated by the various branches of the Armed Forces: the Army, the Navy, and the Air Force. Almost every military and naval installation of any size, both in the United States and overseas, includes a hospital that cares for the servicemen of the installation and their dependents. During time of war, the number and size of military hospitals increase. Certain ones may be designated as specialized treatment centers—tuberculosis, neuro-psychiatric, amputation, etc.—as the number of servicemen requiring such specialized treatment reaches an indicated point. During peace time most military hospitals function as general hospitals, with staff and facilities for treating a broad range of diseases and injuries.

The responsibility for providing recreation services in military hospitals rests with the American National Red Cross. This is a quasi-governmental agency chartered by Congress to provide a program of social services for the members of the Armed Forces and their dependents. In military hospitals, the Red Cross social service program has three main divisions: social casework, recreation, and volunteer services. The administrative head of the Red Cross unit is the Hospital Field Director. She[2] may be either a Recreation Worker or a Social Worker, but has been traditionally a Social Worker. In most cases, she is directly responsible to the Commanding Officer of the hospital for all operations of the Red Cross unit, including the recreation program. Also, she reports to and receives consultative assistance from the Red Cross headquarters staff of the area in which the hospital is located. The four domestic and five overseas area headquarters include, in the division called Services in Military Hospitals, staff who are specialists in social work and in recreation. These Directors and Assistant Directors of SMH report, in turn, to the Director of SMH at the National Headquarters of the American Red Cross.

Traditionally, recreation services in military hospitals provided by the Red Cross have been medically approved but not medically prescribed, nor considered to be a type of therapy. This is in accordance with an agreement reached at the national level with military authorities concerning the division of responsibilities between occupational therapy and recreation.

Other hospitals operated by federal government agencies include those which are a part of federal prisons, those which are under the auspices of the National Institutes of Health and are primarily research institutes, and those operated by the U.S. Public Health Service for specific diseases such as leprosy. The recreation programs in these hospitals are tailored to the specific needs of these specialized hospitals and, to the extent that they are thus individualized, cannot be described in a general way.

State Hospitals

Virtually all state governments have assumed major responsibility for the care of persons suffering from mental illness. State governments have also taken some responsibility for the care and education of children who are blind, deaf, crippled, and mentally retarded. Thus, in most states, one can find a number of mental hospitals, and hospital-schools for the blind, the deaf, and the mentally retarded operated by the state government.

Until recently, mental patients were concentrated in large facilities usually isolated both physically and socially from the rest of society. Although the "State hospitals were clean, humane places and gave good physical care . . . the public mental hospital essentially was a custodial institution that expected to provide lifetime care for the great majority of the mentally ill."[3]

A new approach to the management of mental illness which emphasized treatment and return to the community, and effective treatment *within* the community was given great impetus by a Presidential message of John F. Kennedy, resulting in the enactment of the Mental Retardation Facilities and Community Mental Health Centers Act of 1963. With the help of federal funds, states have been enabled and encouraged to mobilize, integrate, and coordinate in a comprehensive manner, existing as well as new community resources for the prevention, detection, diagnosis, and treatment of mental illness. The various state departments of mental health have approached this task in different ways, depending on the characteristics of each state. At the time of this writing, long-range planning and implementation are still in process. However, it seems evident that recreation is being built into the structures of mental health service in interesting new ways, both in the hospitals and in the comprehensive mental health centers of a district or zone structure.

Unlike VA and military hospitals, the administrative structures of state hospitals may vary from state to state. Within a given state, however, the hospitals are likely to have similar administrative patterns. A pattern found in several state systems places recreation in a service which includes those therapies that involve activity on the part of the patient—occupational therapy, physical therapy, industrial therapy, music therapy, and so on. This may be called "Activitity Therapy Service," "Rehabilitative Service," or some other designation.

The functional structure of the recreation department usually conforms to the functional structure of the hospital insofar as patient treatment is concerned, that is, according to its unit system. Some hospital units are structured on the basis of length of hospitalization (acute, convalescent, continuing, custodial, etc.), others on the basis of age and sex, or the unitization may be based on a catchment or geographical area. An interesting variation of the unit system is represented by the Illinois State Psychiatric Institute in Chicago. Here each unit is housed on one of the eleven floors of this high-rise building. Each of the treatment unit floors is associated with one of five medical schools, or the Institute of Michael Reese Hospital, or the State Department of Mental Health. Each unit has a staff of Activity Therapists, composed of a supervisor and one or more occupational therapists and recreators. Recreation programing on each unit is highly integrated with occupational therapy, and is in accord with the general treatment plan set up for that unit. In addition, a central recreation program is provided for all hospital patients to participate in voluntarily, either individually or with a group from their own unit.

Other state-supported treatment centers, such as schools for the blind, deaf, and mentally retarded, tend to follow the same administrative structure as the state mental hospitals, with recreation in the same administrative position. Recreation programing varies of course in accordance with the treatment and educational aims of the institution and the specific characteristics of the patients or clients served by the institution.

Local Hospitals

A large number of hospitals are owned and controlled by the smaller political sub-divisions, i.e., the county and the city. Within the counties and cities are also found many hospitals which are non-governmental. Such hospitals may be operated by fraternal organizations such as the Shriners, by voluntary health organizations such as the National Easter Seal Society for Crippled Children and Adults, by churches or other religious organizations, by private groups either for profit or not for profit, and so on. Among the community treatment centers are a growing number of nursing homes, or extended care facilities, which are for the most part privately owned and operated for profit.

Probably the majority of the local or community hospitals have no organized recreation program at all for the patients. The ones that do are generally the larger hospitals with separate units for children or for psychiatric patients, or are specialized treatment hospitals such as a rehabilitation institute or a crippled children's hospital. Surveys of local general hospitals show that administrators tend to feel that the short length of hospitalization, the acute illness characteristic of their patients, and the family resources of the patients are such that organized recreation as a part of the hospital services offered is not financially feasible. Nursing homes, however, do tend to provide some type of recreation or social program for their residents. This tendency has increased with the advent of Medicare and its stipulation that such a program be in operation in those agencies eligible for Medicare payments.

The administrative position of recreation in local hospitals and other treatment centers is determined by each insititution individually. No state-wide or nation-wide pattern is established, of course, for these hospitals. The administrative pattern for most of them, however, can very probably be found among those illustrated below.

Patterns of Administration

The simplest structure is illustrated in Figure 1. Many of the smaller hospitals and nursing homes operate in this manner, with each service head reporting directly to the administrator of the institution.

Figure 1

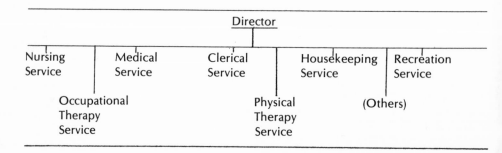

The larger institutions generally follow an administrative pattern which allows for some division of responsibility and authority and reduces the number of persons reporting directly to the administrative head of the institution. One such pattern makes two distinct divisions—administrative services and professional services—with further sub-divisions under each of the two main sections. This pattern is illustrated in Figure 2.

Figure 2

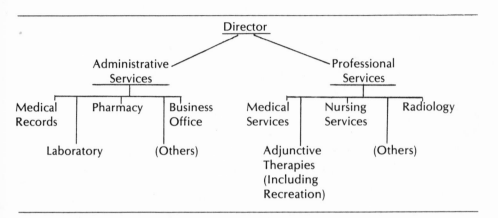

Another pattern followed by some of the larger hospitals is the unit plan. The intent of this plan is to set up a number of therapeutic communities within the larger institution. Each unit is more or less self contained, and has within it each of the professional and administrative services. This pattern is illustrated in Figure 3.

Figure 3

Director			
Unit I	Unit II	Unit III	ETC
Unit Chief	Unit Chief	Unit Chief	
Doctors	Doctors	Doctors	
Nurses	Nurses	Nurses	
Social Workers	Social Workers	Social Workers	
Psychologists	Psychologists	Psychologists	
Adjunctive	Adjunctive	Adjunctive	
Therapists	Therapists	Therapsits	
(including	(including	(including	
Recreators)	Recreators)	Recreators)	

There are, of course, many variations of the basic patterns illustrated in Figures 1, 2, and 3. Further, recreation services may be found in combination with various other services, or as a single department. Recreation may be combined administratively with one, or more, or all of the following: occupational therapy, physical therapy, music therapy, manual arts therapy, industrial therapy, corrective therapy, educational therapy, social work, bibliotherapy, vocational rehabilitation, physical education.

The "chain of command"—the pattern established to indicate successive steps in responsibility and authority—can vary from the very simple to the intricate. Some examples from various hospitals and institutions are given below.

(Fontana Nursing Home, Champaign, Illinois)
Recreation Therapist*—→ Administrator

(Illinois Children's Hospital School, Chicago)
Recreator —→ Activity Coordinator —→ Medical Director of Hospital

(Iowa Methodist Hospital, Des Moines, Iowa)
Recreation Therapist* —→ Recreation Director —→ Assistant Administrator —→ Administrator of Hospital

(Veterans Administration Hospitals)
Recreation Specialist —→ Recreation Supervisor —→ Coordinator of PM&RS —→ Chief, PM&RS —→ Chief of Staff —→ Director of Hospital

(Illinois State Psychiatric Institute, Chicago)
Recreation Worker —→ Unit Supervisor of Activity Therapy —→ Director of Activity Therapy Services —→ Director of Hospital

(Military Hospitals - American Red Cross)
Recreation Worker —→ Recreation Supervisor —→ Hospital Field Director —→ Hospital Commander

(Eastern State Hospital, Lexington, Kentucky)
Recreation Aide —→ Recreation Leader —→ Senior Recreation Leader —→ Chief Recreation Leader —→ Coordinator, Para-psychiatric Services —→ Chief of Staff —→ Superintendent of Hospital

(Western State Hospital, Fort Steilacoom, Washington)
Recreation Leader —→ Recreation Supervisor —→ Activity Therapy Supervisor —→ Superintendent of Hospital

(Department of Mental Health Hospitals, Indiana)
Recreator —→ Therapeutic Recreation Director —→ Coordinator, Activity Therapy —→ Assistant Superintendent, Clinical —→ Superintendent of Hospital

*Term used as job title by this agency.

Bridge between Hospital and Community

Changing attitudes toward the ill and disabled and their place in society were noted in Chapter 1. In recent years, considerable effort has been given to bridging the gap between the hospital and the community, to reducing the isolation that had been imposed on the disabled, the aged, the ill, and the mentally retarded. Recreation has often played a large part in establishing and/or maintaining ties between the patient and his home, family and community.

Several methods of bridging the gap are contained within the hospital recreation program itself. One is to bring volunteers from the community into the hospital to provide or assist with various program activities and entertainments. Volunteers at work in hospital recreation programs is a widespread practice in this country, but varies in scope and effectiveness from hospital to hospital. This is discussed further in Chapter 10.

Another method is to take the patients from the hospital for short excursions into the community to participate in recreation activities, or special events, or to attend entertainment programs. Such out-trips constitute a major portion of the recreation program of certain types of treatment centers, such as rehabilitation centers for the physically handicapped.

One of the most effective means available to recreation for easing the transition from hospital to community living is the camping program. Camp programs for the handicapped and hospitalized vary in range and complexity. In some cases it is a day-camp type of program, an extension to the outdoors of some of the recreation activities ordinarily carried out indoors. In other instances, a camp site is set up on the hospital grounds but away from the main buildings. Patients go to "camp" for an overnight stay or longer where they participate in a regular camping program organized by the recreation staff. Adjustments and accommodations are made, of course, for the abilities and disabilities of each particular group of campers, and necessary medical supervision and medication are near at hand. In still other instances, patients go from a hospital or special school to a camp away from the institution for a period of one or two weeks or longer. In such cases the camp staff is largely made up of hospital personnel, and the camping experience is considered by them to be an extension of the treatment program of the hospital. Nevertheless the camp setting and the greater freedom of movement combined with a democratic yet structured program help to create a "zone of transition" between the institution and community life.

It should be noted that camping experiences also constitute one of the most popular types of programs provided by community agencies for handicapped people after their return to their homes and community.

Bridging the gap between hospital and home is a concern of more than the recreation staff. The chief purpose of the Day Care program and the Night Care program, set up in a number of psychiatric hospitals especially, is to provide support and a testing period prior to final discharge. Day Care Centers are for patients who can benefit most from a daytime experience in the hospital and return home at night. Night Care centers are for patients working in the community during the day who come to the hospital for evening and night treatment and activities. A similar transitional program is that provided by the "halfway house," and the transitional care program. Apartment type living units are provided either on the hospital grounds or in the community where selected patients may try out their ability to live in a fashion more normal than that of the institution. A minimum number of hospital staff is in residence for support and encouragement. In most cases, when the program is carried on outside the hospital, the patients are assisted in finding a suitable job and encouraged to fulfill the responsibilities of the job.

Recreation personnel are frequently assigned to these transitional care programs, to assist the patients in becoming involved in community recreation activities and to gain greater independence in providing for their own leisure.

Another plan to keep intact the ties between the hospital and the community is the type of unit plan adopted by a number of hospital administrations. According to Max P. Pepper, an overriding ingredient of this unit plan is the assignment to each unit of a geographic catchment, a specific community that it serves:

> It involves an attempt . . . to move into the community and particularly so with new . . . services such as pre-care, after-care, home-care . . . hook-up with general psychiatric units in general hospitals . . . day care, night care, and provision for OPD (out patient department) services.[4]

In speaking of the unit systems developed at Anna State Hospital in Illinois, Robert E. Lanier says:

> The recreational therapist has in some cases become the unit leader simply because he was the best suited, as a person and as a professional, for the job. On his unit he has psychologists, social workers, physicians, and others who are in highly skilled roles. . . . The physician is still recognized as the unit member who will be the one to do those things only a skilled physician can best do. Also when it comes to planning for recreation, the recreation worker can give his specialized help. The point is that the physician, for example, may not, in this particular instance, be the person on the unit team who can best relate to the patient toward his re-entry into the community.
>
> Neither may he be the individual, in the particular instance, best suited for the supervisory or administrative responsibility of the unit. What is also of significance here is that the team member no longer confines his base to hospital specialization. His function is to work in the community, to treat patients in the community, to work with community agencies, to help the community develop resources, to prevent hospitalization, and to help patients who have been unable to avoid hospitalization to reintegrate into the community.[5]

Previous mention has been made of the comprehensive mental health centers being developed in many states. In Illinois, for example, these operate within a zone structure. Each of the several zones in the state has a zone center. The zones are further divided into sub-zones. A zone, for instance, may operate both an intramural program for patients in residence in the zone center hospital, and an extramural program with a team of professionals, including one or more recreation specialists, for each of the sub-zones. The cooperation and coordination of the intramural and extramural programs represents a major attempt to bring hospital treatment and community concern and responsibility closer together.

Community Programs for the Ill and Disabled

As full as the treatment centers are, the vast majority of ill or disabled persons in this country reside in the community. There is no ready index to the numbers, locations, and types of ill or disabled persons residing in any given state or community, since there are no state or federal laws requiring the registration of chronic or permanent disabilities. However, some indication of the average number of disabled persons by population count is given in findings released by the Public Health Service. Data collected by the President's Committee on Employment of the Handicapped show that an average of twelve percent of the population, not residing in institutions, reported that they were limited to some degree in their activities as a result of disease or impairment.

There is a growing recognition of the fact that these people have the right to recreation services as much as the general population, and possibly greater need for such services. Efforts are being made by several agencies, institutions, private groups, and individuals to provide recreation services for the ill and disabled in the communities. Such efforts are frequently directed toward specific types of disabilities, independent of or without knowledge of the efforts made by other groups for other types of disabilities. Thus there is no clear picture of the total effort being made.

Some of the types of programs and services that might be found in various communities are discussed here, as well as the administrative structures of the agencies which offer such services.

A number of community recreation programs for the ill or disabled have been initiated and sponsored by various voluntary health agencies. Agencies such as the American Foundation for the Blind, Arthritis and Rheumatism Foundation, Muscular Dystrophy Association, National and State Associations for Retarded Children, National Multiple Sclerosis Society, National Easter Seal Society for Crippled Children and Adults, United Cerebral Palsy Association, and others are concerned with the welfare of their particular disability groups, with not only the prevention and cure of the particular disease but also with making the life of their clients as meaningful as possible. Recognizing that a meaningful life includes recreation, these societies have in some instances set up special recreation programs tailored to the needs and abilities of their clients.

One such program is the Homebound Program of the Chicago Chapter of the National Multiple Sclerosis Society. This program originated as a pilot project of the National Recreation Association to test the feasibility of an organized community recreation program for severely physically handicapped youth and adults who were, to all intents and purposes, homebound. Subsequently the program was taken over by the NMSS and operates within the administrative structure of that society. Figure 4 illustrates the table of organization of the NMSS chapter and the place of the Homebound Program within it.

Figure 4

Chicago Chapter, NMSS
Table of Organization
6-20-69

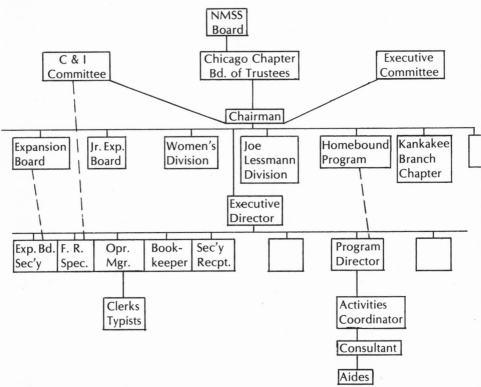

The purposes of the Homebound Program are given in the following statement released by the NMSS Chicago chapter:

> The primary purpose of the "Homebound Program" is to establish a working relationship between the community's public and voluntary agencies. . . . To provide the benefits of therapeutic recreation for persons disabled primarily from Multiple Sclerosis and/or other neurological diseases and those afflicted with Heart Disease and Arthritis. (Although all diagnostic groups are eligible for participation in the program as long as there is available space.)
>
> In order to fulfill this primary purpose the specific goals of the Homebound Program are:

To develop a comprehensive recreation program utilizing community resources for homebound clients.... To guide homebound persons in the use of existing community resources available for recreation purposes. ... To serve as a resource in providing expert planning to communities and agencies desiring to open their facilities to the handicapped and to provide consultation to those communities and agencies in the use of physical resources for recreation for the handicapped.

The description of this program serves only as an illustration of one kind of program sponsored by a health agency. Other programs, some similar and some less broad in scope, may be found in other communities.

Another type of community agency concerned with handicapped persons which includes recreation in its services to the handicapped is the one sponsored by the United States Air Force called the CHAP program. The letters stand for Children Have a Potential. This program represents the combined efforts and resources of the chaplains, medical personnel, and national and local welfare agencies to provide assistance to the large number of Air Force families having handicapped children. Recreation programs designed for these handicapped children are usually under the direction of the Air Force Special Services, but are often operated primarily by volunteers.

Public school officials have in recent years assumed considerable responsibility for the education and training of handicapped children who are unable to receive full benefit from regular classes with normal children. Their efforts have been encouraged by financial assistance from federal funds. Both as an additional method of education and as an effort to expand and enrich the lives of these children, recreation programs, particularly camping, have been instituted by some Special Education Departments and teachers. Cooperation and coordination with the community public recreation department often characterize these programs, with the recreation department providing space, equipment, and sometimes leadership.

Another recreation program for the disabled found in an educational institution is the unique one operated by the Recreation and Athletics Department of the Student Rehabilitation-Education Division at the University of Illinois. This Division provides the services that make it possible for severely physically disabled college students to enroll in college and follow almost any course of study they wish. One of the services provided to enable the disabled students to receive full benefit from campus life is the recreation-athletics service. Professor Timothy Nugent, Director of the Division, has stated that the students are encouraged to participate in all campus recreation activities with able-bodied students which require no change of rules or special equipment. Some activities, such as a number of athletic and sports activities, do require adjustment in order for the disabled students to participate and compete equitably. Therefore, the Recreation-Athletics Department sponsors such activities as wheelchair basketball, wheelchair football, wheelchair square dancing and cheerleading, and judo for the blind. The program has a full-time director and several assistants who are graduate students.

Who should be primarily responsible for initiating and operating recreation programs for the ill and disabled in the community has been an unresolved question for some time. It has been suggested that the tax-supported recreation department of the community should take the initiative in providing recreation opportunities for this special population, as it does for other members of the community. Although many public recreation agencies hesitate to undertake such programs, there are a number that have ventured into this area of programing quite successfully.

The degree to which the public agency has taken full responsibility varies from community to community. As mentioned above, assistance is sometimes given to other community agencies by providing facilities, leadership, transportation, and so on. Programs sponsored jointly by the recreation agency and another agency are increasing in number. Some communities have found it effective for the public agency to pioneer special programs which are later taken over by other agencies. In other communities, the health agency has been the one to pioneer, and then to turn the program over to the public agency for continuation and support.

Another concept is that of a cooperative program among several adjacent communities. The Northern Suburban Special Recreation Association in the Chicago area is an example. Seven suburban communities, none having enough handicapped individuals to warrant providing a full-range recreation program for them, formed the association to consolidate finances and facilities and to provide a combined recreation program for the mentally and physically handicapped.

A good example of a full program of recreation for the ill or disabled, initiated and operated by a single public recreation agency, was developed in Oak Park, Illinois. The organizational chart below shows "Special Recreation" as an integral part of the overall program operation of the Recreation Department.

As indicated previously, the welfare of the handicapped in a community is a concern of a number of agencies including medical institutions, health agencies, special education, and the like. Coordination of the efforts of these agencies is necessary, and it is reasonable that the agency which should initiate coordinating action *in regard to recreation* is the public recreation agency, whose primary purpose is providing recreation.

A public recreation agency, wishing to initiate such a program, might take the following steps:

1. Employ, or appoint from the existing staff, a qualified supervisor to carry major responsibility for the program.
2. Determine the geographical area for whose handicapped citizens the department can feasibly and legally offer services.
3. Conduct a survey to locate and identify the handicapped in the community. Rather than to conduct a door-to-door canvas or a random sample type of survey, it would be more effective to collect information from all the health, voluntary, and government agencies which deal with the varying types of handicaps. Such agencies would include the Office of Special Education, Mental Health Clinic or Department, Visiting Nurses

Figure 5

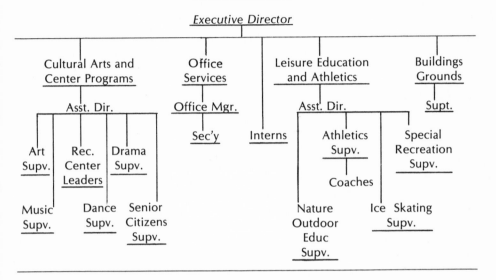

Association, the National Easter Seal Society for Crippled Children and Adults, Mental Retardation Association, and the like.

4. In consultation with the medical and paramedical specialists, make some general determinations about what is a "disability" in regard to recreation. Conditions of illness or impairment are disabling in varying degrees depending on the context in which the condition is being considered. Statistics compiled by various health and government agencies usually refer to conditions which are disabling as they apply to the specific area in which the agency deals, and are not always applicable to recreation. Combining the recreator's knowledge of the abilities required in pursuing the various recreation activities offered by the department with the health expert's knowledge of the handicapped person's disability, some general determinations can be made.

5. Compile information, gained from the above mentioned agencies and other service clubs such as the Lions, the Elks, and others known to have an interest in the handicapped, about recreation activities and services presently provided for the handicapped. Make particular note of any overlapping services which may exist, and areas where service is lacking or scarce.

6. Form an advisory committee with representation from all the agencies concerned, including the recreation department. The purpose of the committee would be to foster coordination of effort, perhaps to divide and

designate specific responsibilities, to investigate the possibilities of sharing facilities, volunteers, and so on.

7. Determine what actual programing responsibilities the recreation department should undertake. The public recreation agency, in fulfilling its responsibility to the community, should take action to initiate services which are not given. It should be in a position to provide what is lacking in the total community effort in meeting the recreation needs of the ill and disabled, whether it be space and areas, facilities, transportation, professional assistance or consultation in programing, leadership training, or leadership itself.

The organizational responsibilities of the supervisor, with the advisory committee, are twofold: (1) to promote the integration of the handicapped into the regular on-going programs of the department's sub-divisions (parks, centers, playgrounds, etc.), of voluntary agencies (YMCA, Boys' Clubs, Scouts, etc.), and of schools; (2) to organize special programs, perhaps on a city-wide basis.

To facilitate carrying out these two types of responsibilities, four additional organizational patterns are needed:

1. Recruiting and training volunteers. This could be a joint project of the recreation department, the health agencies, and other voluntary agencies such as the YMCA and the Red Cross. The cost of such training will be largely in terms of staff time and can be distributed among the agencies that are involved and are providing training staff.

2. Organizing a transportation system. Again, all the agencies concerned with the handicapped can share in the operation and cost of providing transportation. Red Cross Chapters, for instance, are capable of providing a well-organized volunteer motor service. Civic clubs sometimes make arrangements with local taxi companies for transportation of wheelchair patients at reduced rates. Parents and families of the handicapped can form car pools. If the place and time of special recreation programs for the handicapped are properly coordinated, the provision of certain state legislative bills might be utilized, which provide for a certain reimbursement to school districts for the cost of transporting special education students to day care centers.

3. Organizing a lobby-type campaign to promote the removal of architectural barriers in all public and private buildings and facilities used for recreational purposes. The "American Standard Specifications" published by the American Standards Association in 1961 should be used as a guide. According to the researchers who prepared the standards, the cost of meeting the standards in new construction is minimal. The cost of adjustments in existing buildings and facilities should be assessed and borne by the owner, either government or private individuals or business.

4. Organizing a campaign of information and public relations aimed at influencing positively the attitudes of the public toward the handicapped.

Guidelines for Programing

In this chapter's discussion of settings in which therapeutic recreation operates and the administrative patterns of those institutions and agencies providing recreation services, details of the services and actual program content have been mentioned only briefly. There can be no blueprint for a successful program that would apply to all situations. Because patients are people, the same principles for sound recreation program planning that are used with the general population should be applied to therapeutic recreation planning. In planning programs for the ill and disabled, however, there are additional factors which must be taken into consideration. These factors include limitations in the individual's mobility, strength, and physical functioning, length of hospitalization, psychological impact of disease or injury, possibilities for therapeutic application of activities, necessity for coordination with other members of the treatment team, accessibility of facilities in the community, and the like.

Some guidelines for effective programing are given below. The first nine constitute a summary of guidelines which might apply to recreation programing in general, for the able-bodied as well as the ill or disabled. Those that follow have, additionally, particular application to program planning in a treatment center:

1. Considering the range in age, sex, cultural background, and areas of interest of the prospective participants in a given setting, the program should offer recreation opportunities for everyone.
2. There should be provisions for a wide variety of types of activities, including the following:
    a. physical activities, such as games and sports, dancing, camping
    b. intellectual activities, such as reading, studying, writing
    c. esthetic activities, such as music, dramatics, art
    d. social activities such as parties, group games, discussions
    e. creativity, such as crafts, hobbies, photography, art
    f. competition, in games, sports, contests, tournaments
    g. adventure and new experience, such as trips, camping
    h. spectator activities and entertainment.
3. There should be a variety in the duration of activities. There should be some activities intended for immediate and momentary enjoyment, while others should be provided for long term and continuing interest.
4. There should be a variety in the location of activities. There should be outdoor as well as indoor events.
5. There should be variety in group size, with activities provided for the individual, and for small informal groups as well as for large groups.
6. There should be some variety in the degree of assistance and organization provided by the professional staff. The participants should have opportunity for individual expression and initiative, and for participation in the planning and operation of the program.

7. The program should be sustained throughout the year, avoiding let-downs on weekends and following holidays.
8. The program should be flexible, capable of responding to sudden needs for change.
9. There should be provisions for instruction in new skills. The program should provide opportunities for participants to extend the range of their leisure pursuits and gain new recreation experiences.

In the treatment center:

10. There should be provision in the program for degrees of ambulation. The bed patients, as well as the semi-ambulatory and fully ambulatory, should be provided with opportunities for recreation activity.
11. The program should be geared to a tempo and noise level appropriate in a hospital.
12. There should be provision for making adjustments and adaptations of the patient's usual recreation activities necessitated by physical and medical limitations.
13. In adaptations, the components of the activity should be analyzed, and those components preserved which represent the true recreative essence of the activity.
14. The program should be broad, varied, and flexible enough to provide for selection of activities to serve therapeutic goals.
15. The program should be coordinated with other medical and paramedical services.
16. The program should provide for some contact with the community outside the hospital.
17. The program should provide a bridge between the hospital and the community, and/or between the disabled and the able-bodied.
18. The program should have carry-over value. It should promote long-range interests that extend into community recreation activities.
19. One of the aims of the program should be to make the patients recreationally independent.

Notes, Chapter 9

1. Veterans Administration Pamphlet 10-68, revised March, 1968.

2. Most hospital Red Cross workers are women.

3. *Patterns for Change* (Kentucky Mental Health Planning Commission, Kentucky Department of Mental Health, Frankfort, 1966), p. 11.

4. Max P. Pepper, M.D., *The Unit Plan* (Mental Health Association of Southeastern Pennsylvania, Philadelphia, 1963), pp. 8-9.

5. Robert E. Lanier, "Mobilizing Community Resources for Mental Health Through Recreation—A Conference Report" (National Institutes of Mental Health, Technical Assistance Project, 1966), p. 9.

10 | Resources

RECREATION LEADERSHIP AS a profession is based on the fact that people often need assistance in pursuing the leisure activities and experiences which are recreative. It is reasonable to suppose that persons who are disabled and/or hospitalized may need more assistance than others. To the ill or disabled, the professional recreator is a valuable resource in this respect. But the recreator, too, must have some resources on which to call for assistance in providing recreation services. These include both human resources and physical resources such as spaces and facilities, as well as financial and legal resources to support them. One of the tasks of the therapeutic recreator is to marshal all the appropriate resources to serve the needs of the ill or disabled.

Volunteers

Volunteering is a peculiarly American phenomenon. This has been pointed out by Madolin Cannon[1] and was noted by one of the authors during her assignments in both Europe and Asia. The idea of giving one's time, money, and efforts to strangers is a concept difficult for people of a great many cultures to accept. In North America, however, voluntary efforts of some kind are expected of nearly everyone. Voluntary efforts are most often directed toward helping those who in some way are less fortunate than the volunteer. Thus volunteers tend to gravitate toward hospitals and other programs serving the ill and disabled. It is doubtful if any field of human service has greater potential for the use of volunteers than does recreation in the rehabilitation and medical setting. Volunteers do not serve exclusively in the recreation programs, however, but often in every department of the hospital, including administration.

An excellent discussion of volunteer services, particularly the administration of such services throughout a hospital, is given by Cannon.[2] The principles of selection, training, supervision, and recognition she suggests could easily be used in the administration of volunteer programs operating in community agencies with the ill or disabled.

There are a number of different kinds of volunteers. Many hospitals and other agencies have an established corps of volunteers. These are people who are able and willing to come to the hospital or agency regularly, say one-half day each week, to perform an assigned function of direct or ultimate benefit to the patients. Depending on the hospital, these volunteers usually receive some degree of formal training, given either by the hospital staff or by the organization which has recruited them and which they represent. The American Red Cross, for instance, in its long history of volunteer work, has developed an excellent training program for volunteers who wish to work with the ill or disabled.

Properly trained and supervised, regular volunteers become an indispensable part of the recreation department staff. Because of their regularity, dependability, and training, they enable the full-time professional recreation staff to plan and operate a program of greater scope and with more attention to individual patients than they would be able to do without the services of the volunteers.

Another type of volunteer is the person who has a specific skill, interest, or knowledge, and volunteers to assist in the recreation program to use this particular skill for the benefit of the patients. Quite often such service is an expression of the volunteer's enthusiasm for his own hobby or recreational interest and activity. An example from one author's experience is a man whose hobby was photography. He volunteered to set up a darkroom in the recreation building of a military hospital, to assist the patients individually or in groups in the intricacies of picture taking, developing, enlarging, and printing film. His volunteer services resulted in a popular photography club among the patient group. Such volunteers may serve regularly over a long period of time, or may serve a specific need at a specific time according to the interests of the patients.

Other volunteers serve not individually but as groups, and provide services such as social group activities which require a number of people. Often such groups are representatives from established community organizations—civic clubs, garden clubs, church groups, Red Cross Youth groups, college sororities, and so on. The frequency of their services may range from occasional visits connected often with holidays, to organized activities on a regular basis, that is biweekly or monthly.

Another type of volunteer is the college student whose motivation for volunteering may be twofold: (1) the desire to help others, and (2) the desire to gain valuable experience in preparation for professional work. Such volunteers may function as apprentices to the professional staff, and can be a considerable asset to the program. In turn, the professional staff has some responsibility to see that their work is meaningful and of educational benefit.

Professional entertainers, sports personalities, and other major or minor celebrities become volunteers when they come without charge to the hospital to visit with and entertain the patients. The wise recreator will establish good relations with local musicians' union, athletic institutes, and so on, so that such performers' desires to volunteer their services to the hospital will not be impeded.

The therapeutic recreator should not overlook a source close at hand for volunteer assistance. Other members of the hospital staff are often interested in assisting with the recreation program during their off-duty hours. The opportunity to be associated with the healthy and happy aspects of their patients' lives in contrast to the pathological aspects with which they deal in their own professional capacities makes volunteering in recreation especially appealing.

Too, patients themselves become volunteers in many instances. Natural leaders may be found in any group, including a hospital patient population. Patients with leadership ability, special skills, a greater degree of mobility than others, and other such qualifications, are of inestimable value to the therapeutic recreator in planning and operating meaningful recreation programs. In fact, in at least one school for the mentally retarded, one of the specific jobs of the recreation specialist is to train the students with higher IQs to function as recreation aides in working with the students of lower IQs.

Contributions of Volunteers

Some of the contributions that volunteers make to the therapeutic recreation service are obvious and have been mentioned above. They can relieve the professional staff of many small details that do not require specialized training. Conversely, they may provide skills, knowledge, and competencies in certain areas that the paid staff do not have. Or they may supplement and extend the activity and service of the regular staff. Certainly volunteers make it possible for the program to offer more kinds of activity, more frequent activity, and thus greater opportunity for free choice of activity among the patients. The volunteer, by increasing the number of persons at work in the hospital, enables the patient to be individualized to a greater extent.

In addition to these contributions, the volunteers can also provide a bridge between the patient and the community. They help to retain or renew contact with community people and activity. By bringing the hospital and the community together, they may have a positive influence on community attitudes towards the patients, and function as good public relations people.

Further, there is a uniqueness about volunteers which makes their contributions those which only a volunteer can make. The fact that they are people with unhurried and *unpurchased* time for the patient is a tremendous morale factor in a hospital. Helen Padula touched on this in her discussion of the functions of volunteer services:

> Volunteers do need to know something to function well in the hospital. They need to know the rules of the community, something about the nature of its inhabitants and their needs, and enough about the people who run the place to know what they can and cannot do for the patients, and to whom they can turn for information. But volunteers do not need to see the patient through the professional eyes of the staff, or to adopt staff methods. If they do, something of value is lost, and the volunteer comes to disparage what he is, because of what he cannot be. . . .
>
> . . . The volunteer, if she remains just that and does not take over hospital attitudes, can be a gauge for behavior and relationships on the outside. She brings into the hospital by her appearance, her interests, her manners a vivid contrast between hospital and community.[3]

Other Human Resources

Not all volunteer service is in the form of direct service within the hospital or agency. A considerable contribution is made to the recreation program for the ill or disabled by persons or groups who provide or help to provide for patient participation in activities or events outside the hospital. This kind of voluntary effort has a myriad of forms, some examples of which follow: a standing invitation for two or three patients to be guests at the Lions Club weekly luncheon, an invitation for a group of patients to attend the final dress rehearsal of a local little theater production, an invitation for a group of patients to be guests and participate in a church's annual picnic, an invitation for a group of patients to be guests of the local Yacht Club and to witness a sailing regatta.

Other voluntary efforts outside the hospital involve no direct contact with the patients at all. Some individuals and groups make their contribution to the recreation program in the form of materials and supplies rather than direct participation. Some examples are the special interest cooking group of the women's club who provide home-made birthday cakes each month; the 4H Club boys who make playing card holders for patients with one arm in a cast; the lawyer whose hobby is carpentry and who constructs a cart for transporting movie equipment from one ward to another; the local merchants who provide a supply of small items to be used as prizes at a hospital carnival.

The professional therapeutic recreator may at times need assistance of a technical nature, and resources for this are also available. Some states have a state Recreation Commission or some other state-wide consultation service in recreation upon which the recreator may call for consultation on special problems. In some states, the Department of Mental Health maintains a central office which includes on the staff supervisory personnel capable of giving consultative assistance to the recreation personnel in the state hospitals. The American Red Cross has in each of its area offices one or more recreation consultants who give professional assistance to the recreation workers in the military hospitals throughout the area.

The recreator may also turn to local agencies for technical assistance and information. An inexperienced person working in a hospital may consult the community recreation professionals on technical matters in recreation programing. Persons at work in local health agencies can provide valuable information to assist the recreator in understanding the nature of various diseases and disabilities. For the therapeutic recreator working in the community recreation program, such agencies as the welfare department, the visiting nurses association, and the schools are excellent resources for locating the disabled in the community and getting them involved in the recreation program.

Most communities have some kind of health and welfare council. This too is an excellent source for information and consultation.

Because patients' recreation interests are wide and varied, the recreator may find that the best sources of advice and assistance in providing some activities are not necessarily other recreators or medical personnel, but experts in the field of interest. The proprietor of a billiard parlor can give excellent advice on the care of the hospital's pool table; a professional music teacher can help in setting up a record collection for the patients; the local radio and television sports broadcasters, the public librarian, the physical education teacher, and many others can be excellent sources of information in their fields.

Facilities

Recreation denotes some kind of activity, and activity requires facilities—areas in which the activity takes place, sometimes a means of getting to the area, and often equipment or supplies with which to carry out the activity. The same general types of spaces and equipment are needed for therapeutic recreation as for any other recreation program. Certain emphases and modifications are indicated, however, and are discussed here.

Areas

Areas for recreation conducted within a hospital vary greatly, depending on the physical structure of the hospital and on the kinds of patients it houses. Unlike the community recreator, the therapeutic recreator often must take the recreation activity to the patient rather than have the patient come to the activity. A good many patients, either by their physical condition or by hospital regulations, are restricted in their movements to an area very near their beds. For the patient whose movement is highly restricted—a person in neck traction, the victim of a severe heart attack, the post-operative patient—the recreator has only the area immediately surrounding the patient's bed available for recreation activity. Or the area may be a private or semi-private room. Some hospitals have a number of small rooms opening onto a long corridor, with perhaps an open space or lounge area at the end of the corridor. This area is often used for recreation activities, especially in the evenings when other hospital activity has subsided. Other hospitals have sun rooms or porches connected to each ward or floor, within easy reach of the patients. These areas too are used frequently for recreation activities which are brought to the patients. Patient lounges and reading or TV rooms provided on each floor or ward in some hospitals are excellent recreation areas.

Hospitals having patients who are ambulatory, that is, able to move about by walking, on crutches, or in wheelchairs, usually have some special recreation areas. Such facilities vary greatly from hospital to hospital. The facilities may include a central recreation hall suitable for social activities, games, entertainment, dances, and so on. In some hospitals, and particularly in nursing homes, the central dining room is cleared for recreation activities between and after meals. Some of the larger hospitals, particularly the state and federal ones, have a number of areas designated for specific recreation activities, such as a library, music rooms, a gymnasium, craft shop, children's play room, and theater.

Outdoor areas suitable for recreation activity are more readily available in some hospitals than in others. Large single structure hospitals in a congested metropolitan area tend to have limited space for outdoor recreation. On the other hand, some hospitals have extensive outdoor areas, including picnic areas, beach areas, tennis courts, day camp areas, swimming pools, and golf courses. The need for and provision of more or less extensive outdoor recreation facilities depends, of course, on the kinds of patients the hospital serves and the financial resources of the institution.

The recreator who includes in the program trips away from the hospital should consider all the community areas to which trips are taken as available recreation facilities. Also the therapeutic recreator who works with the ill and disabled in the community setting rather than in hospitals should consider all community recreation areas available for these persons, insofar as they are accessible. This specialist should not limit his program to such areas, however. Like the hospital worker, he may, at times, have to take the recreation activities to the disabled person in his home, or to groups of persons in a specially designated place which the disabled persons can easily reach and in which they can function.

Accessibility

The therapeutic recreator necessarily must have greater concern for the accessibility of recreation areas than does the general recreation administrator. Restricted mobility is a characteristic of a large percent of the ill or disabled. In hospitals, as mentioned above, patients with limited strength need to have recreation areas near their beds, so that their strength will not be used up just getting to the activity. Even central recreation areas for the ambulatory patient should be strategically located so as to be easily accessible. For instance, a recreation hall near the dining room makes it easy for the patient to have two pleasant experiences during one trip away from his room. And the way from all bed areas to all recreation areas should be clear—elevators or ramps in place of steps for crutch and wheelchair patients, hard surface paths out of doors, covered walkways from building to building for inclement weather, wide doorways, proper direction signals for the hard of hearing and partially sighted or blind.

One might assume that such considerations are automatically taken into account in the construction of hospitals, but such is not always the case, particularly in institutions built some years ago, and in those which have added recreation services some time after the buildings were built.

The problem of accessibility of buildings and facilities to the physically disabled has been studied extensively, particularly in connection with public buildings which disabled persons residing outside the hospital might need or want to use. With the sponsorship of the President's Committee on Employment of the Physically Handicapped and the National Easter Seal Society for Crippled Children and Adults, and under the auspices of the American Standards Association, a set of standard specifications was developed in 1961 titled, "Making Buildings and Facilities Accessible to, and Usable by, the Physically Handicapped." This document gives the American standard specifications for site development and buildings including grading, walks, parking lots, ramps with gradients, entrances, doors and doorways, stairs, floors, toilet rooms, water fountains, public telephones, elevators, controls, identification, warning signals, and avoidance of hazards. The use of these standards by both community and hospital recreation administrators in designing or remodeling facilities greatly increases the opportunity for the handicapped to participate in recreation activities.

Not only is getting into a building or recreation area of concern to the handicapped, but getting to the area also often requires help. This has been discussed above in connection with hospital recreation areas. The ill and disabled residing in the community find that transportation problems present a distinct barrier to participation in recreation activities. Thus transportation facilities are of major importance to the recreator. In large operations such as the Rehabilitation-Education Division for disabled students at the University of Illinois, specially adapted buses with hydraulic lifts for raising wheelchairs into the bus are used to transport students around the campus and on recreation and athletic trips. Other agencies have specially adapted station wagons or other vehicles. Some agencies have a corp of volunteers who use their private automobiles to transport patients and the disabled to recreation events. Other agencies have arrangements with local taxi companies for reduced rates for disabled persons.

Although mentally ill and mentally retarded persons may have no difficulty getting in and out of conventional vehicles, arranging for their transportation to and from recreation areas still is often a responsibility of the therapeutic recreator, as these persons are ill equipped to cope with the maneuvers involved in public transportation.

Equipment and Supplies

Equipment needed to operate a therapeutic recreation program is fundamentally the same as that needed to operate any general recreation program. A sound administrative principle to keep in mind is that facilities and equipment are a means to an end, and not an end in themselves. They should be considered not as physical exhibits, but rather as tools necessary to provide recreation opportunities for the patients. Thus the equipment needed will depend on the type of patients using the equipment, i.e., physically disabled, mentally affected, children, aged, etc., the type of program that is indicated for the group of participants concerned, and the average length of hospitalization.

In a hospital, it is likely that more equipment for quiet, less strenuous activities will be needed than would be true in a community program. In a hospital such as a tuberculosis sanitarium there is greater need for equipment and supplies that are disposable. Mental hospitals require equipment with minimum opportunity for personal injury.

It is obvious that some equipment needs to be adapted for use by the handicapped. Equipment should not be adapted unless it is absolutely necessary or impossible for the handicapped person to use it as it is. For example, there is no need to lower baskets in order to conduct a wheelchair basketball game. Archery, billiards, and ping pong do not require adaptation in the equipment for wheelchair persons to play. But wheel blocks made for wheelchairs enable bowling to be done from the chair. Prism glasses enable a person to read comfortably while lying flat on his back. Pillow speakers are used in connection with television and radio, so that the sound can be heard only by the individual using the radio or television without disturbing room or ward mates.

Special or adapted equipment is most successful when it is tailored to the needs of individual patients. The recreator may find it helpful to seek assistance in developing adapted equipment from his colleagues in the occupational therapy and the physical therapy departments. It may be found that adjustive devices fitted to the patient, of which the prosthesis is the classic example, are more effective than adapting the equipment that he uses.

One may also consider the feasibility of adapting the rules of the game, or the way a recreation activity is carried out rather than changing the equipment. Changes in rules of play for basketball played in wheelchairs have been carefully worked out and are available from the National Wheelchair Basketball Association.

Whether the adaptation be applied to the person, the equipment, or the rules of the game, the therapeutic recreator should take great care to see to it that the essence of the recreative experience remains in the activity. The authors have found that patients would rather play a genuine game of checkers, for instance, than an adapted, watered-down game of baseball which retains none of the physical challenge or lively competition of a real game.

In summary, the principles applied to the acquisition and provision of facilities for recreation in general may be used as a basis for judging the adequacy of facilities for the ill or disabled. Such principles need to be augmented in some respects to apply most advantageously to therapeutic recreation, as follows:

Location

Recreation facilities should be located near the patient or client's living area—whether in the hospital or the community—to eliminate difficult travel.

Consideration should be given to placing recreation facilities near other facilities used by the patients, again to reduce unneeded travel.

Appropriate facilities should be located outdoors as well as indoors, in treatment centers as well as in the community.

Size

Recreation areas should be of sufficient size to allow for the extra space needed for wheelchair and crutch maneuvering.

Adequate space should be provided for privacy when it is desired, especially in an institutional setting.

Arrangement

In addition to being planned for functional use, recreation facilities should be integrated with the planning of facilities for the remainder of the treatment center, and designed for multiple use. For instance, a swimming pool can have both therapeutic and recreative use.

Facilities should be arranged for easy communication between the leader and participants. The immobility of bed patients, the lack of sight or hearing, and other characteristics of the ill or disabled which increase the difficulty of supervision and control should be considered in the planning of facilities.

Accessibility

Recreation areas and facilities should be accessible to the disabled. It matters little how elaborate, comprehensive, or functional the facilities are if the ill or disabled cannot get to them. The standards set forth by the American Standards Association should be applied.

Appearance

The facilities should be esthetically pleasing and physically comfortable. This is especially important in residential institutions where residents' living and treatment areas tend to be designed for efficiency and antisepsis.

Safety

The normal standards for safety and health should be rigidly applied, and augmented as necessary to accommodate the restricted movements, lowered mental alertness, or weakened physical condition of those who are ill or disabled.

Financial and Legal Resources

Resources for personnel, space, equipment, and other facilities depend to a great extent on the financial resources available to the institution or agency offering recreation services to the ill or disabled:

If a therapeutic recreation service is to be broad and effective, it does require well-based financial support. It is a mistake to assume that recreation services can be provided in a treatment center or elsewhere without the expenditure of money.

With few exceptions, the therapeutic recreator is seldom called upon to carry heavy budgetary and financial responsibilities. This is especially true in treatment centers which are part of a large system, as would be the case in state hospitals or veterans hospital.

In the smaller treatment centers, the budget responsibilities may be somewhat different, and more extensive. Very often, the therapeutic recreator's budget responsibilities begin and end with making budget estimates for his program, seeing to it that funds allocated to him are spent efficiently, and making appropriate financial recommendations as they may be related to the recreation program.[4]

There are a number of different funding patterns in use in various types of hospitals. One system found in some private and voluntary hospitals is a direct charge to the patients for Activity Therapy Services—a certain amount per day from private-room patients and a lesser amount from ward-care patients—from which the Recreation Department receives a certain percentage.

In most tax-supported hospitals the recreation department is financially supported from the hospital's general funds, as all departments are. In military hospitals, the recreation program is supported by the American National Red Cross, which derives its funds from voluntary contributions from the American people. Each hospital unit receives an allocation for expenditures based on a designated amount per patient per month.

It is probably safe to say that most hospital recreation programs derive financial support from a variety of sources. Eastern State Hospital, Lexington, Kentucky, may serve as an example. The recreation department has two major budgets for expenditures from the general hospital funds: the operating budget which provides for equipment and supplies, and the personnel budget which controls number of personnel and their salaries. There is in addition a miscellaneous food account providing for party refreshments. Based on his best estimation of needs, the recreation director submits a budget request periodically as required by the hospital administration. In addition, the recreation department has available certain funds for special equipment from the profits made in the hospital canteen. From time to time restricted donations are received from interested individuals or groups outside the hospital, and are used in the recreation program for the purposes designated by the donor.

It should be noted that many services, supplies, and equipment used by a recreation department in a hospital do not appear on the department budget at all, as they do in an independent agency or department. These include repairs to equipment, use of vehicles, telephone service and other utilities, office furniture and equipment, custodial services, and others.

Voluntary contributions of funds for the welfare of patients are often stimulated and coordinated, as Cannon points out, by a

structured group such as a hospital auxiliary, hospital guild, or hospital community council whose prime function is usually the coordination of community resources, in terms of material and funds, which help meet hospital needs and augment the hospital budget. . . . The fund raising activity may be carried on entirely in the community through bazaars, balls, or special projects, such as thrift shops and benefits. Fund raising projects are sometimes operated within the hospital, for example: TV rental, baby photos, snack bars, and gift shops.[5]

Civic and fraternal groups such as the Elks, Shriners, or Lions Club may adopt as a special project the provision of funds or special equipment for a hospital. These groups, as well as private foundations, are also often interested in helping to sponsor recreation programs for the handicapped in the community. For example, the Joseph P. Kennedy, Jr. Foundation assists communities and private and public local agencies by supplying funds for such demonstration projects as camps for the mentally retarded. The Lions Clubs have sponsored recreation events and functions for the blind for a long period of time.

There is a growing tendency for private, state, and federal agencies to encourage the establishment of recreation programs and services for the ill and disabled in local communities by providing "seed money." These funds are provided so that the need and value of the program can be tested before the local agency takes up the full financial responsibility. Sometimes the grant carries the stipulation that matching funds be provided by the receiving agency to ensure seriousness of intent to carry through the program.

Public recreation administrators and directors of community voluntary agencies who are interested in extending their services to the special population of the disabled might look into the possibilities of assistance to be obtained through cooperative action with other agencies dealing with the disabled. Financial, technical, and advisory assistance offered by both state and federal government in a number of areas might very well be utilized to expand the recreative living of the disabled. These areas include education, programs for the aging, poverty programs, mental health, rehabilitation, and others.

An examination of the current legislation in any state would probably reveal little in the way of specific directives concerning recreation for the ill or disabled. Although there seem to be virtually no laws directly related to recreation with the ill or disabled, a study of legislation in the areas of health, education, and welfare does indicate that the intent of the law is to assist rather than restrict the life and activity of the disabled or handicapped. For instance, a "Facilities for the Handicapped Act" passed by the Seventy-fifth General Assembly of the State of Illinois requires that construction or remodeling of all public accommodations must meet the standard specifications for accessibility and use of the physically disabled.

An example of legislative encouragement of therapeutic recreation is found in the standards set for nursing homes receiving Medicare patients. Approved homes are required to provide programs of "activities," including recreation.

In another area, the Bureau of Outdoor Recreation of the Department of the Interior has made some specific statements about recreation for the handicapped. The following excerpts are found in a Technical Assistance Bulletin published by the Bureau:

> The Bureau of Outdoor Recreation requires that all comprehensive statewide outdoor recreation plans, prepared as a prerequisite to State participation in the Land

and Water Conservation Fund Program, consider needs of the handicapped. The Bureau recognizes that the disabled must be given special consideration if they are to enjoy benefits of the out-of-doors. States and localities are urged, therefore, to consider the needs of the handicapped in both planning and administering programs relating to outdoor recreation.[6]

It seems likely that the meager amount of legislative action concerned with recreation for the ill and disabled is due to the fact that there has been little pioneer effort to establish such programs in communities outside the special schools and hospitals. As more communities expand their recreation programs to include the disabled, no doubt the need for specific legislation will arise as problems related to the lack of such legislation present themselves. Communities sharing the same problems can then join forces to press for laws which will help them and other communities throughout the state.[7]

Notes Chapter 10

1. Madolin E. Cannon, "Volunteer Services," *Modern Concepts of Hospital Administration*, Joseph K. Owen, ed. (Philadelphia: S. W. Saunders Co.), Chapter 35, p. 519.

2. *Ibid.*, pp. 502-520.

3. Helen Padula, "Functions of Volunteer Services—in Specific Pre-Discharge Planning" (proceedings of Technical Assistance Conference held at Allenberry Inn, Boiling Springs, Pennsylvania, April 17-19, 1961).

4. Charles K. Brightbill (from unpublished private papers).

5. Madolin Cannon, *op. cit.*, p. 504.

6. *Outdoor Recreation Planning for the Handicapped* (Superintendent of Documents, United States Government Printing Office, Washington, D. C., 1967), p. 2.

7. The intercommunity program concept, exemplified by the Northern Suburban Special Recreation Association cited in Chapter 9, was given legal authority in Illinois by State Senate Bills 745 and 746 which amended the Park District Code and the Municipality Code to permit districts to join together to provide recreation programs for handicapped children.

Part IV | LOOKING AHEAD

11 | Directions In Research

AS WE LOOK ahead in the field of therapeutic recreation, it is highly probable that we will see research increasing in importance and utilization. Evidence of such a trend can be found in an examination of the research studies done in colleges and universities by students fulfilling the requirements for graduate degrees.[1] In the past twenty years (1950-1970) more than four times as many studies were completed concerning therapeutic recreation and closely related topics than were done in the previous thirty years. And one third of all such studies in the last fifty years have been completed since 1963.

Financial backing of the federal government, expressed in its willingness, through the Bureau of Education for the Handicapped, to support research and development centers for recreation for the handicapped child, indicates the value being placed on this area of the profession. Reports of studies conducted by professional therapeutic recreators in their field of endeavor are finding their way into the professional journals of other disciplines. Further, research efforts are not limited to persons in the academic world. Contributions to research are being made by practitioners in hospitals and treatment centers and community programs, and are being reported to their fellow practitioners and others through professional journals.

The purpose of this chapter is to discuss the importance of research to all recreation people working with the ill and disabled, and ways in which these people may become involved in the research process.

Purpose of Research in the Practice of Therapeutic Recreation

Research is the systematic investigation of a subject in order to discover facts—to gain new knowledge. In order for any discipline to become truly a profession, there must be built up a body of knowledge distinct and peculiar to that discipline.

Through historical studies, research tells us in a reliable and logical way what has gone on in the past as a foundation for the present and future. Carefully conducted surveys and status studies tell us the truth about what currently is, or is going on. Research which follows the scientific method gives us facts about the relations among natural phenomena which may be used to predict and control behavior.

The true value of research lies in the ways in which the results of research are used. The knowledge gained through research in therapeutic recreation should be available to, and usable by, the practitioner to the ultimate benefit of those ill and disabled persons whom he serves. It is, of course, true that many artful recreators practice their profession quite successfully largely by intuition. But intuitive action becomes more reliable when it is backed up by facts.

Research information can give the practitioner a more sound basis for his choice of activity and behavior with his clients than assumptions alone can do. Objective systematic inquiry may reveal reasons for the success or failure of various programs and processes quite different from those which had been assumed. Research findings properly interpreted and applied can give the recreator some assurance that he is indeed doing what he *intends* to do. And certain kinds of research are vitally necessary for solving a variety of problems which have remained insoluble by experience or random experimentation.

Kinds of Studies Useful to the Therapeutic Recreator

The therapeutic recreator looking for completed studies that may help him better understand his clients or solve his problems will find a variety of types of research studies.

Until recent years, the great majority of studies relied on the survey method, and resulted in detailed and important descriptions of the situations being studied. Surveys have been made along many lines, such as camping facilities for handicapped children;[2] the use of volunteer music entertainment in hospitals;[3] the leisure needs of the aged;[4] transportation systems for physically disabled;[5] training practices for therapeutic recreators;[6] leisure activities of the deaf;[7] adapted equipment used by orthopedically handicapped;[8] day care centers for mentally retarded children;[9] recreation opportunities available in the community for the disabled;[10] interests of selected mental patients;[11] recreation background of selected patients;[12] planned programs of aquatics for the handicapped;[13] recreation sources in state institutions;[14] dance therapy among selected mental patients;[15] and so on.

A number of studies have also been conducted which demonstrate the possibility and effectiveness of new programs or techniques. Examples of this type of study include one on the effect of a group discussion program in a home for the aged on the participants' behavior patterns,[16] another on a recreation program for the conduct disorder child,[17] another on the therapeutic use of creative drama with children presenting behavior problems,[18] and one on a community referral program for arthritis and rheumatism subjects.[19]

Certain other studies have been undertaken for the purpose of developing program designs, procedures, and/or manuals, such as a program design for the mental hospitals in the Philippines;[20] the formulation of a drama activities program in a mental hospital;[21] guidelines for programs designed to assist blind children in integrating into non-segregated programs;[22] procedures for conducting rhythm activities on mental wards;[23] procedures for teaching the paralyzed child to swim;[24] a manual for counselors at a camp for the blind;[25] and a planning project for the development of recreation services in rehabilitation centers.[26]

Other studies have adhered to the scientific method a bit more stringently in order to make useful comparisons between phenomena, to discover relationships, and determine the effects of designated variables. Examples of such studies include a comparison of the characteristics of the play of retarded and average children with mother present and absent;[27] the relationship of various play activities to the spontaneous speech sounds of deaf children;[28] the effect of activity group experience on social and emotional adjustment of mentally defective boys;[29] an experimental investigation in rhythm involvement of institutionalized mongoloid children;[30] and comparative play and apparatus usage patterns of Down's Syndrome children.[31]

The examples of research cited above relate directly to recreation with the ill and disabled. Research findings useful to the therapeutic recreator are not confined to those with a primary focus on the ill and disabled, however. Investigation is being conducted related to many problems in the broad field of recreation—programing, activities, the psychological, physical, social effects of leisure, resources for leisure activity, leadership and administrative personnel, and numerous other aspects of the field. The knowledge gained from these studies and investigations can often be applied to the problems arising in therapeutic recreation as well.

Nor should the recreator confine his attention to studies in his own field. Because recreation embraces such a vast range of human activity, almost any of its components may be of interest to various other sciences or disciplines. Much research that is useful to the recreator can thus be found in areas such as physiology, physical education, psychology, sociology, music, art, drama, anthropology, education, and social work. Additionally, and of more specific value to the therapeutic recreator, are selected studies in the fields of medicine, rehabilitation, occupational therapy, music therapy, physical therapy, art therapy, and psychiatry.[32]

Where Research is Conducted and the Results Found

It is possible for research in and related to therapeutic recreation to be carried on almost anywhere ill or disabled people are available. In reality, there are a number of factors which tend to confine the majority of research efforts to a few types of locations. Colleges and universities continue to produce the greatest quantity of research by virtue of:

1. The positive attitude toward the importance of research that prevails in graduate schools.
2. The concentration of expertise in research principles and techniques found in colleges and universities.
3. The resources available in the way of library holdings, computer facilities, and the like.
4. The time made available to students and faculty for research activity.
5. The financial support from federal agencies and foundations that is traditionally granted to colleges and universities for research.

Research institutes, particularly those devoted to medicine and rehabilitation, are another important source. To a lesser extent, the staff of treatment centers, especially rehabilitation centers, teaching hospitals, and the like, are conducting studies, experiments, and investigations both in recreation per se and on an interdisciplinary basis.

National and federal agencies, foundations, and associations, interested in various aspects of recreation or illness and disability, from time to time actively engage in research projects as well as provide financial support for research to be conducted in universities and other institutions.

Most recently research activity concerned with therapeutic recreation has begun to emerge in community settings. These are studies being conducted in most cases by therapeutic recreation specialists in municipal recreation departments and voluntary agencies which are engaged in providing some recreation services for the non-institutionalized ill and disabled residing in the community.

A complaint often voiced by practitioners is that the reports of research find their way only to the shelves of university libraries and seldom come to the attention of practitioners in the field who might benefit from the findings. In this respect, the editorial staffs of the several professional journals published by the National Recreation and Park Association have attempted to bring to the attention of its membership selected reports of research activity. One, the *Journal of Leisure Research*, is devoted exclusively to this. The *Therapeutic Recreation Journal* includes a section, "Research Digest," in each issue, and others of its articles often report or refer to investigative studies as well. The professional journals of societies in other closely related fields present for their readers research reports in their own fields. The recreator will find in these journals from time to time a study of considerable interest and application to therapeutic recreation.[32]

Unfortunately, the majority of research studies are never published. Most masters theses and many doctoral dissertations do indeed find a final resting place on a college library shelf. Yet the practitioner should know that these studies *are* available, at least on loan. A monumental work completed in 1969 by Betty van der Smissen and Donald Joyce is entitled *Bibliography of Theses and Dissertations in Recreation, Parks, Camping and Outdoor Education.* This compilation lists nearly four thousand studies completed in the last fifty years, with brief descriptions of some. A good many of these theses and dissertations are available on interlibrary loan. Van der Smissen reports also that, "almost all doctoral studies in the last ten years and some of the masters studies may be purchased either on microfilm or microcard."[33]

Studies that are funded by federal government agencies, foundations, or other national voluntary agencies are usually reported to the sponsoring agency when completed. Quite often copies of these reports may be obtained merely on request to the sponsoring agency.

The problem of dissemination and interpretation of research findings in the field of therapeutic recreation is recognized by the Bureau of Education for the Handicapped. One of the major functions of the proposed national research and development centers mentioned above would be that of bridging the gap between research and practice. As these centers become operational, practitioners may anticipate wider and wider acquaintance with the work of researchers and more opportunity to apply their findings to the actual practice of therapeutic recreation.

The Use of Research

Another complaint sometimes voiced by practitioners is that the findings of much of the research that is being conducted do not apply to the everyday operation of therapeutic recreation programs. It is true that not many research studies can be lifted *in toto* and fit down snugly over a field situation. Researchers are required to be scrupulously honest in stating the limitations of their studies—the population or geographic area under study, the extent of testing or questioning, and so on—and to be very cautious about making generalized statements based on their findings. But the practitioner is free to make creative use of research findings in his own work, and in many cases may draw from several different studies to reinforce or supplement his ideas.

As an example a recreator in a mental hospital may be looking for assistance in determing the value of recreation to his patients, and in determining what activities will have the most beneficial effect. Some suggestions as to the kinds of activities and the timing of their presentation that were found effective may be found in Thomas McConahey's study. By means of a controlled experimental study, he concluded that

(1) In planning an active recreation program with long-term, schizophrenic female patients, beginning activities should be selected that are more individual in nature. Those activities of a more complex nature that require cooperation and socialization should be added to the program gradually.

(2) A planned active recreation program will improve the hospital adjustment of long-term, schizophrenic female patients. (Activities offered the experimental group were arts and crafts, dance, drama, literary, mental and linguistic activities, music, social recreation, sports and games, nature, discussion, evaluation and planning, and special events.)

(3) Long-term, schizophrenic female patients who participate only in a mass activity program will show a decline in hospital adjustment over a period of months.[34]

Although McConahey's study involved only women, the possibility that the same findings might also apply to men certainly warrants some attention.

Further help for determining what activities may be most beneficial to individual mental patients is found in Martin Meyer's study. Again, by means of a controlled experiment, he concluded that patients having a recreation program that is based on their experience and participation in recreation before the onset of their illness and hospitalization show a more favorable change in behavior than patients participating in recreation activities not participated in during their pre-morbid days.[35]

Another study which offers successful methods and techniques for using play as a learning and developmental process in the management of psychotic children is one conducted by David Park.[36] And should the recreator be interested in knowing the specific effects of specific activities or specific components of activities, he could examine such studies as the one completed by Donald Warder on the responses hospitalized psychotic patients have made to specific music tempos.[37]

Because human behavior is complex, and the forces which affect it are constantly shifting and changing, the recreator must not expect the findings of any one research study to hold true forever. As research in recreation continues and expands, new information will supersede the old, some "hunches" will be proved, others disproved, and some studies will seem to contradict others. The practitioner should not be discouraged but should use research in the way it is intended—to serve as a guide and a catalyst and not as the final answer.

The Practitioner's Responsibility and Opportunity to Participate in Research

Unlike certain of the long established sciences and professions, the field of therapeutic recreation has as yet very few people who are working full time in research. This accounts, in part, for the very modest size of the "body of knowledge" in this profession. Another factor is that the majority of studies have been undertaken by graduate students who, after completing their degree requirements, relinquish some of their enthusiasm for scientific investigation. Recreation practitioners seemingly are particularly reluctant to undertake serious investigations on their own in a proper research study—and rightfully so, perhaps. Certainly one needs to have some preparation and training in the methods of scientific investigation if one expects to gain valid knowledge through research.

But there are several ways in which practitioners can, and should, become involved in the research efforts of their profession. The suggestions below are directed primarily to the therapeutic recreation practitioner:

1. Be curious. Don't accept without question those phenomena in your day to day job operations that you don't understand or don't like. Ask why.
2. Clarify the question or the problem. Extract single specific questions to be answered. Research methods are designed to deal with a clearly stated hypothesis and to accept or reject it according to analysis of the data presented.
3. Get professional help. Many experienced researchers in recreation, or in other behavioral or social sciences, are quite willing to examine a question or problem that is clearly stated, and to advise on methods for undertaking appropriate research.
4. Learn research language. Perusal of an introductory text dealing with social science research will help the practitioner to clarify his own presentation of a problem, to accept and understand the assistance offered by the professional researcher, and to understand the published reports of completed studies.
5. In many instances it may be entirely inappropriate for the practitioner to undertake the investigation of the questions he himself raises. If they are legitimate questions, however, and ones that have some possibility of being generalized (that is, that do not apply only to a single situation or location) the questions might be presented to graduate schools or research centers as suggestions for research topics. Students, particularly, are on the look-out for researchable problems, and those that come directly from current real-life situations tend to have the relevancy that appeals to students.
6. Cooperate with researchers. Even though the practitioner may not initiate or conduct a particular research study, he may be of enormous help to the researcher by virtue of his relationship to the subjects or the situations being investigated. The practitioner may assume considerable responsibility in the collection of data.
7. Be alert to larger comprehensive studies being conducted in the area. The therapeutic recreator can occasionally get information for himself and his practice by "plugging into" a larger study. For instance, a comprehensive survey of the recreational interests and attitudes of a community will probably be conducted by means of a questionnaire. Questions relating to the ill and disabled populations may easily be included in the questionnaire, and resulting data can be processed by computer along with the rest of the study.
8. Be alert also to interdisciplinary studies being conducted in your institution or community. Don't wait for someone else to ask you to become in-

volved. Be alert to any possible relationship of recreation and its facets to the subject of the study, and suggest appropriate involvement. Members of the other disciplines, as well as recreation, may be grateful for additional findings they had not anticipated.

9. Let your colleagues know the results of your research efforts. Any new knowledge should be shared with one's fellow recreators, and with people in related professions. Some of the means of dissemination were listed previously. There are few things more professionally stimulating than communicating with persons engaged in similar efforts beyond one's own institution or community, and sharing exciting new knowledge, experiences, and successes with them.

Notes, Chapter 11

1. Betty van der Smissen and Donald V. Joyce, eds., *Bibliography of Theses and Dissertations in Recreation, Parks, Camping and Outdoor Education*, (Washington, D.C.: National Recreation and Park Association, 1970).

2. Ralph R. Collins, "A Survey of Camping Facilities Available to Handicapped Children in Selected Camps in New England" (Masters thesis, Boston University, 1956).

3. Erleta Covalt, "A Survey and Evaluation of Volunteer Music Entertainment and its Influence on Patients' Behavior at Winter Veterans Administration Hospital" (Masters thesis, University of Kansas, 1958).

4. Janet Lillian Fearn, "The Leisure Time Needs of the Aged" (Masters thesis, University of Toronto, 1964).

5. Gilbert L. Fink, "A Study of the Development and Operation of a Transportation System for Severely Permanently Physically Disabled Students at the University of Illinois" (Masters thesis, University of Illinois, 1962).

6. Vivian P. Griffith, "Current Training Practices for Hospital Recreation Workers" (Masters Thesis, West Virginia University, 1954).

7. Robert M. Knapp, "Leisure-time Activities of the Deaf in Spokane, Washington" (Masters thesis, Washington State University, 1954).

8. Patricia Ann Krenzke, "A Study of Adapted Equipment for the Use of the Orthopedically Handicapped in Sports and Games" (Masters thesis, University of Illinois, 1963).

9. Edward L. La Cross, "A Survey of ARC Sponsored Day Care Centers for Mentally Retarded Children in the United States: A Guide for Future and Present Programs" (Doctoral dissertation, Columbia University, 1964).

10. Martha L. Peters, *Recreation for the Ill and Disabled in Illinois* (Recreation and Park Field Service, University of Illinois, 1967).

11. Lee Edward Meyer, "A Study of the Free-time Experiences and Interests of Twenty-eight Selected Mental Patients" (Masters thesis, University of Illinois, 1965).

12. Martha L. Peters, "A Study of the Recreational Background of 200 Air Force Hospital Patients" (Masters thesis, University of Illinois, 1963).

13. Barbara Ann Potts, "A Survey of Ten American National-Red-Cross-directed programs of Aquatics for the Handicapped and Disabled" (Masters thesis, University of Texas, 1955).

14. Joan Ramm, "A Survey of Recreation Sources in State Institutions for the Mentally Retarded in the United States" (Masters thesis, University of North Carolina at Chapel Hill, 1967).

15. Sondra Zeretsky, "A Survey of Dance Therapy Among Selected Mental Hospitals in the United States" (Masters thesis, University of Illinois, 1957).

16. Wendell Dean Mason, "The Effect of a Group Discussion Program in a Home for the Aged on the Behavior Patterns of the Participants" (Doctoral dissertation, Indiana University, 1964).

17. J. Glavin and Peter Witt, "Recreation for the Conduct Disorder Child" (from Annual Report, Motor Performance and Play Research Laboratory, University of Illinois, 1968).

18. Neith Williamson, "The Therapeutic Use of Creative Drama with Children Presenting Behavior Problems" (Masters thesis, University of Denver, 1946).

19. Rodney Valentine, et al, "A Community Recreation Referral Program" (The Arthritis and Rheumatism Foundation Eastern Pennsylvania Chapter Recreation Pilot Project Report, 1965).

20. Thelma Suzia Castillon, "Program Design for the Mental Hospital and Other Types of Hospitals in the Philippines" (Masters thesis, University of North Carolina at Chapel Hill, 1964).

21. Philip B. Harris, "The Formulation and Direction of a Drama Activities Program in a Mental Hospital" (Masters thesis, University of Kansas, 1963).

22. Edward J. Kramer, "To Develop Guidelines to Assist Specialized Agencies Serving Blind Children to Establish Programs That Will Prepare the Participants to Move into Non-segregated Programs" (Masters thesis, New York University, 1968).

23. Richard Graham, "Suggested Procedures for Conducting Rhythm Activities on Wards of Chronic and Regressed Mental Patients" (Masters thesis, University of Kansas, 1958).

24. Ella Rachel Cabaniss, "Procedures Used in Teaching a Paralyzed Child to Swim" (Masters thesis, University of Alabama, 1944).

25. Lamitsoi Bright-Davies, "A Manual for Counselors at Vacation Camp and Dormitory for the Blind" (Masters thesis, School of Social Work, Columbia University, 1953).

26. Doris L. Berryman, et al, "Planning Project for the Development of Recreation Services in Rehabilitation Centers," *Therapeutic Recreation Journal*, Vol. II, No. 3, (Third Quarter, 1968).

27. Gridth U. Ablon, "Comparison of the Characteristics of the Play of Young Mildly Retarded and Average Children, with Mother Present and Absent" (Doctoral dissertation, Western Reserve University, 1967).

28. Edris L. McCarty, "The Relationship of Various Play Activities to the Spontaneous Speech Sounds of Five-year-old Deaf Children" (Masters thesis, University of Kansas, 1954).

29. Jason W. McCallum, "The Effect of Activity Group Experience on Social and Emotional Adjustment of Mentally Defective Boys" (Masters thesis, University of Toronto, 1954).

30. Marilyn D. Tavares, "An Experimental Investigation in Rhythmic Movement of Institutionalized Mongoloid Children" (Masters thesis, Ohio State University, 1958).

31. Anthony Linford, et al., "Comparative Play and Apparatus Usage Patterns of Down's Syndrome Children" (Annual Report of Motor Performance and Play Research Laboratory, University of Illinois, 1969).

32. Reference is made to publications such as the following: *American Journal of Mental Deficiency*, published bi-monthly by the American Association on Mental Deficiency, Albany, New York; *American Journal of Art Therapy*, published quarterly by The American Art Therapy Association, Washington, D.C.; *The American Journal of Occupational Therapy*, published in eight issues annually by the American Occupational Therapy Association, New York, New York; *Journal of Music Therapy*, published quarterly by the National Association for Music Therapy, Lawrence, Kansas.

33. van der Smissen, *op. cit.*, p. iii.

34. Thomas M. McConahey, "The Effect of an Active Recreation Program on Selected Mentally Ill Female Patients at Cambridge State Hospital" (Doctoral dissertation, Indiana University, 1965).

35. Martin W. Meyer, "The Influence of Recreation Participation upon the Behavior of Schizophrenic Patients" (Doctoral dissertation, New York University, 1955).

36. David C. Park, "Recreation in the Group Treatment of Psychotic Children—a Descriptive Study of Methods and Techniques" (Masters thesis, University of North Carolina at Chapel Hill, 1967).

37. Donald S. Warder, "Response to Specific Music Tempos by Hospitalized Psychotic Patients" (Masters thesis, Purdue University, 1966).

12 | Issues and Trends

Transitions

AN OVERVIEW OF therapeutic recreation as an area of professional service will be aided by looking at some of the transitions or directions of change that have occurred in this facet of the total recreation movement in the United States. Transitions that can readily be identified include movement or development:

1. From support largely by voluntary agencies to governmental (public) as well as voluntary agency support

2. From identification in terms of setting, i.e., hospital recreation, to identification in terms of persons to be served, i.e., recreation with the ill or disabled, or in terms of process, i.e., therapeutic recreation

3. From a concept of service to patients to a concept of services to ill or disabled people including so-called "special populations" such as disadvantaged, aged, etc.

4. From insecurity and controversy concerning the relationships of recreation to treatment or therapy toward more rational examination of therapeutic processes that may be possible through recreative experiences

5. From concepts of recreation in relation to treatment to concepts of leisure habilitation and rehabilitation
6. From settings limited largely to federal and state institutions to an expanding variety of types of public and private institutions and treatment centers as well as to general community and non-treatment settings
7. From a lack of professional identity and standards to professional association at state and national levels and a national program of voluntary registration
8. From a need to establish separate identity to a search for bases of relatedness, e.g., with other disciplines such as occupational therapy, social group work, and physical therapy, as well as with the total field of recreation
9. From separation from public and community recreation to integration with it
10. From no professional fellowship organization, to multiplication of organizations and fragmentation of affiliations, to progress toward professional unity
11. From no specific educational preparation to undergraduate emphasis and graduate specialization in therapeutic recreation as a part of total professional recreation education
12. From a lack of standards for services and programs to progress toward development of evaluative standards, criteria, and instruments for rating or accrediting institutions and agencies relative to their recreation programs and services
13. From minimal and unsophisticated research to beginnings of basic, experimental study as well as surveys, appraisals, demonstration studies, etc.
14. From little or no grant money support to increasing resources of this kind, particularly for educational, demonstration, and research purposes, including both private and public funding, e.g., from the Kennedy Foundation; State Health and Welfare Agencies; United States Department of Health, Education, and Welfare, Social and Rehabilitation Services, Bureau of Education for the Handicapped in the Office of Education, etc.

Issues

Issues currently of concern to therapeutic recreators have been indicated in preceding chapters. Some of these are briefly summarized in the following paragraphs.

Philosophy

A. Philosophical concepts of therapeutic recreation as a process and as an area of professional service appear to be in a healthy stage of examination and development. Progress is evidenced by the willingness of therapeutic recreators to examine critically some of their beliefs and biases concerning therapeutic recreation and to devote concerted effort toward the formulation of new philosophical perspectives. Nevertheless, although statements have been developed by various individuals and small groups within the membership of the National Therapeutic Recreation Society, there remains an apparent need for wider involvement in the discussion of issues in order to achieve the awareness and consensus necessary for effective, consistent application of philosophical tenets.

Leadership

B. Progress in the development and extension of awareness of leisure needs of the ill or disabled—and of their right, as part of the total population, to recreation opportunities—generates increasing demands for personnel to develop and provide programs and services. The gap between demand and supply of qualified therapeutic recreators continues to be a major issue facing the field. Projections of future needs for recreation personnel such as those quoted in Chapter 8 may or may not hold up with the passage of time. However, estimates of total numbers of therapeutic recreators needed now and in the future serve only as gross indicators. Further assessment of needs and of the possible resources and alternatives to meet the needs must take into consideration qualifications required for and appropriate to various types of functions and responsibilities in the total range of therapeutic recreation services, from technician or assistant to administrator, as well as such emerging roles as leisure rehabilitation counselor and therapeutic recreation consultant.

Education and Professional Preparation

C. Closely related to leadership issues are those concerned with educational matters and professional preparation. As a member of the academic family, however youthful, recreation is subject to the scrutiny and reappraisal being applied to higher education generally in the United States. Moreover, all of the issues relative to educational programs in the total field of recreation pertain also to its specialized areas such as therapeutic recreation. In addition, some issues are specific to educational programs and practices in therapeutic recreation. Questions such as the following are indicative of some of these current issues:

   1. Is professional preparation of any kind consonant with educational objectives of undergraduate college education?

   2. How does therapeutic recreation relate to the total recreation (or recreation and parks) curriculum at both undergraduate and graduate levels? What constitutes an undergraduate "option"? "Specialization" at the graduate level? "Core" recreation curricula, both undergraduate and graduate?

   3. What type of preparation or extent of emphasis in therapeutic rec-

reation is feasible in the two-year junior or community college recreation offerings?

4. How much, if any, sub-specialization in therapeutic recreation educational programs is desirable with respect to specific groups such as
the mentally retarded, physically disabled, children, aged, etc.? May
such special focus be appropriate to junior college or certain non-academic training and to high-level graduate study (beyond the master's
degree) but not to the bachelor's and master's levels?

5. How can accreditation both help protect against the proliferation of
inferior, sub-standard recreation and park curricular programs and still
provide for flexibility in according recognition to needed development,
change, innovation, and experimentation in this young educational
field and its special interest areas?

An even larger issue is the matter of recreation-leisure education for all people including the disabled in both informal and formal educational programs.
In the schools the responsibility extends from elementary and secondary
through college and university levels. Park and recreation educators are urging
the recognition of leisure education as a major concern and component of the
total general education program in higher education. Therapeutic recreators
and educators face the additional charge of helping develop understanding and
appreciation among the general population as well as among the disabled,
themselves, of the nature, problems, and importance of leisure and recreation
in the lives of ill or disabled people.

Research

D. The current status, concerns, and progress of research in the field of
therapeutic recreation are documented in some detail in Chapter 11. An
issue which may warrant some attention in this discussion stems from
certain of the conditions governing the awarding and use, in some instances, of grant monies. Objectives as stipulated by the grantor must be in
harmony with the philosophy and principles guiding the professional
field for which funds and support are made available. The burden here
rests mainly with the profession and its representatives to consult and
cooperate with agencies in the development of award programs. The
therapeutic recreation researcher has ethical responsibility both to the
profession he represents and to the grantor in all phases of his study
from the development of the problem and proposal to the dissemination
and application of the findings. This may be a particularly sensitive concern currently in therapeutic recreation because as a new but rapidly
developing field it is in a vulnerable state of being both uncertainly defined and in crucial need of research and of funds to support efforts toward making essential additions to its body of knowledge.

Funds

E. There are few, if any, situations in which all of the funds that might be desirable are available. Therapeutic recreation is not unique in this respect. The issues have to do with: (1) identifying needs and resources to meet them; (2) securing the funds necessary to meet the needs; (3) allocating and using the funds obtained in the most effective way possible. These issues are sharpened for a young field such as therapeutic recreation which is in a period of rapid growth and development at a time when competition to provide for a widening spectrum of high priority needs and programs on the local, state, national, and world scene is straining current and potential financial resources. Therapeutic recreators, like those representing other fields, must be able to justify allocations and expenditures of funds for programs and services in their field. Budgetary issues must be faced realistically and creatively. Effective services and economical practices are not necessarily incompatible. Standards that have been developed for therapeutic recreation programs and services, for qualifications of personnel, for professional curricula must not be deserted or lowered to cut cost corners. Rather, these standards must be subjected to continuing scrutiny and revision in the light of new knowledge and changing conditions. New areas of need that are identified cannot be disregarded because funds are scarce. Financial support is in fact apt to be more forthcoming when it can be demonstrated that effective use is being made of all available resources, particularly personnel and funds. For example, increasing emphasis on the role of the therapeutic recreation consultant may pay financial dividends as well as increase the quality and extend the scope of needed services.

The fundamental issue always as far as funds are concerned is the extent to which the public understands and is ready to commit its resources to a field. The nature and significance of leisure and recreation in the lives of the people and in the total society must be broadly comprehended and appreciated if financial support for recreation is to be obtained. All recreators must address themselves to this purpose. Therapeutic recreators have special, but not by any means exclusive responsibility for interpreting the recreational needs of ill or disabled people.

Quality

F. All other issues are peripheral to this concern: How can the *quality of life* of those who are ill or disabled be enhanced through recreation, or when indicated, through the relating of recreative experience to the therapeutic process? This is the basic question against which the *quality of therapeutic recreation services* must finally be assessed. In this objective lies justification for allocating funds to develop programs and services in therapeutic recreation; for preparing and employing personnel in the field; for mounting studies and research; for promulgating standards; for forming professional societies and associations; indeed, for every aspect of therapeutic recreation as a member of the family of professional recreation services.

Trends

Something of the developments that have occurred in therapeutic recreation and of its current status have been summarized in the above discussion of transitions and issues. There remains a necessity for looking at some of the indications of continuing development or directions of change. Looking into the future is always uncertain. Nevertheless, to be unaware of or to disregard direction pointers as they become evident would be less than prudent. Thus the authors conclude by briefly indicating what appear to them to be some of the trends that are indicative of directions in which therapeutic recreation is moving in the early part of the 1970's.

A. Deeper understandings and broader perceptions of philosophical concepts and of the professional identity and mission of therapeutic recreation are lessening dependency upon the medical field for direction and recognition, and clarifying the nature of relationships between therapeutic recreation and other fields such as social group work, special education, and the various ancillary or paramedical areas.

B. Decreasing emphasis on divisions and differences in areas of concern between therapeutic recreation and general community recreation is affecting educational programs, employment policies, and professional practice.

C. Awareness is developing of the need for a more rational approach to the matter of sub-specializations within therapeutic recreation according to diagnostic groupings or special areas of disability.

D. Growing recognition of the need to provide a broader variety of services and to match individual qualifications and expertise with job requirements is occurring, accompanied by continuing efforts toward refinement in the analyses of roles, functions, competencies, and career opportunities in therapeutic recreation.

E. Interdisciplinary emphases and team concepts are being increasingly applied in recreation education, including therapeutic recreation, and in professional practice in community as well as treatment settings. Recreators, and therapeutic recreators, are in a particularly advantageous position to act as catalysts in initiating concerted, coordinated, cooperative action.

F. Along with re-evaluating, re-organizing, and refining total college curriculums in recreation, from the two year college level (or even the high school) through graduate programs, an increasing tendency is being evidenced toward incorporating a widening variety of approaches to combining work with study. Some examples of such approaches are: (1) exposing all recreation students regardless of area of special interest to field practice in various settings or types of agencies, with the general population and with special groups; (2) providing in-depth exposures in the nature of professional internships for all students rather than a selected few; and (3) greater flexibility in allowing students to intersperse academic programs with periods of employment in the field.

G. Encouraging developments in both the quality and quantity of therapeutic recreation research are being accompanied by growing recognition of the need for wider involvements of people in the field as well as in the laboratories and for more effective dissemination and application of the findings. Therapeutic recreation research personnel, as representatives of an applied rather than basic area of research, are finding the role of the catalyst particularly pertinent in bringing necessary interdisciplinary resources to bear upon problems in therapeutic recreation. Awareness is developing of the need to broaden the kinds of studies currently being undertaken to include longitudinal, sociological, and anthropological problems, approaches, and methodologies.

H. Understanding of therapeutic recreation as an integral, unified part of the total recreation profession is gaining in acceptance and practice in the field, in educational preparation, and in state and national professional societies and organization. Formulation of a joint liaison committee of the National Therapeutic Recreation Society and the American Park and Recreation Society is indicative of a move to provide for more viable interrelationships among various facets of the total recreation and park field as represented by the Branches of the National Park and Recreation Association.

These, then, are some of the issues that must be faced if therapeutic recreation is to fulfill its promise, as yet only dimly perceived and uncertainly pursued. The trends identified above are hopeful indicators of positive direction. Charles K. Brightbill, as he so often did, said it best for us:

> Whatever potentials there are at this point, as the recreative approach to helping us attain, regain, and sustain sound health, they are mainly non-realized. The more we learn about it, however, the more we shall discover how far it can help take us along the road to full existence.[1]

Notes, Chapter 12

1. Charles K. Brightbill, *The Challenge of Leisure* (Englewood Cliffs, N. J.: Prentice-Hall, Inc., 1963), p. 91.

APPENDIX

JOB DESCRIPTIONS

(Developed by Doris L. Berryman for a research project "Development of Educational Programs for New Careers in Recreation Services for the Disabled," supported in part by a grant from the U.S. Department of Health, Education, and Welfare, Office of Education, Bureau of Research)

Recreation Assistant I–(Trainee)

Job Summary

Under close supervision, observes and may assist in a variety of recreation tasks; attends formal training program, either inside or outside the agency; attends staff meetings and conferences as required.

Duties

1. Attends formal training program at specified hours to develop necessary basic skills.
2. Observes and may assist in conducting various recreational activities, especially those which require little specific training.
3. Observes and assists in performing clerical and office tasks, such as maintaining inventory records and issuing supplies and equipment.

4. Assists in preparing and operating equipment for various events, including audio-visual equipment.
5. Assists in maintaining recreation areas, facilities and equipment in good condition.
6. Attends staff meetings and conferences as required.

Recreation Assistant II–Program

Job Summary

Under normal supervision of Recreation Leader, Specialist, or Supervisor, assists in performing a variety of duties involved in carrying out recreation programs, as directed; performs related minor duties, as required.

Duties

1. Assists in instructing and leading recreation activities such as any or all of the following: sports, active and table games, out-trips, special events and programs, social and seasonal events, crafts programs, manual arts, music, art, ceramic, sculpture, dance or other creative activity, camp activities and/or youth groups, e.g., Boy Scouts, Girl Scouts, club groups, etc.; leads programs, as assigned.
2. May assist in organizing and conducting athletic teams.
3. May conduct large group activities, e.g., bingo, movies, entertainment.
4. Assists in preparing and operating equipment for various events, including audio-visual equipment.
5. Stores and maintains recreation supplies and equipment; issues supplies and equipment to program participants; keeps records of supplies and equipment.
6. Prepares and serves refreshments.
7. Performs related routine duties such as clerical work, running errands, transmitting messages, etc., as required.
8. May perform personal services for individual participants such as writing letters or shopping for them.
9. Guides and assists volunteers and/or staff members, when assigned.
10. Attends orientation, in-service training, staff meetings and conferences, as required.

Recreation Assistant II–Clerical

Job Summary

Under normal supervision, performs a variety of clerical duties involved in carrying out recreation programs; may assist in conducting group or individual recreational activities when necessary.

Duties

1. Keeps records, maintains files, and writes reports regarding recreation programs and services, including items such as details of programs planned, activity schedules, participants' attendance and use of facilities, work assignments of staff, payroll time-records, personal records, accidents or other emergencies, inventories of supplies and equipment, correspondence, etc.
2. Issues and collects equipment and supplies; stores and maintains supplies and equipment; requisitions supplies and equipment, as needed; purchases supplies and equipment, as directed.
3. May control the use of certain facilities by participants, issues membership cards and/or admission tickets, if required by the agency, and collects proper fees, if any; schedules use of courts and other facilities.

4. May perform personal services for individual patients such as writing letters or shopping for them.
5. Gives information to participants and visitors; answers their questions regarding programs and services; listens to their complaints and reports complaints to proper superior.
6. Prepares and distributes invitations, notices, weekly schedules, etc. to concerned persons and runs errands, as required.
7. Performs typing and other office duties, if incumbent possesses necessary skills; may assist in preparing publicity release, if qualified; operates duplicating machines.
8. Guides and assists volunteers and/or other staff members, when assigned.
9. Attends orientation, in-service training, staff meetings and conferences, as required.
10. May assist in conducting group or individual recreational activities, when necessary, i.e., in case of temporary staff shortage due to illness, etc.

Recreation Assistant II–Facilities and Maintenance

Job Summary

Under normal supervision, performs a variety of functions to maintain and/or improve facilities required for an effective recreation program; may assist by performing certain clerical duties or in conducting group or individual recreational activities when necessary.

Duties

1. Maintains equipment and facilities in good condition; makes minor repairs to equipment such as movie projectors, record players, tape recorders, etc.; keeps outdoor recreation facilities such as swings, teeter-totters, basketball courts, tennis courts, baseball diamonds, etc. in first-class condition; makes adjustments to and repairs any other type of equipment used in the recreation program such as pool tables, ping pong tables, gymnasium apparatus, etc.; arranges for major repairs, as necessary.
2. Assists in maintaining recreation areas neat and clean.
3. Assists in decorating for special events and seasonal parties; assists in making stage props for shows, and in setting up and operating spotlights and other special lighting effects.
4. Operates equipment such as movie or slide projectors, record players, tape recorders, etc.
5. May assist in swimming pool maintenance; may serve as skating rink guard; may perform any type of guarding assignment; may supervise the use of playground or park facilities.
6. Administers first aid as necessary.
7. Guides and assists volunteers and/or other staff members, when assigned.
8. Attends orientation, in-service training, staff meetings and conferences, as required.
9. May perform certain clerical functions such as controlling the use of facilities by participants, issuing and collecting equipment and supplies, etc., in the absence of the staff member who usually performs such functions; may assist in conducting certain group or individual recreational activities when necessary.

Recreation Leader–Generalist

Job Summary

Under general supervision of Recreation Supervisor, performs a variety of duties involved in carrying out recreation programs in assigned areas; may assist in planning programs, may supervise the work of Recreation Assistants and/or Volunteers; performs related duties, as required.

Duties

1. Instructs and leads recreation activities such as any or all of the following: sports, active and table games, out-trips, special events and programs, social and seasonal events, crafts programs, manual arts, music, art, ceramic, sculpture, dance or other creative activity, camp activities and/or youth groups, e.g., Boy Scouts, Girl Scouts, club groups, etc., may assist in adapting activities and/or equipment to facilitate the participation of disabled persons.
2. Prepares and operates equipment for events, including audio-visual equipment; ensures that adequate supplies and equipment are available as needed.
3. May assist in leading activities such as discussion groups, management and production of a newspaper, grooming and hygiene classes, adult special-interest groups, i.e., bowling, gardening, collecting.
4. May supervise recreation activities such as active and table games, certain sports activities, i.e., roller skating, bowling, nature walks within the agency's grounds.
5. Participates in team conferences, where appropriate.
6. Prepares periodic activity reports and other reports as directed.
7. Supervises the work of Recreation Assistants, Trainees, Volunteers or others; assigns duties and follows up to ascertain that they are performing duties properly; instructs subordinates, as necessary.
8. May adminster first aid to participants who suffer minor injuries.
9. Performs the duties of Recreation Assistant, Trainee or Volunteer, as required, especially in emergency situations.

Recreation Leader–Specialist

Job Summary

Under general supervision, performs a variety of duties involved in planning and carrying out specialized recreation programs; coordinates and supervises approved programs, may supervise the work of Recreation Assistants, Volunteers or other recreation workers; performs related duties, as required.

Duties

1. Develops detailed plans, usually in cooperation with other staff members, for highly specialized recreation programs such as one or more of the following: sports, active and table games, crafts programs, creative activities (i.e., music, art, ceramics, sculpture, dance, drama, etc.) manual arts, large group activities, organizing athletic teams, camping, etc.; may assist in adapting activities and/or equipment to facilitate the participation of disabled persons.
2. Directs, instructs and leads any such specialized activity, as assigned; supervises and leads out-trips, special programs and events, as assigned, supervises the work of assigned staff members and/or volunteers; assigns duties and follows up to ascertain that they are performing their duties properly.
3. Instructs and leads in camp activities and/or other youth groups, e.g., Boy Scouts, Girl Scouts, club groups; instructs and guides in personal appearance and other personal matters; leads adult special interest groups (i.e., bowling, gardening, collecting, etc.); may manage and edit participants' newspaper.

4. May instruct and train staff members and/or volunteers in a specialized activity such as those listed in paragraph 1 above.
5. Participates in team conferences, where appropriate.
6. Maintains various records regarding programs and participants; prepares periodic and/or special reports, as required.
7. Selects appropriate supplies and equipment; requisitions supplies and equipment as necessary to maintain adequate inventory.
8. May contact outside agencies or individuals to arrange for out-trips, entertainers, contributions, etc.

Recreation Supervisor

Job Summary

Under general supervision of the Director of Recreation, plans, or assists in planning, recreation programs; schedules, coordinates and supervises approved programs; assigns duties to subordinate staff members and volunteers, and follows up to ascertain that they are performing their duties properly. May perform the duties of Recreation Leader or other subordinate, if necessary.

Acts in behalf of the Director of Recreation in his absence, if directed to do so.

Duties

1. Develops detailed plans, frequently in cooperation with other staff members and sometimes with participants, for recreation programs such as sports activities, out-trips, special events, social and seasonal events, camp programs, etc.
2. Supervises assigned recreation staff members and volunteers; assigns duties and follows up to ensure that they are performing their duties properly; recommends desirable changes in status including salary increases, promotions, transfers, leaves of absence, terminations, etc; administers equitable and appropriate discipline if necessary.
3. Assists in training of staff and volunteers.
4. Ensures that adequate inventory of recreation supplies and equipment is maintained.
5. May lead discussion groups; may engage in individual recreational counseling.
6. Adapts activities and equipment to facilitate the participation of certain persons, as necessary.
7. Evaluates programs and participants; prepares evaluation reports, accident reports, etc.; prepares observational reports on participants; evaluates the value and usability of equipment and supplies.
8. Participates actively in interdisciplinary conferences and team meetings; disseminates appropriate information to subordinate staff.
9. Meets with visitors and/or relatives of participants; answers their questions and attempts to gain their goodwill.
10. Performs the duties of Recreation Leader or other subordinate staff member as required, especially in emergency situations.
11. Performs the functions of Director of Recreation in his absence, if directed to do so.

Director of Recreation

Job Summary

Under general administrative direction, plans, coordinates, directs and controls all recreational programs and services of the agency.

Duties

1. Develops master plans for the agency's recreation programs and services such as day camp and/or resident camp programs, sports activities, out-trips, special events, social and seasonal events, etc. within the agency's general policies.
2. Plans programs in conjunction with other disciplines (e.g., medicine, psychiatry, physical therapy, rehabilitation counseling, etc.) to help achieve specific treatment goals; cooperates in implementing and/or conducting the activities thus programed.
3. Plans, with individuals who are concerned, for post-institutional or post-program participation in the community.
4. Develops annual budgets for equipment, supplies and personnel; controls expenditures against approved budgets.
5. Administers and coordinates all recreation programs; supervises all planned activities, usually through subordinate supervisors; follows up to ensure that all staff members, field-work students and volunteers perform their work properly; evaluates effectiveness of the various programs.
6. Maintains adequate Recreation Department staff; recruits, selects and hires staff as required; evaluates performance of staff members; approves desirable changes in status, including salary increases, promotions, transfers, leaves of absence, etc.; administers equitable and appropriate discipline as necessary.
7. Organizes, implements and supervises appropriate in-service training programs for professional and sub-professional staff members and for volunteers.
8. Fosters and maintains good public relations; develops publicity releases designed to gain goodwill; assists in educating the public to appreciate the importance of appropriate recreation programs; may give speeches to local organizations such as church groups, P.T.A.'s, etc.
9. Prepares periodic and special reports to be used in the agency and/or in the community.
10. Attends management staff meetings and participates in making policy decisions for the agency which may affect the recreational services.
11. May perform the duties of Recreation Supervisor or other subordinate, when necessary, especially in an emergency.

SHORT-TERM INTENSIVE-TRAINING PROGRAM

(Developed by Doris L. Berryman for a research project "Development of Educational Programs for New Careers in Recreation Services for the Disabled," supported in part by a grant from the U.S. Department of Health, Education, and Welfare, Office of Education, Bureau of Research)

A. Theory
1. Philosophy of recreation service.
2. Orientation to recreation services to special groups through observational trips and class discussion.
3. Understanding of disabilities and their impact on the individual, family and community.
   a. physical disabilities
   b. mental retardation
   c. emotional disturbances
   d. institutionalized aged

4. Understanding of normal growth and development and the range of normal activities for various age groups.
5. Understanding of aging process and orientation to recreation services for older citizens.
6. Principles of program planning.
   a. planning
   b. preparation
   c. evaluation
7. Introduction to activity analysis.
8. Introduction to process of recording.
   a. observational reports
   b. progress reports
   c. activity reports
   d. attendance, inventory and other routine record keeping.
9. Introduction to use and maintenance of audio-visual aids.
10. Introduction to concepts of interpersonal communication.
11. Introduction to first aid and safety.

B. Skill Workshops
   1. Crafts.
   2. Social recreation.
   3. Games of low organization.
   4. Individual and duo sports.
      a. bowling
      b. badminton
      c. table tennis
   5. Team sports.
      a. volleyball (and lead-up games)
      b. basketball (and lead-up games)
      c. softball (and lead-up games)
   6. Music and dance.
      a. group singing and musical games
      b. introduction to music appreciation
      c. social and folk dancing
   7. Dramatic activities.
      a. puppetry
      b. improvisation and pantomime
      c. reading
      d. single dramatic productions
   8. Pre-school activities.
   9. Construction and use of visual aids.
Leadership techniques and the adaptation of activities to suit the interests and capabilities of disabled persons will be presented as an integral part of all activity workshops.

C. Practice Leadership
   1. In the classroom through role-playing and peer evaluation.
   2. On the job, under supervision, evaluation by instructor, agency staff, peers and occasional use of video tape to permit self-evaluation.

JOB DESCRIPTIONS

The following two job descriptions were prepared for a Prototype Grant Proposal, Curriculum in Recreation and Parks, University of Kentucky. The project was supported by a grant from the Department of Health, Education, and Welfare, Office of Education, Bureau of Education for the Handicapped.

The job descriptions are based on information obtained from interviews with a number of persons in administrative and supervisory positions in medical, educational, and recreation agencies and institutions. One of the purposes of the interviews was to determine the actual and/or desired functions of a therapeutic recreation director in each agency, to identify functions common to all, and to arrange the varying job functions into discrete groups which might than serve as one or more representative job descriptions.

Analysis of the data received in the interviews indicated that two distinct types of positions can be described. One is that of Recreation Director operating within a treatment center—hospital, residential school for the handicapped, nursing home—and primarily concerned with the patients or residents of the center. The other is that of a Therapeutic Recreation Director operating from a community based agency and primarily concerned with ill or disabled persons outside the treatment centers. Such agencies include, but are not necessarily limited to, public schools, Comprehensive Care Centers (Mental health and mental retardation), Recreation and Parks Departments.

It is recognized that, in a job description, job functions may be grouped and classified in various ways depending on the kind of work that is performed. Because recreation is a "people-oriented" profession, the functions are grouped, in these job descriptions, according to the kind of involvement with other people.

Director of Recreation in a Treatment Center

It is assumed that the recreation program is provided through an administratively distinct unit or department, and that the Recreation Director has a staff of the size appropriate for the number of patients or residents served.

The Recreation Director's primary functions are those of supervision, training, planning, administration, coordination, and interpretation.

Functions involving direct contact with patients or residents

Face to face leadership of ordinary group activities in recreation is a minor function of the Recreation Director. It may become a major function under the following circumstances:

1. Initiating a new type of program.
2. Conducting activities with special groups of patients or residents.
3. Conducting activities in closed areas of the treatment center.
4. During the expanding or curtailing of current programs.
5. Combining supervision of recreation hall with office work.
6. Initial out-trips.

The Recreation Director may be responsible for conducting or indirectly leading meetings of patient or resident groups such as councils, planning committees, etc.

He may function as a participant-therapist in group therapy.

He may have contact with patients as a participant in medical grand rounds.

Direct contact with individual patients or residents is also a minor function of the Recreation Director, but may become a major function under the following circumstances:

1. Initial contact and individual work with seriously ill patients or ones with unusual diseases.
2. Providing recreation counseling and planning for discharge.
3. Training patients or residents as recreation aides.
4. Initial orientation and evaluation of patients or residents (with other Activity Therapy staff).

Functions involving recreation staff

Recreation staff may include full time or part time recreation leaders and aides, volunteers, and affiliated University students.

The Recreation Director's functions involving the staff as a group may include:
1. Plan and conduct staff meetings.
2. Arrange and conduct in-service training for recreation staff, as needed.

His functions involving staff members individually may include:
1. Explain and assign duties.
2. Confer with staff member concerning his work plans, his job performance and career development, and evaluation.
3. Observe staff member's performance and assist where necessary.

The Recreation Director may be responsible for interviewing applicants for recreation positions, both paid and volunteer.

Functions involving other staff of the treatment center

The Recreation Director's responsibilities may include the following:
1. Representing the recreation department, attend center staff meetings, interdepartmental team meetings, designated committee meetings, and the like.
2. Participate in individual conferences with other department heads concerning coordination of functions, use of space, supplies, and the like.
3. Participate in ward rounds with the medical team.
4. Conduct in-service training sessions in recreation principles, skills, etc., for staff of other departments.
5. As needed, interpret the recreation program to the administrative and other professional staff.
6. Confer regularly with immediate superior concerning administrative matters.

Functions involving persons outside the treatment center

These functions are carried out: (1) on behalf of the patients or residents as a group; (2) on behalf of the individual patients or residents; and (3) as public relations functions.

On behalf of the group, the Recreation Director may be responsible for the following:
1. Make initial arrangements for patient or resident groups to take out-trips.
2. Make initial arrangements for groups from outside the center to come in for visits or entertainment.
3. Develop reciprocal arrangements and programs with other community recreation agencies.
4. When indicated, plan and operate camp programs.

On behalf of individuals, the Recreation Director may be responsible for the following:
1. Arrange for community recreation involvement of patient or resident following his discharge.

2. Confer with patient's or resident's family concerning his recreation.
3. Act as a consultant to personnel of other community agencies concerning the patient's or resident's recreation.

In the area of public relations, the Recreation Director may be responsible for the following:

1. Interpret the center recreation program to the community through various means such as newspaper items, TV interviews, speaking at various community group meetings, and the like.
2. Arrange appropriate publicity of the recreation program.
3. Recruit volunteers.
4. Solicit appropriate contributions (in kind or in funds) for the recreation program.

Functions involving no direct contact with other persons

The Recreation Director's functions involve a certain amount of "desk work" which may include the following:

1. Develop personnel standards and policies for the recreation department.
2. Write job descriptions for all recreation positions.
3. Prepare work schedules.
4. Write evaluations of staff.
5. Determine cost, value, adaptability, and availability of facilities, equipment, and supplies.
6. Prepare requisitions.
7. Obtain equipment and supplies.
8. Adapt facilities, equipment, and supplies for special needs of patients or residents.
9. Arrange for storage, disbursement, inventory, etc. of equipment and supplies.
10. Arrange for maintenance and repair of equipment and supplies.
11. Prepare budget for the recreation department.
12. Compile and maintain records of activity, attendance, and so on.
13. Submit appropriate reports of such statistics to superior, as required.
14. Prepare publicity materials.
15. Prepare miscellaneous indicated correspondence.

Research

The Recreation Director may have, as an additional function, the responsibility to initiate, supervise, coordinate, and/or conduct appropriate recreation research, or to cooperate in joint efforts in research involving other departments.

Therapeutic Recreation Director in a Community Agency

The specific functions of the Therapeutic Recreation Director will vary, depending on the orientation of the agency employing his services. For instance, a medically oriented agency such as a Comprehensive Care Center may rely heavily on his expertise as a recreation specialist, while a recreation oriented agency such as a Municipal Park District may utilize his skill as a therapist.

In general, however, his primary functions are those of planning, training, coordinating, promoting, and research.

The term, "client," is used here to indicate all ill and/or disabled persons receiving the agency's services.

Functions involving direct contact with clients

Responsibilities for direct program leadership are minimal. Direct contact with the clients may be a major function under the following circumstances:
1. Initiate a recreation program in a mental health center for outpatients.
2. Participate in group therapy sessions.
3. Organize a transitional program in recreation from the Center to the community.
4. Plan with clients for discharge from treatment.
5. Analyze recreation needs of individual clients and propose activities or program.
6. Operate a program for clients jointly sponsored by two or more community agencies.
7. Direct an out-of-school program, summer program, and/or camp program for clients.
8. Occasionally directly lead adapted activities for clients on the playground.

Functions involving other staff of agency

"Other staff" refers to classroom teachers, recreation leaders, therapists, aides, volunteers, and any other personnel employed by the agency who work with the clients.
The Therapeutic Recreation Director may have responsibility for the following:
1. Conduct in-service training in therapeutic recreation activities and techniques for personnel who work directly with the clients.
2. Supervise and assist such personnel in program operation.
3. Act as consultant on therapeutic recreation to any staff member.
4. Coordinate recreation activities with other activities provided by the agency for the clients.
5. Interpret the meaning and values of therapeutic recreation.
6. Participate in staff meetings.
7. Confer regularly with agency head concerning administrative aspects of therapeutic recreation program.
If the Therapeutic Recreation Director has a staff reporting directly to him, his responsibilities will include those normally placed on a supervisor, such as conducting staff meetings, holding individual conferences, assigning specific tasks and duties, observing and evaluating programs and staff performance, in-service training, and recruiting staff.

Functions involving persons outside the agency

Depending on the employing agency and the resources and amount of activity in the community, the Therapeutic Recreation Director may have the following responsibilities:
1. Coordinate the agency's therapeutic recreation program with similar programs of other agencies.
2. Serve as a consultant to local hospitals, special camps, community recreation agencies, and any other agencies having special programs for the ill or disabled.
3. Act as a catalyst, stimulus for all community service agencies for developing therapeutic recreation programing.
4. Draw together state, regional, university, and hospital resources.
5. Conduct or assist with interagency in-service training.
6. Educate community re leisure via radio shows, newspaper columns, TV interviews, etc.

7. Initiate and/or coordinate camp programs for clients.
8. Survey community to locate the ill and/or disabled.
9. Survey community to locate appropriate recreation facilities for clients.
10. Recruit and train volunteers.
11. Promote assistance from civic groups, commercial recreation facilities, etc. through appropriate public relations techniques.
12. Supervise university field-work students assigned to the agency.

Functions involving no direct contact with other persons

The amount of administrative "desk work" the Therapeutic Recreation Director is responsible for varies from agency to agency, depending on the orientation of the agency. It is at a minimum in those situations in which the Director functions primarily as a specialist or a consultant, rather than as a supervisor of a specific program. However, he may be expected to be able to carry the following responsibilities:
1. Write evaluations of program content.
2. Write evaluations of staff performance.
3. Assign areas of responsibility to other staff.
4. Propose appropriate budgets.
5. Make appropriate adaptations in facilities, equipment, and supplies.
6. Secure appropriate supplies and equipment.
7. Develop and maintain recreation recordings.
8. Develop grant proposals as needed.

Research

The Therapeutic Recreation Director may have, as an additional function, the responsibility to initiate, supervise, coordinate, and/or conduct appropriate research, or to cooperate in joint efforts in research involving other departments or agencies.

UNDERGRADUATE CURRICULUM IN RECREATION AND PARKS
(University of Kentucky)

Subject	Hours or points
General Studies	
Physical Sciences	6-10
(Astronomy, chemistry, geology or physics)	
Biological Sciences	6-10
Humanities	6-10
(Literature, art, music, philosophy, or foreign language)	
History	6
Social Sciences	9
(Economics, sociology, anthropology, geography, or political sciences)	
Special Studies	
English composition	6
Communications	6
Psychology	6
Physical Education	4

Professional Requirements in Recreation

Introduction to Recreation	3
Program Planning and Leadership	3
Outdoor Recreation	3
Field Work I	2
Field Work II	2
Senior Seminar	3
Space and Structures for Recreation	3
Administration and Organization of Recreation Services	3
Introduction to Therapeutic Recreation	3
Interpretations of Leisure	3
Practicum in Recreation	9

Related Professional Requirements

Introduction to Statistics	3
Techniques of Social Investigation	3

Suggested Electives
(for therapeutic recreation option)

Elementary Anatomy
Abnormal Psychology
Introduction to the Education of Exceptional Children
Human Growth and Development
Behavioral Factors in Health and Disease
Society and Health

SAMPLE PROGRAM OF STUDY
(Therapeutic Recreation Option)

FIRST YEAR

Semester I

English Composition I
General Biology I
Introduction to Recreation
History of the U.S. through 1865
Physical Education Activity

Semester II

General College Chemistry I
Biology I
Basic Public Speaking
Modern Social Problems
Physical Education Activity

SECOND YEAR

Semester I

General Chemistry II
History of the U.S. since 1865
Program Planning and Leadership in Recreation
Art History
English Composition II

Semester II

Human Biology and Health
Introduction to Music
General Psychology
Introduction to Literature
Elementary Anatomy
Physical Education Activity

THIRD YEAR

Semester I

Outdoor Recreation
Field Work in Recreation I
Introduction to Statistics
Behavioral Factors in Health and
  Disease
Introduction to the Education of Ex-
  ceptional Children
Physical Education Activity

Semester II

State Government
Abnormal Psychology
Field Work in Recreation II
Social Change
Survey of Physical and Neurological
  Defects
Human Growth and Development

Semester III (summer)
Practicum in Recreation

FOURTH YEAR

Semester I

Senior Seminar in Recreation
Introduction to Therapeutic
  Recreation
Techniques of Social Investigation
The Nature and Needs of Retarded
  Children
Elective

Semester II

Social Psychology
Space and Structures in Recreation
Interpretations of Leisure
Characteristics of Emotionally Disturb-
  ed Children
Elective

GRADUATE CURRICULUM
(leading to a Master of Science degree)

(Therapeutic Recreation Option)
(University of Kentucky)

DEPARTMENTAL CORE

Educational Statistics	3
Research Techniques Applied to Health, Physical Education, and Recreation	3
Measurement Theory (thesis option)	
or	
Individual Research Project	3

PROFESSIONAL RECREATION REQUIREMENTS

*Interpretations of Leisure	3
*Therapeutic Recreation, An Introduction	3
Organization of Recreation for the Ill or Disabled	3
Therapeutic Applications of Recreation	3
Seminar in Recreation (variable topics)	3
Current Issues in Recreation	3
Practicum	3

*These courses may not be repeated for graduate credit if they have been completed in the undergraduate program.

ELECTIVES

Thesis (optional)	6
Elective courses to be chosen from graduate offering in any department on campus to support the student's special interest in therapeutic recreation	9 or more

SAMPLE FORM FOR INDIVIDUAL CASE RECORD

Page 1   INDIVIDUAL RECORD   Recreator _____
                              RECREATION   Date open _____

General Background

Name of patient _____ Ward # _____ Room # _____

Address _____ Occupation _____

Age _____ Sex _____ Education _____ Religion _____

Marital status _____ Children _____

Medical Information

Admission date _____

Probable length of hospitalization _____

Admission diagnosis _____ Physician _____

Ambulatory status _____ Medical and/or physical

                                                  limitations _____

_____

Projected medical treatment _____

_____

Clinic and treatment schedule _____

_____

Referred by: _____

Referral content:

SAMPLE FORM FOR INDIVIDUAL CASE RECORD (Continued)

Page 2   Activity Preferences and Experience

Games and sports _____   Arts and crafts _____

_____   _____

_____   _____

_____   _____

Music _____   Drama and entertainment_____

_____   _____

_____   _____

_____   _____

Reading _____   Dance _____

_____   _____

_____   _____

_____   _____

Social activities _____   Hobbies _____

_____   _____

_____   _____

_____   _____

Chronological Record

Date	Record of contact with patient

(continue)

NATIONAL THERAPEUTIC RECREATION SOCIETY
1601 N. Kent St.
Arlington, Va. 22209

[January, 1971]

INFORMATION FOR MEMBERS REGARDING VOLUNTARY REGISTRATION WITH THE NATIONAL THERAPEUTIC RECREATION SOCIETY.

Many persons who are responsible for recreation for the ill and handicapped are interested in becoming registered as individuals who meet the standards established by the National Therapeutic Recreation Society. You may want to know more about registration before making application and the following questions and answers have been prepared to help you do this.

1. *What is Voluntary Registration with NTRS?*
A registration program is one under which a professional organization attests that an individual applicant meets the minimum standards it has established for a position classification in the therapeutic recreation field. Registration is initiated by submitting an application along with transcripts and qualifying data to the Executive Secretary of NTRS.

2. *Who may apply?*
Anyone working for compensation in therapeutic recreation with the ill, disabled, handicapped and other special groups, retired personnel and those who were employed in therapeutic recreation in the past.

3. *What does registration cost?*
The registration fee is $10 with a $2 renewal fee every two years. ($7 for registration and $3 for filing fee) Payment is due upon submission of your registration application. While membership in NTRS is strongly encouraged, it is not a pre-requisite for registration. The registration fee is separate from your membership fee.

4. *How should one pay fees?*
A check or money order for registration is required. It should be made out to the National Therapeutic Recreation Society with a note thereon signifying "For Registration NTRS."

5. *How should registration mail be addressed?*
Executive Secretary
National Therapeutic Recreation Society
1601 N. Kent St.
Arlington, Va. 22209
Your name and address should appear in the upper left hand corner of the envelope.

6. *What happens to the Application?*
The Executive Secretary of NTRS checks on the following:
    1. Proper completion of the form.
    2. Inclusion of proper fees.
    3. Transcripts and necessary verifying data.
A letter of receipt is sent to you and if your application and fee are in order, your data are forwarded to the Registration Board for consideration.

7. *How does an applicant know if he qualifies?*
You will receive a letter of qualification along with your registration certificate and card. If you do not qualify you will receive an action form stating why you do not, your transcript and a check for $7.

8. *Does the applicant have a right to appeal?*
Yes! If your application is rejected for the classification for which you applied and you indicated that you would not accept a different classification, you may file an appeal.

9. *How is an appeal filed?*
You may file an appeal by letter to the Executive Secretary, NTRS, within three (3) months of your rejection. Action on your appeal will be taken by the Board of Appeals (The Executive Committee of the NTRS) at its next regular meeting. Action of the Board of Appeals shall be final in all cases. No extra filing fee will be required for appeals and only the $7 registration fee need be returned with the appeal. This $7 will be returned if your appeal is rejected.

10. *How does one update his registration?*
As your qualifications improve, you may apply for a higher classification. This application will be handled as an original one and will require only $3 rather than the full $10 registration fee.

STANDARDS ADOPTED BY THE NATIONAL THERAPEUTIC RECREATION SOCIETY

1. Therapeutic Recreation Assistant

    a. Two years of successful full-time paid experience in therapeutic recreation field.
    or
    b. Two hundred clock hours in-service training in therapeutic recreation field.
    or
    c. A combination of a. and b. may be substituted.

2. Therapeutic Recreation Technician

    a. Associate of Arts degree from an accredited college or university or satisfactory completion of two years of college with major work in recreation or in other fields related to therapeutic recreation. (physical education, music, dance, drama, psychology, and sociology)
    or
    b. Diploma, certificate or other proof of satisfactory completion of two academic years of study in an art or technical field related to therapeutic recreation from an approved or recognized school.

3. Therapeutic Recreation Worker
    a. (Provisional) Baccalaureate degree from an accredited college or university with a major in recreation or field related to therapeutic recreation.
    or
    b. (Registered) Baccalaureate degree from an accredited college or university with a major or emphasis in therapeutic recreation.
    or
    c. (Registered) Baccalaureate degree from an accredited college or university with a major in recreation and one year of experience in therapeutic recreation field.
    or
    d. (Registered) Baccalaureate degree from an accredited college or university with a degree in a field related to therapeutic recreation and two years of experience in therapeutic recreation field.
    or
    e. (Registered) Master's degree from an accredited college or university with a major in recreation or other field related to therapeutic recreation.

4. Therapeutic Recreation Specialist

   a. Master's degree from an accredited college or university with a major in therapeutic recreation.

   or

   b. Master's degree from an accredited college or university with a major in recreation and one year of experience in therapeutic recreation field.

   or

   c. Master's degree from an accredited college or university with a major in a field related to therapeutic recreation and two years of experience in therapeutic recreation field.

   or

   d. Baccalaureate degree from an accredited college or university with a major or emphasis in therapeutic recreation and three years of experience in therapeutic recreation field.

   or

   e. Baccalaureate degree from an accredited college or university with a major in recreation and four years of experience in therapeutic recreation field.

   or

   f. Baccalaureate degree from an accredited college or university with a major in a field related to therapeutic recreation and five years of experience in therapeutic recreation field.

5. Master Therapeutic Recreation Specialist

   a. Master's degree from an accredited college or university with a major in therapeutic recreation and two years of experience in therapeutic recreation field.

   or

   b. Master's degree from an accredited college or university with a major in recreation and three years of experience in therapeutic recreation field.

   or

   c. Master's degree from an accredited college or university with a major in a field related to therapeutic recreation and four years of experience in therapeutic recreation field.

   or

   d. Baccalaureate degree from an accredited college or university with a major or emphasis in therapeutic recreation and five years of experience in therapeutic recreation field.

   or

   e. Baccalaureate degree from an accredited college or university with a major in recreation and six years of experience in therapeutic recreation field.

   or

   f. Baccalaureate degree from an accredited college or university with a major in a field related to therapeutic recreation field and seven years of experience in therapeutic recreation field.

Note: The above standards and registration procedures are subject to revision by the Board of Directors of the National Therapeutic Recreation Society. Applicants should secure current information from the Executive Secretary of NTRS.

Resource Organizations and Agencies

American Art Therapy Association
   6010 Broad Branch Road, N.W., Washington, D. C. 20015
American Association for Health, Physical Education, and Recreation
   1201 Sixteenth Street, N.W., Washington, D. C. 20000
American Camping Association
   Bradford Woods, Martinsville, Indiana 46151
American Foundation for the Blind
   15 West Sixteenth Street, New York, New York 10011
American National Red Cross
   17th and D Street, N.W., Washington, D. C. 20000
American Occupational Therapy Association, Inc.
   251 Park Avenue South, New York, New York 10010
American Physical Therapy Association, Inc.
   1156 15th Street, N.W., Washington, D. C. 20005
American Psychiatric Association
   1700 18th Street, N.W., Washington, D. C. 20000
American Psychological Association
   1200 17th Street, N.W. Washington, D. C. 20000
American Public Health Association
   224 E. Capital, Washington, D. C. 20000
Arthritis and Rheumatism Foundation
   10 Columbus Circle, New York, New York 10019
Bureau of Education for the Handicapped (Office of Education)
   400 Maryland Avenue, S.W., Washington, D. C. 20202
Children's Bureau, Office of Child Development
   300 Independence Ave., S.W., Washington, D. C. 20201
Department of Health, Education and Welfare
   300 Independence Ave., S.W., Washington, D. C. 20201
International Recreation Association
   345 East 46th Street, New York, New York 10017
International Society for Rehabilitation of the Disabled
   219 East 44th Street, New York, New York 10017
Joseph P. Kennedy, Jr. Foundation
   c/o Mrs. Byron H. Pyle, 785 Park Ave., New York, New York 10021
Muscular Dystrophy Association
   1790 Broadway, New York, New York 10019
National Association for Mental Health
   10 Columbus Circle, New York, New York 10020
National Association for Music Therapy, Inc.
   P. O. Box 610, Lawrence, Kansas 66044
National Association for Retarded Children, Inc.
   420 Lexington Avenue, New York, N. Y. 10017
National Association of Social Workers
   2 Park Avenue, New York, New York 10010
National Council on the Aging
   315 Park Avenue, S, New York, N. Y. 10010
National Easter Seal Society for Crippled Children and Adults
   2023 W. Ogden Avenue, Chicago, Illinois 60612

National Institute of Health
9000 Rockvill Pike, Bethesda, Maryland 20010
National Multiple Sclerosis Soc'ety
257 Park Ave., S., New York, N. Y. 10010
National Recreation and Park Association
American Park and Recreation Society (Branch of NRPA)
National Therapeutic Recreation Society (Branch of NRPA)
Society of Park and Recreation Educators (Branch of NRPA)
1601 N. Kent St., Arlington, Va. 22209
Administration on Aging
330 C Street, S.W., Washington, D. C. 20201
Rehabilitation Services Administration (Social And Rehabilitation Service)
330 C Street, S.W., Washington, D. C. 20201
United Cerebral Palsy Association
55 East 34th Street, New York, N. Y. 10016
Veterans Administration (Central Office)
Washington, D. C. 20420

Index